The Image of War

The Image of War

THE PICTORIAL REPORTING
OF THE
AMERICAN CIVIL WAR

by
William F. Thompson

LOUISIANA STATE UNIVERSITY PRESS

BATON ROUGE AND LONDON

Acknowledgments

The author gratefully acknowledges permission to use material from the following publishers and institutions:

Crown Publishers, Inc., for James D. Horan, *Mathew Brady, Historian with a Camera* (1955), and for Lamont Buchanan, *A Pictorial History of the Confederacy* (1951.)

Grosset & Dunlap, Inc., for Otto Eisenschiml and Ralph Newman, *The Civil War* (1956).

Harper & Brothers, for Albert Bigelow Paine, *Th. Nast, His Period and His Pictures* (1904).

Harvard University Press, for Oliver Wendell Holmes, Jr., *Touched with Fire: Civil War Letters and Diary of Oliver Wendell Holmes, Jr., 1861–1864*, edited by Mark A. DeWolfe Howe (1946).

Houghton Mifflin Co., for Frank A. Haskell, *The Battle of Gettysburg*, edited by Bruce Catton (1958).

Indiana University Press, for James A. Connolly, *Three Years in the Army of the Cumberland*, edited by Paul M. Angle (1950).

Alfred A. Knopf, Inc., for Sylvanus Cadwallader, *Three Years with Grant, As Recalled by War Correspondent Sylvanus Cadwallader*, edited by Benjamin P. Thomas (1955), and for Louis M. Starr, *Bohemian Brigade: Civil War Newsmen in Action* (1954).

Macmillan Co., for Virgil Baker, *American Painting, History and Interpretation* (1950), and for *The Diary of George Templeton Strong*, edited by Allan Nevins and Milton Halsey Thomas (1952).

Minnesota Historical Society, for Hazel C. Wolf, editor, "Campaigning with the First Minnesota, A Civil War Diary," in *Minnesota History* (Sept. 1944).

W. W. Norton and Co., Inc., for John Beatty, *Memoirs of a Volunteer* (1946).

Charles Scribner's Sons, for *Home Letters of General Sherman*, edited by Mark A. DeWolfe Howe (1909).

University of North Carolina Press, for George Alfred Townsend, *Rustics in Rebellion, A Yankee Reporter on the Road to Richmond, 1861–65* (1950).

University of Pittsburgh Press, for J. Cutler Andrews, *The North Reports the Civil War* (1955).

State Historical Society of Wisconsin, for Jenkin Lloyd Jones, *An Artilleryman's Diary* (1941), and for the Alexander Simplot Collection.

The World Publishing Co., for Roy Merideth, *The American Wars* (1955).

Yale University Press, for *Marching with Sherman, Passages from the Letters and Campaign Diaries of Henry Hitchcock, major and assistant adjutant general of Volunteers, November 1864—May 1865*, edited by Mark A. DeWolfe Howe (1927).

For
Nancy, Ross, and Susan

Preface

Scholars have written a greater number of books, monographs, and articles about the American Civil War than about any other event in the history of the Republic, and yet new areas of investigation are still available. This book considers two hitherto unexplored aspects of the Civil War. It is, first, a study of the images of the Civil War as created by the wartime illustrators, photographers, cartoonists, and commercial artists, some of whom served as pictorial reporters, while others used pictures as editorials to shape public opinion. Second, this study shows for perhaps the first time how the historian can use journalistic pictures as primary historical documents.

The martial tradition with which most Americans started the Civil War consisted of a number of romantic images. These maintained that Americans fought only in defense of great moral and political principles, and consequently that the free-born militiaman and the volunteer were superior to the professional soldier, that moral fervor was more important than military experience, and that soldiers were crusaders who instinctively performed magnificent feats of heroism. These images were established by artists, most of whom had never accompanied an army into the field. In 1861, for the first time, photographers and sketch artists who provided illustrations for *Harper's Weekly, Frank Leslie's Illustrated Newspaper,* and the *New York Illustrated News* lived constantly with the armies. Like the troops with whom they associated, they soon realized that the stereotyped images were erroneous and meaningless. Gradually they abandoned them, and on the basis of their own experiences and observations they created more realistic images that portrayed the true and full nature of modern warfare.

At the same time editorial artists on the home front used illustrations and cartoons to interpret the issues and meaning of the war. They helped mobilize public opinion to support the war with men and money; they tried to create a climate of conformity around such issues as loyalty and patriotism; they lent support to the campaigns for emancipation and the utilization of Negro troops; and they crusaded for or against the re-election of Abraham Lincoln. The main purpose of the photographers and artists with the armies was to

7

enlighten the public; the editorial artists were primarily concerned with in-doctrination and propaganda.

By the time of the surrender of Appomattox, Americans in the North had witnessed four years of warfare through the efforts of artists, photographers, and cartoonists. Many of their intense feelings about the war were a direct result of having shared in this way the experiences of their fathers, sons, and husbands at the front.

I am gratefully indebted to John Hunter of Madison, Wisconsin, an enthusiastic student of the Civil War who discovered the Alexander Simplot Papers and who shared with me the conclusions of his study of Simplot. It is also a pleasure to acknowledge the assistance of Milton Kaplan of the Library of Congress, whose knowledge of the Waud and Forbes Collections was of great benefit to me, and of Cyrus Nast of New Rochelle, New York, who generously provided me with many insights into the life and personality of his father, Thomas Nast, But most of all, my deepest appreciation to William B. Hesseltine of the University of Wisconsin, whose wisdom and knowledge I have prized above all others.

W. F. T., Jr.

Contents

Illustrations

following page 126

The Image of War

I

The Image Makers

"If you could see me in my rags and dirt . . . you would laugh immensely," Major James A. Connolly wrote his wife late in the summer of 1863, "and if my dear mother could see me she would laugh first and then cry to see me looking so much like a beggar man." Less than two years ago Connolly had left his wife and son and a comfortable law practice to fight for the Union. Since then he had been at Chattanooga, Chickamauga, and Missionary Ridge, and had lived in the mud and rain and dirt of a hundred different camps and bivouacs. His once-fine uniform was in rags: his coat was out at the elbows and the lining was missing, the soles of his boots were "gone up," and his hat was "the very picture of misery and dilapidation." Somehow, this was not what he had expected. He remembered that when he was a young boy "I used to read stories about the Mexican War, and earnestly wished I was a man, so that I could go to war like the men in the pictures, wearing a nice blue coat and red pants, flourishing a great yellow sword over my head, and dashing into the thickest of the fight on a furious, coal black horse." But the pictures had been misleading, and now that he had experienced warfare for himself, he found it "very unenchanting."[1]

Connolly's disillusionment was not unusual. Josh Billings, a private in the Tenth Massachusetts Battery of Light Artillery, recalled that in 1861 the thought of war seemed so strange to him and his companions. "We had nothing in our experience to compare it with. True, some of us had dim remembrances of a Mexican War in our early childhood, but . . . we only remembered that there was a Scott, and a Taylor, and a Santa Ana [sic], from the colored prints we had seen displayed of these worthies; so that we could only run back in memory to the stories and traditions of the wars of the Revolution and 1812 . . . for anything like a vivid picture of what was to occur, and this, of course, was utterly inadequate to do the subject justice."[2]

Like Connolly, he believed that the military artists had misrepresented the real nature of war.

The pictures they thought were so obsolete had been drawn by artists who themselves knew very little about war. Some of them were painters who were primarily interested in demonstrating their skill as artists and not as reporters. They believed that paintings—including battle art—should "refine the mind, enrich the imagination, and soften the heart of man," or as a writer for *Godey's Lady's Magazine* expressed it, "lift the mind above the materialism of common workday life, and . . . urge it to higher aims than those which mere love of wealth or of ease could inspire."[3] Most of them had never witnessed a battle, never seen men cut to the ground by grape shot, nor known the leaden weariness of the forced march. John Trumbull served as an aide on Washington's staff and Charles Willson Peale saw action as a Captain of the Pennsylvania Line during the Revolution, and James Walker was an army interpreter in the Mexican War, but they were exceptions. Most of the painters' battle portraits were created in the snug security of their studios far from the sound of shot and shell.[4]

Battle art reached the man in the street mainly through the pictures of the commercial art publishers. By 1860 there were several hundred picture publishers in the United States, led by the large printhouse of Currier and Ives. Using fast printing and coloring techniques, they sold prints, cartoons, portraits, and many other types of pictures for as little as five cents apiece. Book dealers displayed their prints in their shop windows, pushcart men hawked them in the streets, and Currier and Ives stacked hundreds of their cheaper prints on tables on the sidewalk in front of their New York shop to accommodate browsers. They portrayed a variety of subjects—farm scenes, frontier life, steamboat and railroad races, portraits of hunting dogs and game birds and champion racehorses and prize fighters, and a host of sentimentals for the women. But war pictures and portraits were always a particular favorite with their customers.[5]

Heroic images of warfare stemmed mainly from the American Revolution. Painters and illustrators outdid themselves in heaping accolades on the patriotic and selfless crusaders who sacrificed their fortunes and their lives in the War for Independence. Trumbull's painting of the British, French, and American armies drawn up in parade formation at Yorktown as Cornwallis surrendered his sword to Washington was a masterpiece of feudal pageantry and ceremony. Trumbull also did more than any other artist to immortalize courageous battlefield deaths with his portraits of Montgomery at Quebec, Warren at Bunker's Hill, and Mercer at Princeton. The commercial artists were even less subtle: Washington's Minutemen farmers and mechanics fought in full dress uniforms, marched and wheeled and rallied to the flag with beautiful precision, and despite Valley Forge and scarcely a victory to their credit never showed any sign of exhaustion or discouragement. Heroic postures also came into their own in the battle art of this period. Many artists preferred the resolute equestrian poses. Peale and Trumbull did several standing portraits of Washington that later served as models for the paintings of Thomas Sully and particularly for Emanuel Leutze's "Washington Crossing the Delaware." The printmakers honored the heroes with portraits edged in red, white, and blue bunting and surmounted with a screaming eagle. The chauvinism of these pictures was blatant, yet they were what the public wanted. Many years later, Huckleberry Finn was still fascinated with the pictures he saw for the first time in a typical western home: "Washingtons and Lafayettes and battles and Highland Marys and one called 'Signing the Declaration.' "[6]

Between 1815 and 1860 the Hudson River School of grandiose landscape painting made its impact upon military art. Walker's Mexican War paintings, for instance, were broad panoramas of color and detail. At Lake Chalco, Contreras, Churubusco, and Chapultepec, he set the battles and sieges of the American armies against the brilliant background of the Mexican desert and mountains. Weathered adobe walls and giant Saguare cactus plants stood in mute contrast of the melee of fighting men. But while the painters landscaped warfare, the commercial artists clung to the traditional stereotypes. The generals waved their "great yellow swords" or a plumed hat as they led their men into battle, and the ranks of infantrymen marched so perfectly they resembled long lines of tin soldiers. Cavalry troopers performed amazing feats of equestrian gymnastics, riding, shooting, flourishing their sabers, and huzzahing all at the same time. Even the horses snorted ferociously and reared majestically and pawed the air with their forelegs.[7]

Until mid-century, painters and commercial illustrators monopolized battle art, and their romantic impressions shaped the thinking of the young men who volunteered for the Union and Confederate armies. Little wonder, then, that Connolly and Billings thought their pictures were "utterly inadequate."

17

But by 1861 their monopoly was being challenged. The Civil War was the first opportunity for the artists in two new art mediums—photography and illustrated journalism—to assault the conventional images.

By 1860 photography had become a big business, supporting hundreds of photographers and many supply houses and professional publications. Many factors were responsible. A typical entry in a diary, "Had myself daguerreotyped this morning," indicated the main explanation for its rapid growth. Photographers made portraits quickly and inexpensively, and they provided their customers with as many duplicate copies as they wanted. They also provided the public with portraits of their leaders in greater numbers and with sharper detail than had ever before been possible. A writer for *Harper's Weekly* grieved that there were no photographs of the great men of the past, so "we could have seen them as they really were and not as some preposterous court-painter did them." Nobody believed that the camera could deceive or distort, and the highest praise was that a picture portrayed its subject with "photographic accuracy." Yet some people were not entirely happy with the camera's honesty. Many art students supplemented their incomes by retouching portraits that were too honest. And in the midst of the war Lincoln visited Mathew Brady's studio, and when Brady showed him the proofs and suggested they looked very natural, he remarked. "Yes, that is my objection. The cameras are painfully truthful."[8]

By 1861, however, cameramen had had only a few opportunities to photograph war. In 1846 and '47, a Mexican photographer made several daguerreotypes, one of which may have been a view of the battlefield of Buena Vista, and in the following decade several European photographers accompanied the armies during the Crimean and Italian wars. Each of them faced the same basic problems. The size and weight of their cameras and tripods restricted their ease of movement. The necessity of having a portable darkroom right at hand to prepare the plates for exposure and then to develop them immediately afterward was a distinct handicap. The long exposure time of the early cameras also prevented them from photographing any subject in motion. The operation costs for field photographers was exceedingly high, especially since newspapers and magazines, prior to the development of photo-engraving, did not cover their expenses. For these and other reasons, Brady and his photographers were not serious competitors to the sketch artists. But they did force them to try to duplicate the accuracy of the camera.[9]

In the long run, the single most significant factor in establishing new images of war was the development of illustrated journalism in the United States. Broadsides and scattersheets illustrating news events appeared in Europe as early as the 16th century, and in the first half of the 19th century a few metropolitan newspapers occasionally published crude woodcut illustrations. But the real advent of illustrated journalism came in 1842 when an English newspaperman, Herbert Ingram, founded the *Illustrated London News*. In the following year, *L'Illustration* and *Illustriete Zeitung* made their debut in Paris and Leipzig. The problems faced by these pioneers were immense, but in one way or another they found the answers, and they prospered. They also profited from the work of the regular newspaper publishers in stimulating advertising, developing sales and distribution techniques, acquiring cheap newsprint and fast rotary presses, and achieving favorable postage rates from their governments. By the Fifties, illustrated journalism was a firm success in western Europe.[10]

It came later to America. The obstacles were manifold. The United States did not have enough trained artists and engravers, and distance and isolation compounded the problem of communications. The expense of acquiring and preparing news illustrations required that an illustrated newspaper have a national distribution, and this in turn meant that the pictures had to illustrate events of nationwide interest. The strayed cow, the wedding of the banker's daughter, the new building on Main Street, and all the items that formed the bulk of the daily news were capable of illustration, but interest in them was purely local and the resultant sales could not have covered the costs of artists and engravers. In short, illustrated journalism was not successful until there was a steady supply of news items that were of general interest throughout the nation.[11]

Phineas T. Barnum, the showman-promoter who sponsored General Tom Thumb and introduced Jenny Lind to the United States, rarely misjudged what the American public wanted, but in 1852 he made a premature attempt to establish an illustrated newspaper. He and two partners each invested twenty thousand dollars to establish the *Illustrated News*. Frank Leslie, a veteran artist and engraver from the *Illustrated London News,* supervised the engraving of the illustrations and portraits. At one time circulation approached fifty thousand, just enough to meet publication expenses. By November of 1853 Barnum and his partners were anxious to abandon the entire enterprise. They sold their investment to *Gleason's Pictorial,* an illustrated magazine that occasionally published news pictures, and the *Illustrated News* quietly went out of business.[12]

Yet only two years later Frank Leslie established the first successful American illustrated newspaper. In that short interim, events, largely political, occurred which created a sustained national market for news pictures. In 1854 the Kansas-Nebraska Act shattered the complacency that had characterized American public affairs since the Compromise of 1850. In rapid succession there followed guerrilla warfare in Missouri and Kansas and the resurgence of bitter political sectionalism. For the first time Americans consistently followed the same news reports and thus had a common desire to see the same pictures. Also new methods of engraving now made it possible to prepare illustrations in only a few days' time. The result was *Frank Leslie's Illustrated Newspaper.*

Leslie grew up with illustrated journalism. His real name was Henry Carter and he was born in Ipswich, England in 1821. Soon after the establishment of the *Illustrated London News* he submitted some drawings to Ingram under the *nom de plume* of Frank Leslie. Ingram recognized his talent and within several years promoted him to superintendent of the *News'* engraving department. In 1848 he came to the United States to prepare an illustrated catalogue of Barnum's American Museum. After establishing the engraving department for *Gleason's Pictorial,* he became managing foreman for Barnum's ill-fated *Illustrated News.* By 1855 he was ready to establish his own publication, and the first issue of *Frank Leslie's Illustrated Newspaper* appeared in December, "a weekly miscellany to be featured by news pictures. . . ."[13]

Leslie was a man of huge ambition. He was short and broad in appearance, but he gave the impression of great physical strength. His black-bearded face was animated and intelligent. He was respected and admired, but not beloved. Many associates and employees were victims of his deviousness in personal relationships and were cast aside in his ruthless drive to wealth and position. But friend and foe alike admitted that he was the foremost publisher of illustrated journalism in America—he himself would have said "in the world." He had an intuitive touch on the public pulse, which he tempted with vivid and sometimes lurid illustrations. Murders and shipwrecks, prize fights and political scandals, ship races and foreign wars were all grist for his picture mill. If there was a dearth of news, he created crusades to fill the vacuum. In 1857 he excited the mothers of New York City with graphic pictures exposing the swill milk scandals. Before the campaign was over, he had established himself as a leader of local reform, and incidentally also sold a lot of newspapers.[14]

The key to Leslie's success were his illustrations. Corresponding artists and photographers in every section of the country sent him pictures. He also supported a large staff of sketch artists to illustrate important news stories as they occurred. They made rapid pencil sketches on the spot, interviewed people who could contribute useful information, and then rushed their material back to Leslie. Above all else, he demanded accuracy in his illustrations. He often editorialized with cartoons, but he insisted that his news pictures be unimpeachable. His requirements were rigorous, but their value was apparent, for from his staff came most of the outstanding cartoonists and sketch artists of the Civil War.[15]

The center of *Frank Leslie's Illustrated Newspaper* was a five-story white marble building at 19 City Hall Square. Here he employed 130 craftsmen. On the upper floors engravers copied sketches from the field artists onto hard blocks of boxwood, and then cut out the uninked sections. Ordinarily this process consumed several weeks if only one engraver did the work, but Leslie had devised a system by which he cut the boxwood blocks into twelve to forty smaller squares and assigned each piece to a separate engraver. If the illustration was important enough, he could have copies of it on the streets within forty-eight hours of receiving the original sketch. In 1860 he created a sensation when his artists cut the illustrations of the Heenan-Sayers heavyweight championship fight in England while returning on the first ship to New York. That particular issue of *Leslie's* sold 347,000 copies. Under ordinary circumstances, however, Leslie had illustrations in circulation within two weeks, which at the time far surpassed the efforts of any other paper. After the engravers were finished, an electrotyped metal copy of the woodcut went down to the cellar for printing on huge rotary presses. Workmen then folded the uncut papers and either wrapped and mailed them to subscribers or rolled them into packs of one hundred and distributed them to newspaper agencies throughout the country. All of this was expensive. By 1860 Leslie was paying $168,000 a year for paper, nearly $7,000 for a special ink he imported from England and Germany, and $72,000 in salaries to editors and artists. But it was also profitable. Circulation was near a hundred thousand copies a week, and annual receipts amounted to nearly a half-million dollars.[16]

Leslie's success encouraged others to enter the field. In 1857 the giant publishing firm of Harper and Brothers established *Harper's Weekly*. From the beginning, the *Weekly* was the pet enterprise of Fletcher Harper, the most able of the four brothers. He was a slender clean-shaven middle-aged man with deep-set eyes, a sharp straight nose, and high sloping forehead. He had extensive experience in general publishing, but illustrated journalism was a new enterprise for him. Nevertheless, he selected each item, approved every expression of policy, and personally supervised the work of his artists and engravers. In line with his professional background and the promise of the *Weekly's* subtitle, "A Journal of Civilization," he at first published mainly illustrated fiction. But he soon found that news pictures boosted circulation, and in 1859 he entered into active competition with Leslie.[17]

By 1860 *Harper's Weekly* was potentially the strongest of the American illustrated newspapers. The House of Harper on Franklin Square, a cluster of seven-story buildings housing 750 employees, represented an investment in personnel and equipment far surpassing that of Leslie. Harper was quick to recognize and reward artistic skill, and he could attract talent to the *Weekly* with handsome salaries and commissions. His main disadvantage at the beginning of the war was that he did not have enough competent sketch artists and engravers. As late as 1860 an illustration of a Union meeting in New York appeared six weeks after the event, and until well into the war the quality of the *Weekly's* engravings was definitely inferior to *Leslie's*. Nevertheless, the public received the *Weekly* well. Within two years of its establishment, its circulation was near ninety thousand copies each week.[18]

In 1859 John King, a veteran publisher, established the *New York Illustrated News*, and for several years the prospects were bright. The engravings rivaled those in *Leslie's* for general excellence, and three of the *News'* wartime artists, Alfred R. Waud, Theodore R. Davis, and Arthur Lumley, were among the best in their profession. The *News* might have prospered in peacetime, but the limited resources of its owners were not sufficient to meet the wartime demand for expanded facilities. In 1861 King despaired of the effort and sold the *News* to T. B. Leggett.[19]

Evidence of the success of the illustrated weeklies came with the war. Several of the larger metropolitan dailies, including the *New York Herald* and the *Philadelphia Inquirer,* occasionally published simple woodcut portraits, illustrations, and maps. Furthermore, when southerners were cut off from the northern pictorials they attempted to establish an illustrated weekly of their own. In September 1862 Ayers and Wade, Richmond publishers, established the *Southern Illustrated News*—"A News and Literary Journal for Southern Families." But the attempt to found an illustrated press when the Confederacy lacked sketch artists and cartoonists, engravers and die-makers, paper, ink, and presses (shortages that also plagued the Confederate Post Office and Treasury Departments) was doomed from the start. In July 1863 the *Southern Illustrated News* ran the following plaintive advertisement: "Engravers Wanted. Desirous, if possible of illustrating the 'News' in a style not inferior to the 'London Illustrated News,' we offer the *highest salaries* ever paid in this country for good engravers." There were no takers. Illustrations became something of a rarity—a portrait of a Confederate general now and then, sometimes a crude wood engraving or a cartoon. Leslie delighted in calling attention to the "whitey brown wrapping paper" and the "wonderfully bad woodcuts" of his southern competition. In November 1864 Ayers and Wade gave up the struggle. The *Southern Illustrated News* was just one more casualty of the war.[20]

In 1861, however, the men in illustrated journalism had not had any experience illustrating wars. Leslie, Harper, and Leggett had no idea of the expense or the personnel problems involved. Of the several dozen artists who went into the field during the next four years, only one had ever sketched under fire. In 1860 a nineteen-year-old illustrator, painter, and cartoonist named Thomas Nast joined Giuseppe Garibaldi's army in Italy as a representative of the *New York Illustrated News,* the *Illustrated London News,* and *Monde Illustrie* of Paris. Nast was an enthusiastic supporter of Garibaldi even before he arrived in Italy, and his illustrations were frankly partisan. He delighted in illustrating tumultuous street scenes where Garibaldi moved like a saint among the cheering populace, and his battle pictures were grand panoramic views of a suppressed people struggling against tyranny for independence and democracy. In spirit and in style there was little to distinguish his Italian sketches from the heroic paintings of Trumbull, Peale, and Walker.[21]

23

THE IMAGE OF WAR

The advent of illustrated journalism and photography by the beginning of the Civil War gave artists at least two mediums to provide the public with fresh images of warfare. But the artists themselves were encumbered with an antiquated artistic concept of war that sacrificed realism for stereotyped heroics. Like Major Connolly and Private Billings, they were due for a rather rude shock.

II

The Crusade

In the winter of 1860–61, Americans north and south watched the succession of events in the city of Charleston with anxiety and yet with exhilaration. After Lincoln's election in November, the South Carolina Legislature called a convention which late in December withdrew the state from the Federal Union. Thereupon, the main symbol of Federal power in South Carolina was the small garrison of troops in three forts in Charleston under the command of Major Robert Anderson. Secession leaders demanded the immediate surrender of the forts. The government in Washington refused. On Christmas Eve Anderson concentrated his small forces at Fort Sumter on an island in the harbor. For the next three months a virtual stalemate ensued, during which the military forces on both sides postured themselves in apparent readiness for action. The great majority of Americans did not want war, did not really think there would be a war, but as they waited they were enthralled as if they were watching a great tragedy on a far-away stage.

Fletcher Harper and T. B. Leggett were anxious to illustrate the drama at Charleston, but neither could afford an artist. Harper had the money, but he lacked an available sketch artist; Leggett had neither the money nor the artist. Moreover, there was some doubt whether representatives of the *Weekly* or the *Illustrated News* would be welcome in Charleston. Early in 1860 Leggett had published several illustrations showing an angry mob tarring and feathering a northern woman accused of teaching Negroes, and thereafter he suspected that any *News* artist would be *persona non grata*. For the time being he was satisfied to publish photographs of the city and to instruct his staff artist to illustrate the news reports as they came off the telegraph. Harper had antagonized southern extremists with several critical editorials in the *Weekly*, as he discovered when he went to Charleston early in 1861 and again when southern postmasters in many towns stopped the distribution of the *Weekly*

25

through the mails. But he had arranged with Captain Truman Seymour, a former instructor in drawing at West Point, and several other officers of Anderson's command to provide the *Weekly* with sketches. Their work was limited to the forts under Anderson's command, but within that small area they sketched practically every man and object, including even Anderson's candle-holder. Harper was satisfied. At least he could claim the only on-the-spot illustrations from within Sumter.[1]

Frank Leslie, on the other hand, had won the confidence of the Carolinians. During the presidential campaign of 1860 he had edited every word and picture that might have offended his southern subscribers, and they were appreciative. After Lincoln's election, Leslie sent William Waud to Charleston, confident that he would be well received. Waud was an English free lance artist who had emigrated to the United States in the mid-fifties, and his British citizenship gave him an additional advantage over any "Yankee" artist. Moreover, Leslie instructed him to use the greatest discretion in making his sketches and to avoid giving the impression of being a northern investigator. If necessary, he was to err in favor of the Carolinians.[2]

Waud enjoyed following Leslie's instructions. He was a bright though cynical individual who always preferred conviviality to serious work, and the holiday mood of the Charlestonians was entirely to his liking. He spent much of November, December, and January making the rounds of the rallies, meetings, parties, and regimental reviews at which the Charlestonians celebrated their new independence. The high-pitched fervor of secession filled his sketches and his reports to Leslie. A sketch of Mrs. Governor Pickens and her daughter reviewing the "gallant volunteer soldiers of South Carolina" recorded "a pleasant incident . . . one to be long remembered." He spent two "delightful and charming" days with the Richland Guards, a "gentlemanly and hospitable group . . . well uniformed, well drilled and well officered," and he even had a "dashing" little adventure of his own one evening when an alert sentry challenged him and demanded the countersign. He titillated Leslie's readers with thoughts of what might have happened to him had he not been saved by the officer of the day.[3]

But there was also serious work to be done. He sketched many of the enthusiastic rallies supporting independence, and he scoured the city for portraits of secession leaders. In February he went to Montgomery to sketch the inauguration of Jefferson Davis as the first President of the Confederate

States of America; Leslie shrewdly published these sketches in the same issue with the illustrations of Lincoln's inauguration in Washington. Back in Charleston, Waud illustrated the mobilization of men and munitions. State officials granted him permission to sketch all the Confederate installations around the harbor, the entrenched guns on Morris Island, the regimental preparations, the Charleston armory, and particularly a floating battery complete with sleeping quarters and a hospital that the Carolinians planned to use at close range against Fort Sumter. He would have liked to portray the activities of Anderson's garrison within Sumter, but the hospitality of his southern hosts was not quite that liberal. Nevertheless, he was present when Confederate batteries fired on the *Star of the West,* a relief ship sent to provision Sumter, and several days later he showed one of Anderson's men protesting the unwarranted attack. He also sketched the evacuation of the women and children of the Sumter garrison. Then he waited for the climax.[4]

Waud's portrayal of the bombardment of Sumter on April 12 and 13 was one of the outstanding pictorial exclusives of the war. A few days earlier, Leslie had sent a young art student, Eugene Benson, to join Waud. Benson arrived just in time to sketch the hysteria of the cheering and dancing crowds in the city as they watched the cannonade. But the real triumph was Waud's. He moved quickly to the various places he had earlier decided gave him the best views of Sumter. On Morris Island he showed the furious work of the gun crews as they fired salvos of hot shot across the harbor. At the floating battery, he sketched the perspiring gunners stripped to the waist as they cleaned, loaded, and fired their guns. The shells spiraled in a high arc and oftentimes exploded in the air, leaving only a small white cloud as a momentary remembrance. The gun crews were enshrouded in a heavy pall of black smoke that streaked their naked arms and backs. But they had done their work well. Waud's final sketch was a dark and somber picture of Fort Sumter gutted with flames.[5]

The officers within Sumter were much too busy for sketching. As reports of the bombardment filtered into New York, Harper passed them on to his engravers. One of the unlikely pictures they produced showed the men and women of Charleston weeping in sorrow as they watched the attack from their rooftops. Another recreated the scene in the fort, the Sumter garrison calm and unruffled as shrapnel exploded in every direction. A third picture of

27

one of the Confederate forts showed the damage supposedly done by shells from the Sumter batteries.[6]

The first pictures of the bombardment in the *Illustrated News* were also New York creations. But the following week, Leggett published three sketches by a man who had been an eyewitness. B. S. Osbon was a reporter for the *New York World* who had signed on one of the ships sent to relieve Anderson. Returning to New York, he drew three sketches for Leggett showing the massed destruction at Sumter. Like all the other artists, he featured the torn and shredded flag waving from a makeshift flagpole, a symbol of the hopeless heroism of the small garrison.[7]

A day or two after Anderson's surrender, Benson visited the battered fort and made two quick sketches of the shattered ramparts and the huge mass of rubble scattered in the inner courts. Then with his own and Waud's sketches, he took passage for the North. Waud remained behind in Charleston.[8]

The bombardment of Sumter, Leslie reported, worked a "wonderful transformation" throughout the North. All good patriots rallied together in devotion to the Union and the Flag. The cry of every man and woman was: "Are you for the Union?" Preachers searched Scripture for appropriate texts; more than one minister chose Joel, 3:9, "Prepare war; wake up the mighty men; let all the men of war draw near." New York City seemed to have "gone suddenly wild and crazy." Citizens flocked to huge mass meetings in Union Square to listen to speakers exhort them about their duty to God and nation. For the thousands of northerners who could not attend the rallies, artists and photographers pictured the eager thrust of the crowds, the bunting on carriages and wagons, and the flags flying from every building. One prominent New Yorker exclaimed: "God be praised for the unity of feeling here! It is beyond, very far beyond, anything I hoped for. If it only lasts, we are safe."[9]

Americans were a martial but not a militaristic people. They were suspicious of standing armies and the professional militarists of the service academies. But at the same time they delighted in the symbols and pageantry of warfare, the parades, the reviews, and the flag, and they gloried in the martial tradition of a nation that had managed to win most of its wars under the leadership of inspired amateurs. America's best loved military heroes were not her professional soldiers so much as the militia, the Minutemen of Concord and Lexington, and the frontier fighters who rallied to Andy Jackson at New Orleans. The volunteers, the "peaceable" men who cast aside their plows and pitchforks and picked up their muskets, had always been victorious in the past. In 1861 everyone was confident they would win again.

Lincoln's call for seventy-five thousand militia troops to serve for three months met an enthusiastic reception. The picturemen helped keep the excitement at a high pitch. Lithographers and engravers illustrated the eagerness with which young men put on the uniform of their country. A number of sentimental prints portrayed wives and mothers making their last farewells. Church women prepared Bibles for the troops and pasted paper flags in them, each with an appropriate verse—"Fight the good fight" or "Endure hardness as a good soldier of Jesus Christ." Children waved flags and wore cockades in their caps and bonnets, and little boys in uniforms watched their fathers parade in company maneuvers. With such help, the quotas for volunteers in most states were soon oversubscribed.[10]

Readers of the illustrated weeklies were not surprised to see their soldiers adopt the pageantry and ceremony of crusaders. Mothers, wives, and sweethearts sacrificed their men, and like the fair ladies of Camelot, they tearfully presented them with elaborately decorated regimental flags and many personal favors and remembrances. The crusaders pledged their faith. In late April, artists for *Leslie's* and the *Illustrated News* sketched Colonel William Wilson's New York Zouaves brandishing daggers as they gathered about the flag and vowed "Death to Secessionists." In Indianapolis, James Gookins sketched his own Eleventh Indiana kneeling in front of the state house and swearing to remember Buena Vista, because there during the Mexican War Jefferson Davis had once insulted the Indiana troops. It was unthinkable that any soldier would not recite the oath of allegiance. The *Illustrated News* published a picture of two Albany soldiers who refused; their former companions promptly shaved their heads and drummed them out of camp.[11]

Every town dispatched its regiments with an orgy of speeches, flag presentations, and long parades down Main Street. Artists and photographers recorded many of these scenes for the rest of the nation. In Providence, Arthur Lumley, a sketch artist soon to be employed by Leslie, pictured the departure of Ambrose Burnside's regiment. New York throbbed to the beat of marching feet as Scotch Highlanders in kilts and the New York bullies and toughs of Wilson's and Ellsworth's Zouaves paraded down Broadway. New Yorkers turned out in "immense crowds" to cheer the departure of Gotham's special pride, the Seventh New York. Artists for *Leslie's, Harper's,* and the *Illustrated News* sketched the Seventh as it appeared far up Broadway, "a bluish steel-grey light on the blackness of the dense mob that filled the street. . . ." Few people, including the artists, seemed to notice that some of the soldiers lacked uniforms and that others marched without weapons. Rather, their eyes were "filled with tears" and their hearts "half choked in sympathy with the contageous excitement."[12]

The publishers of the illustrated newspapers also began a mobilization of their own. They knew that their peacetime staffs of sketch artists were not large enough, but as long as they thought the war might last for only six weeks or three months, they were willing to use part-time amateur artists from the army. Fletcher Harper appealed to Federal officers serving in the South, promising to pay them liberally for any sketches he might use, and he offered the *Weekly* gratuitously for six months to any officer who sent his address to the New York office. Leggett also offered to pay for any sketches he used, no matter how roughly they were drawn. Leslie solicited sketches from officers and soldiers alike, and he offered a year's free subscription to anyone in the service who submitted a small sketch as a sample of his ability as an artist. Whenever regiments passed through New York, he asked any volunteer who could sketch to call on him at his office. By July of 1861 Leslie claimed to have over fifty corresponding artists with the northern armies. Harper had a similar number.[13]

Leslie and Harper also expanded their contacts among civilian artists and photographers. Troop movements in the West encouraged several young artists to submit sketches. Henry Mosler, a young Cincinnatian who combined wood-engraving with landscape painting, received a commission from Harper as Special Artist for Ohio and Kentucky. Alexander Simplot, the scion of a prominent Dubuque family, sent Harper a sketch of the departure of the Governor's Grey's, and in return Harper sent him a commission as Special Artist for the Trans-Mississippi West. Arthur Lumley had been an occasional contributor to *Leslie's* while studying at the National Academy of Design. In April Leslie assigned him to the Army of the Potomac.[14]

Many artists and art students declined the opportunities to become sketch artists. Some avoided the war, leaving the country for France or Italy. John Ross Browne, a traveling writer and artist for *Harper's Monthly,* was on assignment in Europe at the outbreak of the war and did not return to the

United States until 1863. A short time later he left for the Orient. In early 1861 August Sontag, an artist for the *Weekly*, joined the Hayes Arctic Expedition as recording artist, and four months later he froze to death. Others enlisted to take advantage of the bounties. In early May the National Academy converted its gallery into a drill hall for a military company in which a half dozen art students had enlisted. Moreover, the army itself had need of artists. James Hope, a painter, and David Strother, widely known to readers of *Harper's Monthly* as "Porte Crayon," served in the Topographical Engineers. The Engineers also enlisted several of Mathew Brady's photographers, and repeatedly offered commissions to a number of sketch artists.[15]

Nevertheless, the publishers secured the services of a considerable number of artists. The field corps of the *Illustrated News* was always the smallest simply because Leggett could not afford to support more than a single full-time artist at the front. But by the end of 1861 both Harper and Leslie had a half dozen special artists with the major northern armies. They tried to utilize the particular experience of each artist. Harper assigned Mosler and Simplot to areas familiar to them. Arthur Lumley had personal contacts in a Rhode Island regiment and he accompanied it to the Army of the Potomac. Only a few artists, like *Harper's* Theodore Davis and *Leslie's* William Waud, got roving assignments, which in four years took them from Vicksburg and New Orleans in the West to the Peninsula and Petersburg. But whatever their assignment, all the sketch artists came to know warfare as intimately as the men they sketched.

Photographers found that the mobilization brought them long hours and large profits. Mathew Brady's business had never been as good. The photographers at his New York and Washington studios worked late into the nights to keep ahead of the rush of orders. In the outcountry, itinerant photographers and one-man studios were busier than ever before. Tens of thousands of young men got into their uniforms and went to the nearest Photograph Salon, many for the first time. The procedure there was relatively easy. They carefully posed themselves while the photographer adjusted his camera and checked the lighting. Ordinarily the enlisted men leaned on their long muskets, and the officers comfortably seated themselves with their legs crossed and their sword hip turned toward the camera. The Zouaves ballooned the fullness of their trousers, and the Michigan lumberjack troops posed full face to call attention to the bright plaids of their tunics. Each portrait usually cost about twenty-five cents and was mounted on a small card with the name of the soldier printed across the bottom. Each man usually bought many copies to give to his mother, sisters, and wife or sweetheart.[16]

In addition to preparing portraits, photographing Lincoln's inauguration, and taking innumerable pictures of Union rallies and regimental parades, Brady was also considering making a complete photographic record of the war. The idea was not exclusively his own. In June a committee of the American Photographic Society broached the project to the War Department, but without success. Brady persisted. He hoped to get financial assistance from the government, or failing in that, to sell enough stereoptic views to cover the costs of the project. The most immediate problem was to secure permission to take photographs within the army. In July, General Winfield Scott, an old friend who was General-in-chief of the Union armies, and General Irwin McDowell, who had the field command of the army, gave Brady their blessings. With this assurance he began to train his assistants and to gather the equipment, supplies, and transportation that would be necessary for action in the field. For the time being, he also decided to finance the project from his own resources.[17]

Many of the photographers and artists began their assignments by accompanying regiments to Washington. Life aboard troop ships was not always as relaxed and easy as they portrayed it, nor were boxcars and flatcars the most comfortable of conveyances for the troops moving south by rail, but there was no questioning the men's exuberance and confidence.[18]

On April 19 one regiment moving south to Washington marched into Civil War immortality. The Sixth Massachusetts was changing trains in Baltimore, but as the men passed through the city they were stoned by an angry mob of southern sympathizers. In the resulting panic, some of the soldiers opened fire. Men of the mob seized muskets from the soldiers, and several minutes later four soldiers and nearly a dozen citizens were dead. Many others were wounded. The North had its first martyr-soldiers, and artists and photographers hurried to commemorate them. There were no artists with the Sixth when it fought its way through Baltimore, but several artists had sketched the regiment when it passed through New York. With these pictures as guides, the engravers translated the telegraphic reports into vigorous illustrations. *Harper's* sketch showed the crowd pelting the troops with a hailstorm of stones and brickbats from the streets and rooftops. The

32

Illustrated News featured the frantic hand-to-hand struggle between mob and soldiers.[19]

Frank Leslie best appreciated the news value of the Baltimore riot. He published several detailed sketches of the fight, and then assigned one of his artists to follow the bodies of the martyrs to their final burial place in Massachusetts. He also sent Francis H. Schell and C. S. Hall to portray the Federal occupation of the turbulent city. Hall produced a series of pictures illustrating Baltimore's continued Confederate sympathies, including several pictures of a cache of weapons found in the marshal's office, and a delightful sketch showing the impertinence with which feminine Confederates flirted with Federal officers on the streets of the city.[20]

Most of the artists moved south without real incident. Alfred R. Waud, a handsome man in his early thirties, carried all the front-line hopes of the *Illustrated News*. Like his younger brother, William, Alf was born and trained in England and had come to the United States to work as an illustrator. Of all the sketch artists, he had perhaps the best combination of talents: a quick and imaginative hand, a huge capacity for work, and a lively personality and sense of diplomatic tact that gained him many friends within the army. He could write as well as he could draw. As he proceeded from New York to Washington, he complained jestingly to Leggett about the crowded railroad cars and the poor steamship service. But the only casualties he suffered were the loss of three nights' sleep and a "miserable breakfast" at Annapolis.[21]

He made his headquarters at Willard's Hotel, a popular hostelry on Fourteenth Street that attracted nearly every important person in the capital. Generals anxious for field commands and businessmen hungry for government contracts squeezed their way to the tables and bars to share Willard's good food and liquor with congressmen and senators. Waud knew that here was the ideal place to pick up information and to make friends with people who might help him. He particularly wanted an interview with one of Willard's more famous patrons, General Winfield Scott. A veteran of the War of 1812 and the Mexican War, Scott was crippled with gout and dropsy at seventy-five, but there was still a stiff and determined pride in his huge frame. For a moment, he was the hero of the day. Picturemen sold thousands of copies of his portrait, and cartoonists delighted in portraying him as a bulldog who defied the Confederates to trespass on his property. Scott reluctantly agreed to let Waud sketch him signing orders in his office, but he told him he would "as lief be taken out and shot at ten paces, as be sketched." Waud wrote Leggett: "I had the honor of shaking hands with him, and can safely say that his lion eye is still as imposing as ever." His portrait added to the impression.[22]

From May to July Waud was often in the company of Mathew Brady. They were interested in the same subjects, and Brady often supplied Waud with portraits of generals and politicians for publication in the *News*. They worked well together, Ward making a quick outline sketch in about the same time it took Brady to prepare his plates, make the exposure, and then wash and develop his picture. The results often bore a striking similarity.

Together they showed how the army trained the fifty thousand young recruits gathered about Washington. Their pictures of the camps showed rows of white tents formed in squares around well-patrolled drill fields where fully uniformed and equipped soldiers marched in perfect formations. They recorded how the volunteers learned to maneuver in formation, load and fire their muskets and heavy artillery pieces, and make a straight-line bayonet charge. Other pictures showed soldiers stringing telegraph wires, digging entrenchments for the protection of the capital, and driving beef on the hoof into Washington. They often crossed the Long Bridge from Washington to Virginia to sketch the countryside or the scene of a patrol skirmish, and they portrayed pickets stationed along the roads and railroad tracks leading into the capital with little more to do than to examine the passes of Virginia farmers bringing their crops to market. Back in the camps they showed how the men worshipped at outdoor chapels they had built and decorated themselves. Brady also made dozens of portraits of soldiers at ease, reading newspapers, washing clothes, or sitting on a box writing letters. If they idealized camp life it was more a matter of omission than of intentional misrepresentation. Brady and Waud and the other artists recorded scenes which they thought best explained the training of the volunteers, and if they neglected to record the overcrowded barns which sometimes had to serve for temporary shelter or the breakdown of an antiquated supply system that resulted in a lack of food for a day or two, they considered these incidents exceptions to the generally efficient routine.[23]

Inevitably some regiments received more attention than others. The New York City regiments never lacked good picture publicity. Most of the sketch artists thought the cavalry was more glamorous than the infantry, and they paid little attention to the ponderous artillery. But Brady more than compensated for their neglect by making hundreds of photographs of field batteries, cooks and teamsters, and the other essential non-combat units. Sometimes it also appeared as if the sketch artists portrayed the ordinary soldier only in direct proportion to the sartorial imagination of the regimental tailors. They were fascinated by the Zouaves. By the end of 1861 some readers of the illustrated weeklies possibly believed that the men in the baggy pants and the impractical fezzes had borne the entire brunt of the early skirmishing. Bare-chested Zouaves made gallant and sometimes foolhardy bayonet charges, but Billy Yank in drab regimental blue guarded railroads and dug trenches. Not until Winslow Homer sketched the Army of the Potomac in 1862 did the ordinary soldier find an artist who preferred him to the heroics of bedecked New York plug-uglies or the headline-snatching exploits of well-publicized officers.[24]

But in the summer of 1861 the public wanted heroics, and on May 24 they got another martyr. Elmer E. Ellsworth was a former student in Lincoln's law office who had raised a Zouave regiment among the New York City firemen and taken it south to Washington. On the 24th he led his men across the river to Alexandria, and seeing a Confederate flag flying over the local hotel, he dashed up the stairs to cut it down. As he came down with the flag, James W. Jackson, the hotel-keeper, emptied both barrels of a shotgun into his chest. Ellsworth died, and a President and a nation mourned.

The artists had contributed to Ellsworth's fame while he was alive, and they rushed to add their tributes after his death. Photographers and artists had pictured his Zouaves as they drilled and trained in New York, marched triumphantly down Broadway, swaggered through the streets of Washington, and then in early May endeared themselves to the city by putting out a fire that threatened Willard's Hotel. As a result, they were national heroes long before they crossed the Long Bridge to Virginia. Artists hurried to Alexandria to sketch the hotel, the flag, and the now-famous staircase.[25] With the help of eyewitnesses, they recreated the scene of Ellsworth's death. Printers issued stationery and envelopes with his portrait edged in black. Corporal Francis Brownell, who had avenged his colonel by killing Jackson, also became a hero. Artists asked him to replay his part and to pose for portraits. Everyone delighted in his terse account of the incident: "Col. Ellsworth was killed this morning. I shot his murderer dead." Leslie published a picture of Ellsworth's coat with a gaping hole in the front. Then for balance he also printed a sketch of several Zouaves comforting Mrs. Jackson as she wept over the body of her husband. National attention focused on Ellsworth's body as his Zouaves bore it to Washington for a funeral at the White House, and then on to New York for burial. Only then did the nation turn back to the war.[26]

The reaction to Ellsworth's murder reflected the traditional ideas about warfare. His death was a distinct shock to Northerners. Although their minds knew better, their hearts told them it was not right that young men like Ellsworth had to die, even if they died a martyr's death. They preferred to envision warfare in terms of handsome officers leading vigorous young men to the ultimate test of their strength and courage. Ellsworth was for them the perfect volunteer, strong and handsome and representing Young America anxious to serve the nation in the confidence that moral superiority and a righteous cause were the only essential ingredients for success in war. One New York diarist expressed these basic attitudes when he wrote: "Colonel Ellsworth was a valuable man, but he could hardly have done such service as his assassin has rendered the country. . . . His murder will stir the fire in every western state, and shows all Christendom with what kind of enemy we are contending."[27]

Consequently, northerners were ill prepared for the lessons of the next several months.

III

The Picnic War

The crusading fervor demanded vigorous action. Northerners hungered for revenge after the bombardment of Fort Sumter, and they enthusiastically supported the mobilization for war. Thousands of young men enlisted for a good fight. But from April to June they only marched and countermarched, stood on picket duty, perhaps skirmished on patrol—everything except carry the war into the South. They found it difficult to understand the inactivity. The common belief was that one great overwhelming victory would crumble the Confederacy and restore peace and unity to the nation. But only a few people comprehended the problems of mounting a major offensive against a resourceful and dedicated enemy. The ease with which Northerners adopted the rallying cry "Forward to Richmond" indicated they envisioned an easy advance, indeed even something of a picnic excursion.

Meanwhile, the picture industry prospered. Lithographers and engravers sold thousands of portraits and pictures of army camps, military installations, and ships of war. Stationers did a big business in envelopes engraved with cartoons or regimental insignia. Photographers pressed to meet the demand for portraits. The illustrated weeklies profited from a steady increase in circulation. Leslie's prewar circulation had been well over a hundred thousand each week, but in July he reported that despite the loss of the southern market, his circulation had increased by many thousands and his subscription list had doubled. A month earlier Fletcher Harper boasted a circulation of a hundred fifteen thousand for the *Weekly,* and figures for the *Illustrated News* approached the hundred thousand mark. For the picture industry, the war was a blessing.[1]

But at the front the sketch artists were restless. The routine of the camps seemed a poor substitute for the challenge of the battlefield. In their eagerness for action, the artists sometimes inflated the importance of insignificant incidents. Alf Waud sent Leggett an elaborate story about a Union soldier who tried to steal Waud's horse at pistol point and failed only when Waud kicked his horse into a run and dragged the soldier along the ground. He and the other artists spent many days scouting with the cavalry in the hope they would stumble into a real skirmish. But they were seldom fortunate enough to witness any of these unplanned clashes, and for their sketches they had to rely upon the accounts of the participants. The results were oftentimes big pictures of little skirmishes. On May 31, for instance, Lieutenant Tomkins and B Company of the U.S. Dragoons galloped through Fairfax Court House. "Fifteen hundred secession troops" fired on them from the streets and the windows of nearby buildings. Tomkins' spirited dragoons were mounted on angry snorting horses running in a flying gallop,[2] and they waved their sabers and fired their rifles at the same time, momentarily forgetting their reins. A few minutes later they had killed thirty Confederates and taken five prisoners. A "brilliant cavalry charge," concluded the readers of *Leslie's* and *Harper's Weekly* when they had seen the illustrations of this "dashing little affair."[3]

Pictures such as these only whetted the appetite. By June many people were demanding a more concerted movement against the enemy. Every report and picture indicated the army was ready. Brady recorded the self-assurance of the men who posed for him. Artists captured the enthusiasm of the volunteers as they trained, and their illustrations of corps reviews showed an army that was well equipped and well drilled. Generals Scott and McDowell, however, did not think the army was ready for a general advance. Consequently, the first major battles occurred on the flanks of the Eastern Front—along the coast and in the steep hill country of western Virginia. Frank Leslie had special artists at both places.

Frank Schell had become a familiar figure around Fortress Monroe on the James River. He was a short stocky man with a closely clipped beard, conspicuously attired in the loose white frock coat and slack-brimmed hat usually worn by art students. Leslie had first assigned him to Baltimore after the riots, and then moved him to Monroe. Schell was particularly interested in the Negroes who drifted into the army lines to work as contrabands digging entrenchments and doing other odd jobs for the army, and he had a good series of illustrations for Leslie portraying their early apprehensions and then their delight with their new freedom. But like Waud, Schell was also anxious to sketch the army in combat.[4]

On the night of June 9, Schell accompanied troops from Monroe as they boarded long river rafts, ferried across Hampton Creek, and moved inland against Confederate positions at Little and Great Bethel. The Federal plan called for two columns to surprise the enemy at Little Bethel with a daybreak attack. But owing to an "unfortunate mistake" in the darkness and the "utter incapacity" of several civilian appointees to high command, one of the columns fired on the other. Fully warned of the attack, the Confederates fought stubbornly at Little Bethel and then repulsed the Federal army at Great Bethel.

Schell quickly discovered that combat sketching presented problems he had not met previously. There was no place from which he could get a full view of the battle; if he moved away from the fighting, the terrain interfered with his view; but when he followed on the heels of the advancing troops, the dense smoke of battle obscured everything in sight. The best he could do was portray isolated incidents: an artillery battery during the futile assaults against Great Bethel and the charge of Duryea's Zouaves. He tried to show the ferocity of the fighting in the faces of the men, and he did not hesitate to show the extensive Federal casualties, but the full scope of the battle escaped his best efforts. Harper's artist was not as frank. He boasted that he had been in the thick of the fighting, that men were cut down at his side, but he did not show these things in his sketches. Both artists retreated with the army and saw men exhausted with fatigue and sunstroke fall off to the side and collapse. Everyone who returned to Fortress Monroe was disheartened.[5]

Nevertheless, the defeat did not undermine the popular faith in the volunteers. Nobody blamed the troops. Schell had illustrated their bravery under fire, and they were still untarnished heroes. The "miserably managed skirmish" was the responsibility of incompetent and inexperienced officers, according to Leslie, who suggested that the authorities in Washington apparently regarded a political partisan more qualified for command than an experienced officer. He appealed to General Scott to save lives by giving field commands to professional officers who would turn the politicians back into the ranks. Thomas Nast did a bitter cartoon for the *Illustrated News* showing a political brigadier general leading his men to slaughter, and other cartoonists adopted the same theme. Furthermore, proof that the volunteers could fight well came from General George B. McClellan's army in western Virginia.[6]

Henri Lovie was the senior veteran of Leslie's corps of artists. In his early thirties, tall and strong, with a dark handsome face, he was one of the most mature of all the sketch artists. He supported his mother and father, a wife, and several children with a lithograph business in Cincinnati and by sketching for Leslie. There were several sketchers with more talent than Lovie, but none with as much skill or experience in the field. He knew what Leslie and the public wanted in their news pictures. Because he also knew that he could rely upon Leslie's engravers to finish and polish his rough field sketches, he seldom bothered to submit elaborately detailed illustrations, and consequently his sketches usually arrived in New York many days before those of his competitors. In February of 1861, Leslie assigned him to follow Lincoln from Springfield to Washington. After the inauguration, he joined McClellan's army.[7]

Lovie knew from previous experience that the sketch artist should make a full and complete view of a scene and then supplement it with close-up views. His sketches of the battle of Philippi at the beginning of McClellan's campaign showed how he worked. He avoided the melee of the battle and took a vantage point near a battery far up on a hillside. The sketch he made there was a large panoramic view of the battle and also of the rough and heavily-timbered west Virginia terrain. When the fighting was over he went down onto the field and made several sketches of the battle debris, and then he toured the Federal camp and interviewed and sketched the exhausted soldiers. Every movement had been planned ahead of time and demonstrated his mastery of his craft.[8]

Yet even a veteran artist had much to learn. Several days after Philippi, he was roaming the countryside when several Union sentries saw him in the distance, and mistaking him for a spy reconnoitering their camp, hailed him to stop. The next thing he knew a bullet whizzed by his head. He broke for cover, which only increased the suspicion of the sentries, and they sent a volley of musket balls after him. In desperation he finally identified himself. Back in camp he grumbled to a newspaper friend from Cincinnati that although he had no objection to running reasonable risks from the enemy, it would be damnably unpleasant to be killed by mistake.[9]

McClellan's campaign was a masterpiece of quick movement and sudden assaults. But at the beginning of the war the sketch artists seldom bothered to show the army on the march because they knew the public preferred battle illustrations. Lovie was no exception. A week after Philippi he illustrated a skirmish at Romney, and on July 8 he made a drawing of the fight at Laurel Hill. Still McClellan pushed his army ahead. Four days later, Lovie found himself entrapped in the midst of the battle of Rich Mountain. He made some quick sketch notes of the heavy hand-to-hand fighting near an overrun Confederate battery, and then quickly moved back to higher and safer ground to capture the whole scene as McClellan's men chased the enemy from the field. The following day he wandered out to a quiet sheltered site on the ridge of Rich Mountain and sketched the graves of the men killed in the battle. The fight at Corrick's Ford on the 13th brought McClellan's campaign to a successful end. A week later Lovie rode into Grafton, ragged and tired after a frenzied month in the field. "There should have been another artist here to sketch his appearance," his Cincinnati newspaper friend told the folks at home. "It was decidedly more comic than anything in *Vanity Fair*." Lovie was too exhausted to care.[10]

McClellan's victories dispelled the disillusionment of Great Bethel and restored confidence. Once again everyone was in "great spirits." Northerners now had a new hero; already the publishers were rushing to fill orders for McClellan portraits. Moreover, his success bolstered the clamor for a general advance against Richmond. Public attention had continued to focus on McDowell's army in front of Washington. Congressmen, editors, and armchair generals everywhere demanded that it get into the field. McClellan's campaign seemed to prove that with competent field commanders Federal troops were invincible. So "Forward to Richmond!" In early July Lincoln and Scott capitulated to the pressure. McDowell reluctantly started the army south.[11]

During the several days of the advance a holiday crowd bumped over the rough Virginia roads. Congressmen and senators bearing picnic baskets rode down from the capital with their wives and daughters. Their brightly-decorated carriages fought for space on the narrow roads with lurching army wagons. The volunteers in new uniforms and with full packs were confident and gay as they briskly marched along, joking and singing and waving to pretty girls in the carriages. By the second and third days, however, they began to wilt under the hot sun. Latecomers along the road to Manassas followed a trail of coats, canteens, packs, and other abandoned equipment.

By all accounts the most unusual vehicles on the road were two canvas-covered wagons aptly nicknamed "whatisit wagons." These carefully-designed portable darkrooms were Mathew Brady's answer to the problem of photographing the army in the field. Inside were shelves loaded with cameras, tripods, photographic plates, and bottles of chemicals. Ned Hause, one of Brady's darkroom assistants, drove one of the wagons, while on the lead wagon with Brady was Alf Waud. All of Waud's equipment, several pads of artist's paper and a fistful of pencils, was jammed into a large portfolio that jounced at his hip.[12]

By the evening of the first day's march, the army reached Fairfax Court House. While the troops cavorted in the streets and looted houses for souvenirs, and their officers struggled to restore discipline, Brady and Waud made pictures of quiet orderly scenes about the town. On the second evening the army entered Centreville. While the men bivouacked, Brady and Waud drove out to picture the abandoned Confederate earthworks just beyond the town.[13]

Yet Waud was merely keeping busy. He knew that Leggett probably would not publish illustrations of supply wagons and abandoned trenches if he could print battle illustrations instead. In those bonny days of the early summer of 1861, Leggett's readers envisioned war in terms of the shock of battle, the inspired leadership of mounted officers, and the heroic deeds of courageous volunteers. By July they were surfeited with pictures of camps and equipment. The public pressure that compelled McDowell to advance to Centreville also impelled Waud to produce pictures of a combat army. Competition also added to the pressure on Waud. Leslie's artist with the army was Arthur Lumley. Twenty-four years old, he was born in Dublin and came to the United States in the late Fifties. For several years he supported himself as a student at the National Academy of Design by doing illustrations for the weeklies. Leslie assigned him to the army around Washington, and like Waud he had spent the past several months in the camps and on the picket lines. He too was anxious to test his skill under fire.[14]

The Confederate army was entrenched some five miles outside of Centreville, astride the Warrenton turnpike just beyond Bull Run Creek. On July 18 McDowell sent advance units of the Federal army forward to reconnoiter.

Brady followed in one of the whatisit wagons, and witnessed a short but stiff fight at Blackburn's Ford. He nearly lost all his equipment in the hasty withdrawal, but the experience made him aware that during a battle the front lines were no place for a photographer; he would take his pictures when the fighting was over.[15]

As a result of the reconnaissance, McDowell saw hope of victory in a flank attack. Early on the 21st he ordered a diversionary attack down the Warrenton turnpike after sending the bulk of his army on a wide arc to attack the Confederate left flank. The halting march delayed the main attack until well into the morning, so that the element of surprise was lost. Nevertheless, the initiative of the early fighting lay with McDowell's troops. They fought better than many of their commanders had expected. There were no signs of hesitation, rather much enthusiasm when orders passed along the line to rush the enemy. They also fought well in repulsing some of the early Confederate counter-attacks. By early afternoon it appeared that victory was within their grasp. But Confederate reenforcements arrived to bolster the sagging Confederate lines. The tide of the battle changed. A general Confederate counter-assault broke the back of the Federal defenses, and the volunteers began to withdraw. Some of the teamsters and other superfluous spectators became frightened by enemy artillery fire, and they started a stampede that quickly spread to the retreating troops. By late afternoon, a mad mass of men that was once a Union army fled in panic for the protection of the entrenchments surrounding Washington.

Lumley and Waud were frantically busy. Lumley's large panoramic illustrations showed the Federal army in the flush of victory. One sketch made early in the day portrayed soldiers, artillery, wagons, and cavalry pushing forward into battle. All were in proper formation. On a slight elevation to one side, other troops waited in reserve, and several officers and a few civilian spectators watched from a safe distance. Later in the day he made another sketch of several waves of Union soldiers in the hard run of the bayonet charge, every regiment in formation except where Confederate artillery fire had blown holes in their lines. Other troops waited for orders to advance, a battery fired in support of the attack, and in the immediate foreground he showed the remnants of earlier fighting in the dead horses, shattered wagons, and wounded men calling for help. His one close-up sketch of the bayonet charge of the New York City Fire Zouaves was a masterpiece of heroic war art. On

43

their faces he portrayed the gamut of emotions, anguish and pain from searing wounds, hatred for the enemy, and exaltation in the moment of victory.[16]

Waud also portrayed the volunteers on the offensive. He made several rapid sketches of Union batteries bombarding the enemy prior to the forward rush of the infantry. His large battle sketches showed how the men fought from behind whatever cover they could find to protect themselves from the withering fire of the enemy. Shells exploded in the air, musket balls clipped tree branches and buried themselves in soft bark, and a heavy acrid battle smoke hung over the field. On every side he recorded the heroism of the volunteers, the courage of officers who exposed themselves to the bullets of the enemy as an example for their troops, and the men of the New York Irish regiment who fought with muskets and bayonets against Confederate cavalry. Victory seemed imminent in each of his sketches.[17]

Brady avoided the melee of the battle and in one of his whatisit wagons roamed behind the lines making pictures as the opportunities allowed. He made one superb picture of several Confederate soldiers lying dead in a clearing in the woods, their bodies and the trampled grass a quiet reminder of the battle that had passed by. When in the late afternoon the retreat of the Federal troops became a rout, he was again in danger of losing his equipment. But despite the rush of the fleeing mob, he managed to save the whatisits from being trampled and also made several pictures of the panic.[18]

During the retreat from Bull Run, Waud tried without success to rally some of the volunteers. His sketch, however, included no signs of panic, and portrayed an orderly withdrawal, showing mounted officers directing the fire of a line of infantrymen who had taken shelter behind a rail fence to cover the retreat of other regiments. Lumley, on the other hand, did not ignore the breakdown of morale and discipline. In one of the most vivid pictures yet to come out of the war, he portrayed all the signs of hysteria in the rush of panic-stricken troops. Officers fled with their men. A white-suited civilian, maybe a Congressman who had come down to watch the picnic battle, stumbled to the rear. Frightened and confused men milled about without organization or leadership. In every direction the field was littered with broken wagons and artillery, packs and muskets, and the abandoned trampled bodies of wounded and dead comrades.[19]

A violent Virginia thunderstorm relieved the withdrawing Federal army from the pressure of pursuit, but the stormy darkness only added to the confusion. Many officers tried unsuccessfully to bring some order to the melee. Regiments were hopelessly scattered, and in many instances soldiers lost all contact with their comrades. Teamsters and civilian spectators abandoned their wagons and carriages along the few roads leading back to Washington, thus making the retreat even more difficult. Waud followed the army back to Centreville and fell to the ground to get some sleep. Early the next morning, two newspaper friends warned him that the army had evacuated the town while he slept, and he continued on to Washington. Brady got lost in the surrounding woods, spent a wet night in one of the wagons, but sometime the next day he stumbled back into Washington, exhausted and discouraged but still in possession of his precious pictures. When he showed them several days later at his Washington studio, critics of the campaign pointed to them as indisputable proof of the panic and terror that had gripped the raw army.[20]

Reaction to the defeat was immediate and vehement. "Total defeat and national disaster on the largest scale," one man wailed. Harper, Leslie, and Leggett demanded an unqualified prosecution of the war. Harper called for an aggressive suppression of the rebellion without regard to cost. He urged Scott to shoot every deserter, hang every spy, degrade all insubordinate officers, and replace every political brigadier with a professional expert. Bull Run demonstrated that peace was impossible without a definite conquest by one side or the other; the "sword *must* decide this radical quarrel." Leslie thought the attack at Bull's Run was "a tremendous error," but that the public pressure for an active campaign had been justified. The slogan "Forward to Richmond," he said, "did not mean forward and fail . . . it did not prompt a battle unprepared, without plan or foresight; but it did suggest the utmost activity, the most rapid concentration of all the available forces, to the end that the rebels should be crushed. . . ." "The call remains," he concluded, " 'Forward to Richmond'—and this time—go there."[21]

Artists and reporters agreed that responsibility for the defeat lay with the politicians and generals, and not with the troops. Waud's and Lumley's pictures showed that the volunteers had fought well; the implication was that with better officers they would have won the battle. The retreat became a rout, they thought, because of lack of training and the complete breakdown of the command system.

Another explanation of the panic was that the Confederate troops had attacked the retreating Yankees with ferocious savagery. In the anguish of the casualty lists it was also easy to believe that the enemy had committed atrocities. Excited citizens repeated stories of how the cowardly southern "felons" had with "artistic fertility" murdered the wounded Union soldiers they found on the field. Harper's artists in New York prepared a picture, supposedly based upon the reports of a number of reliable witnesses, showing the fiendish enemy plunging their bayonets into helplessly-wounded men. A cartoon in the same issue of the *Weekly* showed Confederates shelling a field hospital; the accompanying caption was taken from a southern newspaper: "Our artillery are improving rapidly in their firing; they practice constantly at targets." Leggett also published a picture showing the enemy bayoneting wounded soldiers. But the following week he admitted that he had been deceived by "sensation mongers" of the daily press. Waud provided part of the proof when he sent Leggett a sketch of the field hospital at Sudbury Church, which was reported to have been burned to the ground by the Confederates. His sketch and accompanying letter explained that the church had not even been damaged by the fighting, much less burned, and that the enemy had not "roasted" the wounded inside, but on the contrary had treated them "with the humanity becoming a Christian people."[22]

Leslie was equivocal in his handling of atrocity stories. In an editorial he referred to "the wanton and fearful atrocities [that] are too shocking and revolting to place before our readers," but his only illustration on the subject merely showed a solitary Confederate shell exploding in the air over the heads of several wounded Union soldiers. When in early October, the Confederate government released some of the Bull Run prisoners at Fortress Monroe, he and Leggett had artists present on the docks. Their sketches showed the wounded and crippled prisoners cramped into the hold of the ship. Amputees rested on the deck or supported themselves pitifully on crutches. Others sick with disease or with serious head wounds lay quietly until doctors could attend to them. In an angry editorial accompanying the sketches, Leslie was indignant at the Confederate treatment of the prisoners and at a war that "sent back its legless and armless men . . . to become the ornaments of society." He renewed his demand for unrelenting warfare against this barbarous enemy.[23]

Bull Run destroyed many of the romantic images of war. Neither the artists nor the public was prepared for such a disaster. Waud and Lumley were the first of the artists to realize that the traditional images were useless as an indication of what actually occurred in battle. In the swamps and underbrush along Bull Run they saw for the first time that mounted officers did not win battles alone, that Billy Yanks fought fully as heroically as the Zouaves—also that Johnny Reb could fight hard too—and that the cost of war was always measured in the faces of the wounded and in the blood and flesh of the dead. It would take more battles and more defeats to bring that realization home to Schell and Lovie and the other sketch artists. But once they had discarded the old images, they would be free to create new ones.

Nevertheless, confidence in ultimate victory remained high. The volunteers were still heroes. Pictures from Bull Run proved they had fought exceptionally well. George Templeton Strong, a prominent New Yorker, reaffirmed his faith on the day after Bull Run: "If the North be not cast down and discouraged by this reverse, we shall flog these scoundrels and traitors all the more bitterly for it before we are done with them."[24] Thousands of other northerners came to the same conclusion. They now knew the volunteers needed more training. Because of the ferocious nature of the enemy, the army and the nation would also have to toughen their attitude. The war would undoubtedly be more costly in life and material than anyone had predicted; every loyal Unionist would have to make some sacrifices. But the most necessary reform was an essentially simple one: bring to the command of the army a general who had proved his ability to lead the volunteers to victory. Nearly everybody had the same man in mind. His popular nickname "Little Napoleon" indicated their great faith in his leadership.[25]

Perhaps the sobriquet also betrayed the lingering strength of the old images.

IV

McClellan in Command

George B. McClellan assumed command of the Division of the Potomac within a week after Bull Run, and immediately he began to stamp his personality upon the army. His first task was to insure the safety of the capital. The soldiers who huddled about Washington after Bull Run were "undisciplined, ill-officered and uninstructed . . . demoralized and ready to run at the first shot." He strengthened the fortifications around the city, established strict discipline among the troops, and reassigned them for more training to the camps, where they were joined by fresh recruits who had enlisted for three years rather than three months. For more than six months they drilled and studied the rudiments of soldiering. His second task was the organization of a professional command system that ultimately concentrated all military power in his own hands. Wherever possible he replaced political appointees with officers from the regular army. He expanded the staff organizations, particularly his own, the Engineer, Signal and Medical Corps, and the Commissary and Ordnance Departments. On November 1 he forced the retirement of General Scott and accepted the over-all command of the Union armies. Only by the spring of 1862 did he believe his men were ready to take the field against the enemy. By that time, he commanded an army nearly four times as large as the one he inherited in July, and he had imparted to it a large measure of his own superb self-confidence.[1]

Nobody thought more highly of McClellan's capacity for command than McClellan himself. Second in his class at West Point, he had served in the Mexican War and with the Engineers, toured the Crimean War as an observer, and then resigned to become a railroad executive. By June of 1861 he was back in the army as a Major General in command of the Department of the Ohio when he undertook his successful campaign in western Virginia. His rapid rise to supreme command—he was only thirty-four in 1861—

suggested an obvious comparison with another young general. To many Northerners he was America's Napoleon.[2]

Both McClellan and the picturemen relished the comparison. Like the Corsican, McClellan compensated for his small stature by assuming a number of striking postures when he appeared in public. Posing for a Brady portrait early in the war, he carefully brushed his heavy forelock over his brow and inserted his right hand in the front of his tunic. On another occasion, he stood with his arms crossed, glaring belligerently into the camera. Lithographed copies of these portraits filled the shop windows. *Harper's Weekly* and the *Illustrated News* published large equestrian portraits of McClellan astride Dan Webster (what better name for the charger of the Union general-in-chief?) and encouraged their readers to clip and pin them on their parlor walls. Stationers sold thousands of envelope packages and *cartes de visite* with his portrait. The vogue reached down even to the children. Several Currier and Ives prints portrayed youngsters dressed in uniforms and pretending to be "Little Mac."[3]

As the training progressed, Arthur Lumley and Alf Waud resumed a familiar routine in the camps. Occasionally there were grand reviews of the Army of the Potomac for the edification of Lincoln and other government leaders, but ordinarily each day followed the ordered pattern of the previous day. Waud shared a tent with a colonel, sleeping on a hospital stretcher with a valise for a pillow. Each morning he arose, slipped into his working clothes —dark-colored shirt, coat, and trousers, knee-high jack boots, and a broad-brimmed black hat—shaved in a mirror nailed to a pine tree back of the tent, and then sat down to a breakfast of beefsteak and potatoes, bread, poached eggs, pancakes, and coffee. He planned his day's sketching while smoking his after-breakfast cigar.[4]

Both he and Lumley felt they had done enough sketches of army training, and consequently they looked for subjects with a human-interest value for the folks at home—a sharpshooting contest, the return of a foraging party, or a number of soldiers touring Mount Vernon while on furlough. With the approach of winter they showed how the troops built winter quarters and celebrated the Christmas holidays. Waud thought that life on the picket line was the most picturesque of all the soldiers' duties, and he showed how the pickets skirmished through the brown cornfields in autumn and huddled inside their branch and bough huts when winter came. He sketched them taking baths in shallow pools of water and then warming themselves at a small fire, or smoking and playing cards as they roasted stolen pig on a spit. To vary the routine, he and Lumley sometimes joined scouting parties on quick rides behind the enemy lines. Late in December, Lumley sketched a skirmish at Dranesville, and on one occasion Waud escaped capture only by hiding behind a woodpile when two hundred Confederate cavalry thundered by.[5]

Yet these were poor substitutes for sketching major battles, particularly when artists with Fremont's army in Missouri and Burnside's army along the Carolina coast were submitting a regular supply of combat illustrations. By early 1862 Lumley and Waud were restless. Lumley made a series of sketches on the conditions in the women's section of the Washington jail, where minor offenders were confined in the same cells with professional criminals. But this unsuccessful attempt to start a little reform crusade was actually more a testimony to the lack of any real war activity along the Potomac front.[6]

Waud was particularly dissatisfied with his association with the *Illustrated News*. Leggett expected him to cover the entire front from Fortress Monroe to the Shenandoah Valley and all the scattered army camps in addition to sketching political and social events in Washington. On one occasion, Leggett even hinted that he should distribute copies of the *News* to the troops in the front lines. From Waud's viewpoint the work load was too heavy and the pay was scanty and unreliable. Moreover, he did not like the way Leggett's engravers copied his field sketches. Sometimes the illustrations in the *News* hardly resembled the sketches he had submitted. For all these reasons, he was ready for a change.[7]

Early in 1862 Fletcher Harper came to Waud's relief. At that time, Harper had only two artists east of the Appalachians—Angelo Wiser on the Carolina coast and Theodore Davis on roving assignments—and he had been looking for another artist to cover the Army of the Potomac. In February, he made one of the great coups of his career when Waud left Leggett and signed on with *Harper's Weekly*. Harper took full advantage of Waud's experience and contacts within the army, and kept him on the Potomac front. Waud was delighted with the change; he remained with the *Weekly* until his death some thirty years later.[8]

There were immediate repercussions at *Leslie's* and the *Illustrated News*. A few weeks later, Leggett filled Waud's place by hiring Lumley away from *Leslie's*. Temporarily at least, Frank Leslie was the loser. It was probably to be expected that as the publisher with the largest staff of artists, he would bear the brunt of raids such as these, and certainly before the war was over he was to lose several other artists to his competitors. Yet in 1862 his resources were so great that he could lose an artist like Lumley without permanent injury. He immediately transferred C. S. Hall to the Washington front, and the next month he sent a newcomer, Edwin Forbes, to serve as a second artist with McClellan's army. When in April McClellan launched his offensive, Leslie recalled Frank Schell from the stalemated North Carolina campaign to assist Hall and Forbes, and a month later they were joined by William Waud, who had just returned from sketching Farragut's capture of New Orleans. By the time McClellan threatened Richmond, Leslie had as many artists with the Army of the Potomac as both of his competitors.[9]

Mathew Brady was also busy. The success of his Bull Run photographs convinced him that his project of compiling a photographic history of the war was worth the financial gamble it entailed. Secretary of War Edwin Stanton had approved Brady's plan to send teams of photographers into every theater of the war, but with the definite understanding that Brady would bear the complete financial burden. Brady accepted because he believed the public would purchase enough stereoptic copies of his war pictures to cover all the costs of their production. During the winter he selected his field photographers from among the operators at his galleries, purchased cameras, tripods, plates and plate holders, chemicals and chemical tanks, and negative boxes for his fleet of whatsit wagons, and established supply bases in every sector of the war. He continued to manage the affairs of his two studios, supplied thousands of soldiers with their portraits, and also made several trips to the Potomac front for new army views. By April of 1862 he was ready to accompany McClellan's army to the Peninsula.[10]

McClellan's strategy was simple enough. Late in the winter of 1861–62 he transferred nearly a hundred thousand men to Fortress Monroe. From there he planned to advance up the peninsula between the James and York rivers, defeat the Army of Northern Virginia, and end the war by capturing Richmond. Early in April he sent his army toward Richmond. C. S. Hall rode with the troops, stopping to sketch the men waving their hats and cheering for McClellan as he galloped to the head of the column. Several days later, the army reached a line of Confederate fortifications based on Yorktown and stretching across the peninsula to the James River. But rather than assault the defense line, which was actually much weaker than he imagined, McClellan ordered the army into a siege. Transports brought in hundreds of long-range battery pieces, and the soldiers abandoned their muskets for shovels and dug gun emplacements. For nearly a month, the campaign stalled at Yorktown.[11]

The artists and photographers had ample time to see how McClellan's army functioned in the field. The spring rains had begun, and Brady took full advantage of the few bright days and the sunshine he needed to expose his plates. Everyone in the army, from McClellan and the corps generals to the lowest privates and teamsters, was willing to pose for group portraits. He photographed the river boats and wagons that supplied the combat troops. He showed how engineers and shovel-soldiers repaired and rebuilt bridges and planked the muddy roads around Yorktown by stripping the countryside of timber and laying the logs sideways across the roadbeds. But his pictures of hundreds of unused pieces of field artillery also testified to the idleness of a large part of the army, and his photographs of the clean white tents, hobbled cavalry horses, and white-gloved staff officers in the camps behind the lines portrayed a parade-ground formality that did not seem to have much to do with winning the war.[12]

Lumley had thrown off the torpor of winter on the day McClellan's army took to the field. At Yorktown he ranged up and down the lines sketching every aspect of the siege operations. In the camps he showed how the men relaxed after a day in the trenches and cooked their meals and bought newspapers and tobacco from army sutlers. Nothing escaped his attention. The only thing that discouraged him was the weather: "Nothing but rain, rain" to make sketching more difficult. He was particularly anxious to make the large panoramic illustrations so popular with the public. The main problem was to get the long view. Field glasses were an indispensable help. He also climbed trees and church steeples for a better view, and he often used the stations that the Signal Corps constructed atop high towers or perched precariously in tree tops. And when S. T. C. Lowe arrived at Yorktown, Lumley immediately cultivated his friendship.[13]

Lowe was the official aeronaut of the Army of the Potomac. From a small basket suspended below a gas-filled balloon, he informed the army about enemy positions and troop movements. Lumley made his first ascension with Lowe during the siege of Yorktown, and his sketch showing the swamps and heavily overgrown terrain surrounding Yorktown and the long jagged lines of Confederate and Union entrenchments fronted with rifle pits was one of the most unusual illustrations of the war. Several months later he made another aerial sketch from Lowe's balloon just four miles from Richmond. The evening was quiet in the basket of the "Constitution," and a thousand feet below, the Confederate army gathered around the flickering light of hundreds of small campfires, while on the near horizon the foundries and spires of Richmond were silhouetted against the dusk.[14]

On May 4 the Confederates abandoned Yorktown and fell back toward new defensive positions around Richmond. Rain and muddy roads continued to slow McClellan's advance. Lumley, Waud, and Hall made cruel sticky pictures of soldiers pushing gun carriages ensnared in the oozing earth of the Peninsula. By the end of the month, McClellan's army straddled the Chickahominy River north of Richmond. On May 30 General Joseph E. Johnston threw his Confederate army against McClellan's right flank at Fair Oaks. For Lumley and Waud, this was the first chance since Bull Run to sketch the Union army in battle. They rushed from one point to another behind the lines, filling their notebooks with hurried shorthand sketches of the furious Confederate charges into the tearing shot and shell of the Union artillery. Federal counter-attacks with bayonets finally blunted the edge of Johnston's assaults. Casualties on both sides were horrendous. Finally on the evening of June 1 the battle came to an end. Johnston's troops fell back into their trenches before Richmond. Nevertheless, they had halted McClellan's advance.[15]

Brady and Lumley spent several days making pictures on the field at Fair Oaks. Brady photographed the now-cold field batteries which had stemmed the Confederate advance, their crews standing aimlessly by as if uncertain what to do next after so many hours of unrelenting work. He also made several pictures on the slaughterfield where two frame houses stood like empty tombs in the midst of the carnage that had taken place around them. Lumley sketched soldiers evacuating wounded men from the field and quietly burying dead comrades in long, shallow, anonymous slit trenches.[16]

Neither army resumed the offensive for another month. Robert E. Lee assumed command after Johnston was wounded at Fair Oaks, and began to rebuild the badly-mauled Army of Northern Virginia. McClellan again settled his army down in stable positions while he methodically established his bases and brought forward more men and supplies. But near the end of June he abandoned the Chickahominy and swung his army around to the east and south of Richmond toward a new base on the James River. Brady and the artists investigated the new country and found a terrain covered with forests of scrub pine and white oak laced with a thick undergrowth of brush and deadwood. When the guns were silent it was awesome and fascinating. But even the best of the artists' drawings could not portray the rush of the swollen streams or hint at the dank odors and portentious stillness of White Oak Swamp with the stark clarity of Brady's photographs.[17]

It was over this terrain that Lee attacked McClellan in a series of battles from June 25 to July 1 known as the Seven Days. At Mechanicsville, Gaines' Mill, Savage's Station, White Oak Swamp, and Malvern Hill, Lee's army suffered unusually heavy casualties as the price of forcing McClellan to relinquish ground before Richmond. Frank Schell and William Waud were now on the scene for Leslie, but like Alf Waud and Lumley, they faced almost insurmountable problems. The heavy forest and undergrowth cover, particularly at White Oak Swamp, could not have been a worse hindrance to sketching. There were no stable battle lines; units from both armies were hopelessly entangled and oftentimes isolated for many hours from the rest of the army. Except at Malvern Hill, where McClellan finally halted Lee's rush, the sketch artists were unable to make any satisfactory illustrations of the fighting. Brady made only one striking photograph—a harshly-realistic picture of wounded and dying men lying on the ground outside a field hospital. He spent most of the Seven Days enmeshed in the disorganized retreat of the wagon trains, pushing his whatisit through the mud, catching a few hours' sleep in abandoned barns or on the seat of the wagon, witnessing none of the battles and hearing only the rumble of the fighting from a distance.[18]

At the end of the Seven Days exhaustion fell over the Peninsula. Lee had suffered heavy casualties. McClellan's army missed thousands in killed and wounded, and many more were too ill or tired for immediate service. Lincoln conferred with McClellan and decided to abandon the campaign. He also transferred the command of the Army of the Potomac to General John Pope, thus leaving McClellan without an active field command.

The campaign had also taken its toll among the artists. "Seven days almost without food or sleep, night and day being attacked by overwhelming masses of infuriated rebels, thundering at us from all sides" was too much for

Alf Waud. He had an attack of "billious remittent fever" brought on by "exposure to the damned climate in the cussed swamps." William Waud suffered from sunstroke in addition to an attack of the fever. Lumley was "worn out." Finishing a superhuman effort on the Peninsula, in which the number of his published sketches equaled that of all four of his competitors, he returned to New York to direct the engraving of the last of his sketches and to recuperate. Like the others, he was glad to see the last of the Peninsula.[19]

Their publishers were delighted with their sketches but disappointed with the inconclusive results of the campaign. Leslie shuddered when he thought that after eighteen months of fighting the army was again at Manassas, worrying once more about the safety of Washington, and considering "grand Napoleonic schemes" to crush the rebellion. Such the state, he wrote, to which "incompetence, treason and half-heartedness in camp and cabinet have reduced the nation." Leggett argued that "the monstrous incompetency and incapacity that have marked the leadership of our splendid army" justified Lincoln's removal of McClellan from active command. Only Harper defended McClellan. He suggested that it would be better for stay-at-home critics to withhold criticizing a general who had made a brilliant record even though he had not taken Richmond. His artists indicated that McClellan was still very popular in the army; one illustration showed a dozen tough veterans of the Peninsula singing "McClellan is our man." They were not ready to abandon their hero.[20]

Two months later Lincoln had little choice but to restore McClellan to active command. In the interval, Lee had shattered Pope's attacks at the second battle of Bull Run, and Stonewall Jackson had beaten another Union army at Cedar Mountain. On September 5, Lee crossed the Potomac and launched the long-anticipated Confederate invasion of the North. McClellan was the only available man who had the confidence of the army.

The men were delighted to be fighting under "Little Mac" once again. "Shouts, yells and cheers of appreciation rent the air" as he left Washington to join the army. Farmers in the Maryland countryside threatened by Lee's army were more confident when they learned that McClellan was in command. Edwin Forbes, the young sketch artist Leslie had sent to take Lumley's place, was at Frederick when McClellan rushed through, and in a quick sketch he pictured the delighted expressions of relief and joy. Despite the debacle of the Peninsula, the troops loved this proud little man with his contageous self-confidence. They were comfortable in the familiarity of his leadership. They felt that whatever they knew of soldiering had been learned under his command, and if ever the Army of the Potomac won a victory it would be because of the training he had given them. Perhaps this was the occasion.[21]

Most of the artists with the army had already served with McClellan. They came in from many different directions as McClellan gathered his forces. Brady was a thoroughly-familiar figure; his arrival at headquarters from Washington did not cause even the slightest stir. Frank Schell sketched cavalry skirmishes near South Mountain as Lee moved from Frederick towards Sharpsburg, where Alf Waud pictured the flight of the inhabitants. Theodore Davis, Harper's artist on roving assignments, rushed down from New York to portray the mobilization of troops at Harrisburg and the Confederate occupation of Hagerstown. Only Edwin Forbes was a newcomer to McClellan, but he had nearly as much front-line experience as any of the others. Since joining the army early in 1862 he had sketched most of Jackson's campaigns in the Shenandoah and also Pope's repulse at Second Bull Run. Like the others, he was eager to see how McClellan met Lee's challenge.[22]

On September 17 Lee attacked at Antietam Creek just a few miles north of Sharpsburg. During a day of the hardest fighting of the war, the artists had a superb opportunity to show their skill. From their viewpoint the battle was ideal. The open rolling terrain allowed them to see large areas of the battle in comparative safety without missing any of the significant details. The charges were as brave and gallant as any artist could hope for. Even the weather was clear and bright for Brady's camera. Scenes on the field after the battle were some of the most vivid the artists had yet produced. Years later Forbes still thought it was the most "picturesque" battle of the war.[23]

Forbes scanned the field through his binoculars from the heights well back of the lines, laying them down only to make hurried penciled notes. In the morning and early afternoon he sketched the charges of Hooker's and Sumner's corps, and toward the end of the day he was the only artist present to make a picture of the assault of Burnside's Corps as it funneled across the stone bridge over Antietam Creek and reformed on the other side. Alf Waud sketched many of the same scenes, but from a closer vantage point, and his finished illustrations were a triumph of detail in picturing the frenetic confusion of hand-to-hand fighting. Early in the day Brady made what was probably the only photograph of the war showing men actually under fire, a section of Sumner's Corps seen through a wall of smoke drifting back from a battery of artillery. As parts of the battlefield came under Federal control, he moved his cameras down onto the field. At a sunken road where D. H. Hill's Confederate brigades had repulsed several Federal charges, he photographed "a ghastly array of dead"; abandoned packs and clothing, empty cartridge cases, shattered muskets, and the bodies of Hill's veterans huddled behind the meager protection of a rail fence. Everywhere he worked that day he photographed the twisted and contorted remains of men lying in fields swept clean by the fury of the fighting. He entitled these pictures "The Dead of Antietam" when he exhibited them to the complacent and curious citizens who later flocked to his studio to see his most recent work.[24]

On the following day as Lee retreated back to Virginia, the artists joined Brady on the field to examine the frightful sights of destruction. After the slaughter of the previous day, they apparently did not care what effect their pictures would have on the sensibilities of their readers. After Antietam, they had witnessed enough fighting to be interested in more than the heroics of the combat hours. Frank Schell, for instance, was appalled by what he saw. He had been sketching for Leslie since the mobilization, but mainly in the backwaters of the war at Fortress Monroe and Great Bethel, on the North Carolina coast, and behind the lines on the Peninsula. His experience had trained him to look for the small and seemingly unimportant incidents that seldom made the headlines but which he sensed would remain etched in the memories of the veterans. On the day after Antietam he found what he was looking for as special squads of men began the grisly work of burying their dead. What particularly attracted his attention was the behavior of the Maryland farmers who brought their families to the battlefield. Many of them roamed about looking for cannon balls, guns, canteens, bayonets, swords, or any other relic to take home as a souvenir. He noticed that while some of them were genuinely appalled at what they saw, others seemed utterly indifferent and interested only in satisfying their gap-mouthed curiosity. Josiah Favill, a young officer in charge of one of the burial parties, compared the farmers to vultures hovering over corpses. Schell made several sketches of the battlefield tourists, and when Leslie saw them he caustically wrote that he hoped the farmers realized that "to these sacrificed men, on whom some of them gazed with such callous indifference, the safety of their lives and home-steads is owing."[25]

The significance of Schell's sketches at Antietam was that after a year of fighting such "callous indifference" still existed. This indicated that as yet many Northerners had not the slightest understanding of what war was really like, but still thought in terms of the heroic images of the picnic war before Bull Run. But Schell's sketches also indicated that at least the artists themselves had been learning. McClellan had taught them that the modern army was a huge complex organization of technicians and engineers as well as fighting men, indeed almost a society within itself. On the Peninsula they saw the influence of weather and terrain, and most of them knew from personal experience how illness affected the morale and strength of an army. They were still entranced with the combat army, but their pictures of other army units indicated they were also aware that the bayonet charge was only one scene in the story of any battle. Their picture reporting at Antietam was more mature than it had been six months earlier, and it indicated they had acquired a new and balanced set of values with which to instill new images in the public mind.

V

The Western War

At the same time that Waud, Lumley, Schell, Forbes, and the other artists with McClellan were illustrating the necessity of rigorous training and discipline, the valuable services of the Engineers and the other auxiliary branches, and the impact of weather and terrain, different artists with the Federal armies in the West were making their special contributions to the new war images. In the sixteen months between Fort Sumter and Antietam, the eastern artists had tested and then discarded the traditional concepts of the Heroic War. Artists with the western armies eventually had to abandon two legacies—the heroic images and also the conventional notions about the West.

Over the years the images describing the West had become thoroughly stereotyped. For the most part, they reflected the eagerness of eastern writers and artists to equate the West with the frontier. Many people envisioned an untouched scenic wonderland. American painters of the Hudson River School had suddenly discovered the magnificence of America's hinterland. George Catlin and Seth Eastman painted Indian life on the Great Plains, and John Banvard and Henry Lewis manufactured their panoramas of the Mississippi River. Currier and Ives and the other commerical lithographers portrayed the romance of the frontier with prints showing wagon trains going west, hunters shooting buffalo on the plains, rivermen rafting and steamboating on the Mississippi, and miners panning gold in California. According to the pictures, westerners were hardy men; they fought duels, wrestled bears, and waged a ceaseless struggle with the Indians. Moreover, western warfare was hard and savage. It involved sudden ambushes and forced marches over great wilderness distances. No quarter was asked and none was granted. Everyone knew Indians scalped their victims and slaughtered helpless women and children. Consequently, many northerners were only momentarily surprised when in the mid-Fifties they read reports of similar atrocities during the border wars in Missouri and Kansas. The frontier also produced its military heroes—Anthony Wayne at Fallen Timbers, William Henry Harrison at Tippecanoe, Andrew Jackson at Horseshoe Bend and New Orleans, Davy Crockett at the Alamo, and many others. Most of them were bold and audacious men; they came from humble origins, and had fought their way to the top often against unfavorable odds. Their exploits were part of the great legend of the West.[1]

With this legend in the background, the westerners started the Civil War with a period of heroic warfare under the leadership of Nathaniel Lyon and John C. Fremont. Both men aroused great expectations, but their campaigns ended in frustrating defeat and stalemate. Then in 1862 Ulysses Grant and William T. Sherman took command. In six months they had neutralized Missouri, pushed the Confederates out of most of Kentucky, and made a deep penetration into Tennessee. The great battle of Shiloh marked an early culmination to the western war, comparable in its impact to Antietam in the East.

At the beginning of the Civil War, the current hero in Missouri was Nathaniel Lyon. Soon after Fort Sumter, he forced the surrender of the Confederate militia in St. Louis and then enlisted his own corps of volunteers. In July he chased the enemy troops out of Jefferson City and pursued them as far as Springfield in the center of the state. Northerners were delighted; cartoonists immediately portrayed their hero as a lion who held the Confederate jackals at bay. But Lyon's position at Springfield was precarious; he was 120 miles from his nearest base of supplies, his men were exhausted after weeks of marching, and a reenforced Confederate army which outnumbered his own by more than two to one was approaching Springfield from the southwest. Nevertheless, Lyon foolishly decided to force the enemy into a pitched fight.[2]

On the night of August 9, Henri Lovie followed Lyon's army ten miles out of Springfield to Wilson's Creek. At the conclusion of McClellan's campaign in western Virginia, Lovie had recuperated with his family in Cincinnati, and then accepted another assignment from Leslie to sketch the war in Missouri. He had spent several weeks at Cairo, Illinois, sketching the myriad activities in the two near-by army camps and along the busy water front of the shabby little river town. But when he learned of Lyon's predicament at Springfield, he immediately left to join him. He must have had a sense of foreboding as he watched Lyon divide his small army and send part of his troops to strike the enemy from the rear. They failed, and the remainder of his army had to bear the full weight of the Confederate counter-attacks. Both sides took fearful casualties, but within an hour a third of Lyon's men were out of action. Lovie ranged back and forth behind the lines, making hurried sketches of scenes he glimpsed through the heavy smoke—shells exploding and maiming many men while others instinctively threw their arms across their faces, several soldiers evacuating a wounded companion by draping him over their muskets, and a cannon ball buried harmlessly in the trampled Missouri turf at the side of a dead warrior. Lyon desperately tried to salvage a victory, riding along his lines, waving his plumed hat, and calling for one more charge. His men rallied to follow, when a Confederate bullet struck him in the chest. The charge faltered, and when Lyon died a few minutes later, the battle was lost.[3]

Lyon's death made him a hero rather than just another defeated general. Americans had seen dozens of engravings showing valiant battlefield deaths, and perhaps Lyon had seen the same pictures and so died as Lovie portrayed the scene, lying in the arms of his aides, his eyes turned heavenward, still firmly grasping his sword and plumed hat. In either case, Lovie and the other artists who immortalized the death scene elevated Lyon into the company of Ellsworth and the martyrs of the Sixth Massachusetts.[4]

In the month following Lyon's death, Lovie was further exposed to the capricious nature of the Western Picnic War. He joined another expeditionary army in a futile and exhausting march through southeastern Missouri, and then he hurried back to sketch the occupation of Paducah, Kentucky. In neither case was there any contact with the enemy. Somewhat discouraged, he went home to Cincinnati. He came back to Missouri in a hurry when he learned that a Confederate force was besieging a small Federal garrison at Lexington on the Missouri River. By the time Lovie arrived, the garrison had surrendered and then secured release on parole. He was too shrewd, however, to admit failure. When he heard that Franc Wilkie of *The New York Times* had watched the entire siege from the Confederate camp, he persuaded him to make a sketch of the siege for *Leslie's*. Their joint effort was so successful that several soldiers who had been present later testified that it was "as correct as [could] be had on paper." Nevertheless, Lovie was disappointed, despite the knowledge that Harper's western artist had not accompanied a single one of these campaigns.[5]

Alexander Simplot was twenty-four in the summer of 1861, but his slender physique, bright eager expression, and naive attitude made him appear much younger. He had gone to school at Rock River Seminary, where he was a schoolmate of John Rawlings, Grant's Chief of Staff, and then at Union College in New York. After graduation he taught school. He became a sketch artist largely by accident. Ten days after Sumter he was on the wharfs at Dubuque to cheer the departure of a regiment of home-town boys. Everybody's eyes were "dimmed with mistiness and hearts throbbed with painful yet tender thoughts." Excited by the "thundering hurrahs of the crowd and the roar of artillery," he made a sketch of the scene and sent it to *Harper's Weekly*. A few weeks later he was in Cairo with a commission as the *Weekly's* special artist in the West. He repeated his Dubuque theme with variations, sending Harper dozens of routine illustrations of fortifications, gun emplacements, and steamboats. He traveled up and down the river, stopping at St. Louis and Cairo to make sketches, but never to join an expedition. He was in St. Louis when three steamboats embarked to reenforce the garrison at Lexington, but he merely sketched the departure. Harper nevertheless paid him from five to twenty-five dollars for the sketches he published, and Simplot unabashedly submitted the sketches Harper rejected to the *New York Illustrated News* under the pseudonym of A. S. Leclerc. Harper continually urged Simplot to get into the field with the armies. In early September Simplot promised to accompany the next important campaign, and a few days later he learned that General John C. Fremont was readying the western army for a blow against the enemy.[6]

Like most northerners, Simplot was impressed by Fremont's reputation—"Pathfinder of the West," senator from California, and in 1856 the Republican Party's first candidate for president. In May Lincoln gave Fremont the command of the Department of the West. Fremont arrived in St. Louis with a flourish, and soon he made known his grand plans for winning the war—and for restoring his own political fortunes. In August he issued a proclamation confiscating the slave property of every rebel in Missouri, a move that made him the darling of northern abolitionists but which proved highly embarrassing to Lincoln and his administration. That same month he announced an audacious plan to end the war. He would lead his army through

Missouri and Arkansas to the Mississippi River at Memphis and then on to New Orleans to sever the Confederacy and open the river for the Union. He blithely told his friends he would spend the winter in New Orleans and be back home the following summer.[7]

The gathering point for the army was Jefferson City. In mid-September Simplot joined Lovie and the other newspapermen who had assembled there to report the progress of the grand campaign. The army camped on the edge of town, and Simplot and Lovie made several sketches of the huge stores of supplies and equipment stacked in readiness for the march and the impressive semicircle of tents that marked Fremont's headquarters. Everywhere there was an air of optimism and anticipation.[8]

Simplot stayed at the Virginia Hotel, a ramshackle tavern and hostelry that served as a temporary officers' club. There he joined the fellowship of the Bohemian Brigade, a group of New York, Chicago, and Cincinnati newspaper reporters extended to include Lovie and Simplot, who personified the romantic illusions of the Heroic War. Henri Lovie, Franc Wilkie, and several of the other westerners in the Brigade undoubtedly had their reservations about how bohemian an environment the prairies of Missouri would provide, but Simplot was delighted with the company. Though he neither drank nor gambled, which meant that many times he was a spectator rather than a participant, he reveled in the free-for-all brawls in one of the second-floor bedrooms of the Virginia Hotel, the wild horse races in the gullies outside of town, and the pseudo-sophisticated discussions on metaphysics and poetry, art and opera, and women and the war. The former school teacher from Dubuque wanted very much to be a real Bohemian.[9]

Early in October, Fremont sent his army toward Springfield. Each day his troops marched across the prairies with the dignity and measured tread of a royal procession. Simplot and Lovie sketched the long infantry columns flanked on both sides by wagon trains and cavalry escorts and followed by a herd of beef cattle churning the dust of the dry grassland. At night the army quartered the Bohemians in one of the large tents in the headquarters semicircle. They ate their meals at the officers' mess. A Negro servant spread straw over the ground before they turned in for the night. The cacophony of sounds and colors at headquarters each evening resembled the camp of a medieval king. An army band serenaded the general. A bodyguard of Zouaves hovered in the background immediately behind Fremont's tent. His huge glittering staff of foreign officers with yellow-trimmed trousers, white leggings, and soft hussar hats tried to look busy. The whole scene reminded Franc Wilkie of a "brilliant flower garden."[10]

Simplot had several "novel and exciting" adventures on his own. Twice during a delay of several days at Warsaw he accompanied a secret detail of soldiers searching for contraband weapons. During the silent rides into the enemy country he was apprehensive of an ambush, but the touch of a holstered pistol at his hip and a saber brushing his thigh bolstered his courage. He particularly relished the secrecy to which he was sworn and the insistent questions of the other Bohemians when he returned from his nightly forays. Several days later he and Lovie joined Jim Lane's newly-arrived army. Lane was a veteran of the Kansas Wars, a man with wild dark hair, matted mustache, and stringy chin whiskers who looked like a border ruffian. Simplot did a portrait of Lane for Harper. He also saw Indians for the first time, and he was fascinated with Lane's scouts who wore incongruous white top hats decorated with feathers. They provided good material for a series of sketches. In further contrast to the formality at Fremont's headquarters, evenings with Lane's army were spent playing poker and drinking peach brandy in the general's tent. Simplot was the eager spectator.[11]

Henri Lovie on the other hand, was disgusted. At one of the poker sessions he remarked that he thought Fremont should have been given a colonelcy and a troop of cavalry, because an army command was too much for his limited capacity. He was frankly bored, and each quiet day without sight of the enemy convinced him that Fremont was leading the army on a false chase. He was not at all impressed with brass bands, bright uniforms, and special bodyguards. He sent Leslie sketches, but he was too experienced an artist to believe he was illustrating anything really significant. Franc Wilkie was also discouraged. He thought that Fremont's expedition was nothing more than a "gigantic picnic, whose main qualities were display, vanity, ostentation. . . ."[12]

In Washington, Lincoln decided that politically as well as militarily, Fremont was a liability to the government. His emancipation edict, which Lincoln had had to countermand, had embarrassed Lincoln's policy of appeasement toward the border states. There were also widespread charges of corruption concerning Fremont's handling of government contracts. Fremont's enemies in Washington demanded his scalp. In October Lincoln relieved him of command.[13]

Nevertheless, Fremont relinquished control of the western army only after he had won what he called a "glorious victory." On October 25 at Springfield, his advance cavalry skirmished with the rear guard of the Confederate army. The troopers huzzahed for Fremont and charged. Lovie and Simplot arrived too late to see the action, but they re-created it from second-hand accounts. Simplot showed the cavalrymen waving their sabers as they charged in five separate ranks. Lovie sketched the charge as one single line of cavalrymen who held their reins in one hand and braced and triggered their rifles with the other. A soldier with the army sent Leggett a sketch; he favored sabers. Fletcher Harper described the skirmish as a "brilliant victory," despite the fact that the main enemy army was sixty miles away. Frank Leslie, on the other hand, was not at all sympathetic. One of his cartoonists showed Fremont reaching for the presidency with his sword, while Lincoln commented: "Well, Master Fremont, that's rather a long reach, ain't it? You might fetch it with your sword, perhaps, in the proper time, but it isn't right yet."[14]

The Picnic War in the West was over. Simplot, however, did not know that, and still fresh from the "rigors" of the Fremont expedition, he was ready for more adventure. Lovie took a short furlough with his family. He wrote Leslie that his life was certainly not "one of elegant leisure. I have spent more than three months in the open air, sleeping in tents on bivouacs, and have ridden nearly 1,000 miles on horseback." But he added that he liked action, had no objection to a "spice of danger," and he was ready to take the field again. Recalling Fremont's strategy, he said he expected to be in Memphis by this time. Nevertheless he hoped the government would allow the western army to "sail in."[15]

During the winter of 1861–62 the nature of the western war changed radically. The armies shifted from the dusty prairies of Missouri to the muddy waters of the western rivers. For the moment at least, army wagons, artillery caissons, and cavalry regiments played a subordinate role to steamships and gunboats. It was a new kind of warfare for the westerners because it required an extensive use of naval power. But it also appealed to them because it called for commanders with a gambler's personality. The stakes were high; control of the rivers meant dominance of their hinterlands and direct access to the heart of the western Confederacy.

Artists and photographers soon acquainted the public with all the ships and ordnance of the river squadrons. The sternwheelers that plied the Mississippi and the Ohio had always been a favorite subject for the print-makers; now they became troop transports and hospital ships. Not so familiar were the gunboats and mortar boats, the floating artillery designed to reduce Confederate forts along the rivers and to serve in support of the armies. Simplot spent some time in the St. Louis shipyards following his return from Springfield, preparing a series of illustrations for Harper. He showed carpenters building the wooden hulls of the gunboats prior to mounting the heavy armor plate. When completed, they looked like slant-sided blockhouses with a smokestack and ports for the guns. The mortar boats were huge rafts supporting a six-sided enclosure for the mortar gun and its crew, or as Simplot explained to Harper, they could also be used as troop carriers. They were ugly ducklings, to be sure, but as Simplot and Lovie were to show, they made fully as great a contribution to the winning of the war as the more graceful full-rigged ships of the ocean fleets.[16]

The western naval war opened with a combined land-river assault against the Confederate strongholds on the Tennessee and Cumberland rivers. By February 5, Ulysses Grant and Andrew Foote, the flag officer in command of the Mississippi squadron, had transported nearly fifteen thousand troops up the Tennessee to a point several miles from Fort Henry. Lovie and Simplot made the trip with Grant and his staff aboard the *New Uncle Sam,* a large New Orleans steamer "affording all the accommodations of a hotel": comfortable sleeping quarters, meals with the general, and when Foote's gunboat batteries began the bombardment of Fort Henry on the morning of the 6th, a leisurely stroll to the hurricane deck to view the action. The only disadvantage was that the heavy smoke from the guns hung like a shroud over the river and obscured their view.[17]

The small garrison inside Henry made only a token resistance and then surrendered. Lovie and Simplot inspected the fort and the prisoners—among whom Simplot found two schoolmates from Dubuque who had enlisted in the Confederate army. Lovie gathered information for several sketches showing how the bombardment might have appeared to the defenders of the fort. In one illustration he showed a large mounted battery taking a direct hit from one of the gunboats, the gun shattered, most of the crew killed, but a few survivors rushing for cover. The startling feature of this sketch was Lovie's detailed portrayal of dismembered Confederate dead. Previously artists had avoided this subject, but in the foreground of his illustration Lovie showed one Confederate minus his lower arm and another with his head and both arms blown off. Frank Leslie published Lovie's sketch as a double-page illustration, and in the following months he exposed his subscribers to several more similar pictures. His readers were getting their first introduction to the real horrors of war.[18]

Encouraged by his easy victory, Grant marched most of his army from Fort Henry to Fort Donelson on the Cumberland River and sent the remainder around on the transports with the gunboats. By the evening of the 14th, Grant had encircled Donelson, and Foote's flotilla opened a bombardment. But the shelling from the fort's batteries crippled the gunboats and forced them back down river. Grant realized that the navy could not force a sur-render as at Henry, and he reluctantly settled his army down for a siege. On the morning of the 15th, the large Confederate garrison sallied out of the fort and struck the right wing of Grant's army, rolling it back on the center. There the westerners held their positions, closed the gap, and then launched an assault of their own against the Confederate breastworks on the Federal left. The following day they overwhelmed the fort.[19]

The westerners had won the first great northern victory of the war, but both of their artists had missed most of the fighting. Simplot did not leave Fort Henry until the morning of the 15th, and although he heard the heavy rumbling of the artillery throughout the day, it was late afternoon before he reached the army. He sketched Grant's headquarters and a field hospital well behind the lines, but rather than walk another mile to the area of the fighting, he found a nearby farmhouse, had his dinner, and went to sleep. The next morning, he sketched the interior of Fort Donelson, and then boarded the *New Uncle Sam* to join Grant's staff in a victory celebration. But as he listened to the story of the previous day's battle, he suddenly became aware of the full extent of his own failure.[20]

Lovie had relied upon a repetition of the Fort Henry bombardment and surrender, and had stayed with the river squadron. The retreat of Foote's flotilla took him so far down river from Donelson that he missed the heavy fighting on the following day. He got back to Donelson on the morning of the 16th and made one magnificent sketch showing several thousand men disembarking from their transports and marching into the fort, and another of the prisoners "looking more like a mob gathering than warriors," their "guilty . . . stupid" faces and wretched equipment comparing poorly with the proud bearing of the Federal soldiers who guarded them. But Lovie knew these pictures were poor substitutes for sketches of the battle.[21]

Both artists turned to the reporters who had been with the army on the 15th and tapped them for information they could use in their sketches. They inspected the places where the heaviest fighting had occurred and filled their notebooks with quick sketches. Simplot prepared one illustration of the gunboat bombardment of the 14th, though he had been at Fort Henry that day, and another of a hand-to-hand fight on the 15th. Harper published them without question. Lovie was appalled to find the charred remains of three Union soldiers who had fallen wounded and helpless to the ground and then burned to death in a brush fire. He re-created the scene, showing the three men watching in horror as the flames crept toward them. From his collaborator at Lexington, Franc Wilkie, he got a description of the Federal assault on the 15th for a sketch which was so complete and accurate that the soldiers who made the assault were sure he had been with them. "The western army has gained a place in history," he wrote Leslie, adding, "I hope that you will find room for all the sketches that I have sent, as they illustrate the principal events with great truthfulness." Leslie was convinced. He printed Lovie's sketches and praised him as "one of the most accurate and faithful artists in the country."[22]

The capture of Henry and Donelson forced the Confederates to withdraw down the Mississippi to their stronghold at Island No. 10 opposite the Kentucky-Tennessee line. In March Foote's river squadron began a siege of the island. No artist ever portrayed a campaign with such ease. The river was straight and unobstructed for several miles upstream from the island where the fleet of troop transports anchored and waited. Simplot and Lovie were delighted to find they could watch the reduction of the island in comfort from the rear cabin of their steamer. Mortar boats hugged the shores and gunboats maneuvered in midstream as they bombarded the enemy defenses. Shells spiraled in a long arc until they struck the island with a dull thud or exploded in the air in tight little puffs of smoke. At night the scene was like a Fourth of July celebration, the sparks from the fuses of the shells tracing a fiery course through the sky. For variety, they sketched the bombardment at close range from the gunboats, and on several occasions they ran past the island and pictured the scene from downriver. Yet by the end of the month Lovie felt he had illustrated the siege from every possible vantage point, and late in March he abandoned Island No. 10 and rejoined Grant's army on the Tennessee. Simplot remained until the surrender, and he sketched the landing of the Federal troops and the battered remnants of the Confederate defenses. He was convinced he had been wise to stay for the moment of victory.[23]

Also in March, another of Leslie's artists sent him a dramatic series of pictures from the lower Mississippi. William Waud had been inactive since illustrating Fort Sumter, but in the spring of 1862 he sent Leslie several sketches from Florida before joining Admiral David Farragut's naval expedition against New Orelans. Farragut planned to run his ships past Forts Jackson and St. Philip south of New Orleans, engage and destroy the Confederate river squadron, and with the capture of New Orleans deprive the Confederacy of its greatest port. The three-day battle began on April 23. Farragut's sailors tried to camouflage their ships by tying tree boughs to the masts, and although the trick fooled nobody, it did provide Waud with a good sketch. That evening the enemy sent fire rafts downstream with the current to try to set the fleet ablaze. In a brilliant night scene, Waud sketched Farragut's men pushing the burning rafts away with long poles and dousing the flames with fire hoses. On the following day he climbed the mainmast of the *U.S.S. Mississippi* and drew a superb series of illustrations of the fleet as it ran past Forts Jackson and St. Philip. He portrayed the desperate shelling from the batteries in the forts, especially picturesque as evening brought darkness for a backdrop to the sparkling shells. Still in his vantage point, he sketched the attack of the Confederate monitors and rams and their repulse and annihilation by Farragut's gunners. The next day Farragut anchored at New Orleans. From the deck of the *Mississippi,* Waud made one sketch of the water front in flames and another of a Federal truce team rowing ashore to demand the surrender of the city from a crowd of angry citizens.[24]

Leslie featured Waud's New Orleans illustrations in several supplements to his regular editions. But even they were overshadowed by a series of sketches from another of his artists. While Waud awaited the gathering of the fleet at the mouth of the Mississippi, and Simplot sketched the surrender of Island No. 10, Henri Lovie was with Grant's army at the battle of Shiloh.

Someone once said that the South never smiled after Shiloh; he could have added that neither was there much joy in the North. On the morning of April 6, 80,000 young men began a brutal indoctrination to war, and by the evening of the 7th, 20,000 of them were wounded or dead. Yet on April 5, nobody really suspected that the quiet fields and orchards around Shiloh Church and Pittsburg Landing would be the scene of a battle of such huge proportions. General Albert Sidney Johnston with 40,000 Confederates planned to strike the northern army encamped near the landing, but he was hoping for a surprise attack and a quick victory. Several days earlier he had ordered his army forward. Despite the cracking of musket fire as the recruits tested their weapons for the first time, the westerners were unaware of their danger. They were disembarking from troop transports and bivouacking on the bluffs over the river, more concerned with hardtack and stale coffee than with the enemy. William T. Sherman had not ordered the 40,000 men already at the landing to dig entrenchments. At his headquarters six miles downriver, Ulysses Grant awaited the arrival of Don Carlos Buell and an additional 20,000 men from the Army of the Ohio. Everything seemed quiet and routine. Double-decked river steamers pulled up to the landings and unloaded troops and supplies. Two lonely gunboats patrolled aimlessly in midstream.

Shortly after dawn on the morning of April 6, the forward units of Johnston's army cracked through the Federal picket lines and overran the outlying camps. Some regiments from the Missouri campaigning held firm for several hours and momentarily halted the Confederate onrush. During those precious hours, thousands of young men who had never before been in a battle became veterans, learning the business of war under the worst possible conditions. On every side, they saw their companions slaughtered by enemy musket balls and grape shot. Some fled in terror, but many more rallied and stayed to fight.[25]

Lovie was with Grant as he rushed up to Pittsburg Landing to organize the defense. As he disembarked he saw a scene of indescribable chaos. Hundreds of frightened men had fled from the field and climbed down the steep bluffs to the landing, and there they huddled in silent and sullen groups, ignoring orders to return to their regiments. Some of them tried to get aboard the steamers, but officers with drawn revolvers blocked their way and threatened to shoot them. Climbing the single road that led to the top of the bluffs, Lovie saw even greater confusion. Stragglers, deserters, and wounded men surged toward the river, blocking the way of the reenforcements moving to the front. Ambulances, ammunition wagons, and field artillery jammed the road. As he pushed forward he saw dozens of independent battles raging at one and the same time, the armies hopelessly mixed together without any apparent plan or method. He realized it would be impossible to illustrate the entire battle, yet he began sketching at once to record specific incidents that caught his attention. One sketch showed part of the battle in the background, but primarily it portrayed the men of the Ambulance Corps tenderly lifting wounded soldiers into wagons and driving them to the rear. To show the destructive power of the artillery, he sketched the trees where the grape shot tore sore gashes in the soft bark and cracked the dry winter branches and hurled them to the ground.[26]

By late afternoon, Grant's army was perilously close to the bluffs. But he had brought up his artillery and it poured a heavy fire into the enemy. The westerners held on for the rest of the day, and during the night they reorganized. That evening Lovie sketched the two gunboats that continued to shell the Confederate army throughout the night. By the following morning, Grant had brought forward 5,000 men from downriver and Buell had finally arrived with 20,000 fresh troops.

The next day the initiative was in the hands of the westerners. Reenforced by twenty-five thousand men, they began to regain lost ground. Johnston's men were tired and had suffered unusually heavy casualties, but they fought stubbornly until mid-afternoon. Lovie sketched the turmoil of the final victorious charge of the westerners, the soldiers firing, reloading, and firing again as they forced the enemy back. "The scene was a fearful one," he told Leslie, "our artillerists worked with the utmost rapidity, branches torn by the enemy's shots, who fortunately fired too high, flying in every direction; shot and shell rushing through the timber, while the road close by was covered with an inextricable confusion of wagons, ambulances, wounded, stragglers, mules, and horses, struggling to gain the transports on the river." The enemy pulled back, formed into columns and retreated toward Corinth. The northern army was too badly mauled to give pursuit. The battle was over.[27]

Lovie continued to gather information and impressions. He tramped over the battlefield again, getting soldiers to show him places where the fighting had been particularly intense. He visited most of the regiments and listened to accounts of the battle from anyone who cared to talk about it. Every significant detail went into his portfolio. When he was finished, he compared all his new information with the notes he had made during the battle, and then prepared nearly a dozen large drawings to rush off to New York.[28]

His picture report of Shiloh was outstanding. He was the only artist who illustrated the full two days of fighting. W. R. McComas and Henry Mosler, Leslie's and Harper's artists in Kentucky, arrived on the 7th with Buell's army, but neither made much of an effort to sketch the fighting. Simplot's pride in his Island No. 10 sketches was shattered when he heard the first reports of the battle; he left immediately for Shiloh, but he did not arrive there until a week later. Harper's New York artists prepared an illustration that was so fantastic in conception, showing six ranks of Federal soldiers in perfect marching order charging five perfect ranks of Confederate soldiers, as to be completely ridiculous to the men who had been there. Leslie celebrated Lovie's triumph with a sixteen-page supplement issue devoted exclusively to Lovie's drawings. They were superb examples of what was possible when an expert sketch artist worked with talented engravers. Lovie had drawn with vigor, filling each sketch with vivid detail, and the engravers had prepared the illustrations with magnificent skill. They proved that Lovie and Leslie formed the outstanding artist-publisher partnership of the war.[29]

Moreover, Lovie had sketched many of the scenes that were etched in the memories of the soldiers at Shiloh. His picture of the "mass of cowards" huddling under the bluffs reflected the anger of men who had not fled the field. William Bircher, a drummer boy with a Minnesota regiment, thought that only a great artist could portray the horrors of Shiloh: "I had frequently seen pictures of battle-fields and often read about them; but the most terrible scenes of carnage my boyish imagination ever figured fell far short of the dreadful reality." Yet Lovie's illustrations of casualties expressed the "perfect horror" most of the veterans felt when they saw the thousands of wounded and dead. The stench of death filled his sketch showing soldiers burning dead horses in acrid pungent pyres. Every soldier at Shiloh remembered the deafening noise, and Lovie did a remarkable job of silently portraying the "screaming and bursting of shell, the swishing sound of canister, the roaring of volley firing, the death screams of the stricken and struggling horses and the cries and groans of the wounded. . . ." No other artist in the war illustrated a battle as well as Henri Lovie sketched the battle of Shiloh.[30]

Shiloh gave maturity to the westerners. The casualty lists told the price they had paid. Nor were they ever quite the same after Shiloh. They were cleansed of the cocksureness they had acquired at Henry and Donelson, and though they were more confident than ever, this was a solemn confidence born in sacrifice. Shiloh was the battle they never forgot.

Shiloh was also the turning point for the western artists. Once again Henry Lovie proved that he was more valuable than all the other western artists together. Shiloh was the beginning of the end for Alex Simplot. The Picnic War attitudes he acquired with Fremont repeatedly misled him throughout the rest of his career. He never fully realized that success as a field artist demanded hard work and the sacrifice of personal comfort. This was all the more unfortunate because he was a skillful artist. But to miss Shiloh was a bitter disappointment, and he was not to have such an opportunity again. Simplot was the unluckiest artist of the war.

By the summer of 1862 northerners knew the western army well enough to abandon many of the stereotyped images. In only a few ways were the westerners still unique. A string of victories gave them an air of assurance that was expressed in the exuberant sketches of their artists. They continued to dislike formality, and they seldom held inspections or reviews. But they marched and fought with an efficiency that excited admiration everywhere. Actually, easterners and westerners were not significantly different.[31] They fought their battles, made their camps, and passed their leisure time in much the same way. Eastern artists transferred to the western army did not find the adjustment very difficult. By mid-1862 artists on the Mississippi as well as the Potomac were joined in a common effort to erase many of the distinctive images and attitudes so strong only the year before.

VI

Artists at Work

Henri Lovie's triumph at Shiloh sprang from his mastery of his profession. When he first joined McClellan's army in western Virginia, he was unfamiliar with warfare, but he did know the picture business. He had his own lithographing shop in Cincinnati, and he also acquired valuable experience as a pre-war sketch artist for Leslie. He knew how to meet people who might assist him in his work. He was aware that successful news sketching required acute observation and a retentive memory as well as artistic talent. As an engraver himself, he prepared his sketches with the problems of Leslie's engravers in mind. They, after all, were the men who translated his sketches into illustrations. Mastery of these and many other skills explained why he had a distinct advantage over his competitors.

But even veteran news artists like Lovie encountered many new problems during the war. They were dependent upon the army for subsistence and for other favors, but they also had to try to remain free of army bias. For the first time they met the challenge of a controlled press. The army and the government established a censorship and enforced it by expelling artists. Artists also faced the rigors of campaigning in the field, physical exhaustion and illness, and the possibility of being captured, wounded, or killed. The process of creating new images depended on more than just open-minded observation. Unless the field artists met and overcame the obstacles that faced them, they were not able to convey their impressions to the public.

The Civil War artists were a group of widely divergent personalities, but in many respects they were remarkably alike. They were young and penny-poor. War sketching for most of them was a mere interlude, a temporary means of livelihood, until they decided upon permanent and more remunerative careers. Simplot was the only one from a well-to-do family, and he was unique also because he had graduated from college. Henri Lovie and Henry

74

Mosler had businesses in Cincinnati. Most of the artists, however, were dependent upon sketching for their income. Only a few of them had family responsibilities. Theo Davis supported his mother; Lovie and Thomas Nast were married and had children. But most of the artists could not afford marriage and a family.[1]

The one factor most in their favor was their youth. In 1861, Arthur Lumley and Alex Simplot were twenty-four; Edwin Forbes was twenty-two; Theo Davis was just twenty-one; and Thomas Nast and Henry Mosler were only twenty. The strength and endurance of youth were advantages for survival in the field. Lovie and the Wauds were in their early thirties, and they were usually the ones who suffered the most from sickness and exhaustion. But all were young enough to have flexible minds, open to the impact of new experiences.

They all had some art training. Alf Waud had studied at the Royal Academy in London, and his brother William had been an apprentice to the English architect, Sir Joseph Paxton. Davis and Forbes studied painting under private instructors. Lumley, Nast, Winslow Homer, and Eugene Benson[2] were students at the National Academy of Design. Forbes and Benson had been trained exclusively in the fine arts, but Lumley, Davis, Homer, Nast, and Frank Schell were also skillful commercial illustrators, and Homer, together with Henri Lovie and Henry Mosler, had been apprentice engravers. Only Alex Simplot lacked both formal training and commercial experience.

Many of them also had some experience in news sketching. Alf Waud and Theo Davis worked for the *Illustrated News* before the war. In 1860 Davis sketched the tour of the Prince of Wales through Canada and the United States for the *Illustrated News.* He then transferred to *Harper's Weekly,* and in April and May of 1861 he accompanied William Howard Russell, special correspondent of the *London Times,* on a tour through the south.[3] William Waud and Henri Lovie were the mainstays of Leslie's pre-war staff of artists. Arthur Lumley and Winslow Homer had contributed to *Harper's Weekly.* These veterans started the war with distinct advantages over newcomers like Alex Simplot and Edwin Forbes, who had to learn the skills of the craft in a hurry. Thomas Nast, though only twenty years old, had the greatest variety of sketching experience. By 1860 he had already worked for *Leslie's,* the *New York Illustrated News,* the *Illustrated London News,* and *Le Monde* of Paris, and after Garibaldi's Italian campaign, he was the only artist who had sketched under fire. But Nast's real talent was as an editorial cartoonist, and he was to sketch very little action in the field.

The war posed a number of new problems for these artists. This was particularly true of their relations with the army. As *ex officio* camp followers, they were subject to military law. There were several provisions in the Articles of War which the army used to define the activities of newspapermen, but in practice every reporter and artist was subject to the particular interpretation which each commanding officer gave to the regulations, and these interpretations varied radically from camp to camp. Some generals, particularly the political brigadiers, welcomed the journalists because they were anxious to establish good public relations. The West Point professionals, on the other hand, oftentimes looked upon the reporters and artists as arrogant snoopers. Under these circumstances it was common sense for the artists to cultivate the goodwill of each individual commander, and given time, tact, and a normal allotment of good luck, they usually became experts in headquarters diplomacy.[4]

As a practical matter, the artists were dependent upon the army for their subsistence. The army provided them with food and shelter. On the march, they shared the common supply. In camp they joined a mess made up of several officers and maybe a reporter or two, and contributed their share of the expenses. They provided their own horses, and a veteran artist like Henri Lovie had three or four horses stationed at various points throughout his theater of the war. But they were dependent upon the quartermaster corps for forage and feed for their animals. The army also provided them with indispensable services. Brady's photographers had the use of the army's transports and railroads, and the photographers who did special work for the army also enjoyed the protection of Allan Pinkerton and the Secret Service. Artists with good contacts could get passes to move about with practically unlimited freedom, permission to accompany units on every kind of mission, and even small military escorts for their protection. They sat in on conferences and strategy sessions, and to all intents had the full privileges of staff officers. In fact, Theo Davis and Alf Waud several times declined commissions for staff appointments.[5]

In return, the artists and photographers repaid their debts in a number of ways. Sometimes they were directly useful to the army. The Engineers learned a good deal about the construction of roads and bridges in other theaters of the war from Brady's photographs, and the Topographical Engineers used several of his operators to make photographic duplicates of maps. Alex Gardner, a former Brady photographer, assisted the Army Secret Service to detect Confederate spies by photographing groups of soldiers. In the summer of 1863, General Quincy A. Gilmore assigned W. T. Crane, Leslie's artist in South Carolina, to illustrate the army's systematic demolition of Fort Sumter, and he included Crane's sketches in his official report to the War Department. Ulysses S. Grant once asked Theo Davis if he could see the sketches he had made of some army operations in Charleston harbor, and after studying them, he remarked that "these clear up the situation far better than printed descriptions that have reached us."[6]

Both Crane and Davis were masters at using the technique of the "testimonial." After Davis completed an excellent series on the ironclad *Monitor,* he showed his sketches to the officers in command, and then asked them to write a letter testifying to their accuracy. The officers were only too willing to praise his work. Everyone was happy; Davis had a testimonial, and the officers had received some good free publicity.[7]

Officers also welcomed the sketchers because they knew that army units with artists were assured of good coverage in the illustrated newspapers. The artists showed their gratitude by sending portraits of their benefactors to their editors, and by making more pictures of their own outfit than of other divisions engaged at the same action. They also filled their letters to New York with praise for the men and officers of their own units. Davis was undoubtedly guilty of the charge, often levied against the reporters, of boosting a particular officer in return for special favors. Other artists were usually more subtle, though in the long run no less successful, than Davis in currying the favor of the army.[8]

Neither the artists nor the army was deceived by their mutual efforts to remain on good terms with each other, and the men in the ranks soon got into the spirit of the game. George Alfred Townsend, a reporter for the *New York Herald,* remembered the snide greetings he often got from the privates and corporals: "Our Special Artist!", "Our Own Correspondent!", "Give our Captain a setting up, you sir!", and "Puff our Colonel!" Sometimes the remarks were more caustic: "Where's your pass, bub?" and "Ef I had a warrant for the devil, I'd arrest that feller." Making a plan of the Cedar Mountain battlefield, Townsend was accosted by a soldier who asked him if he was making a sketch of the Federal positions. "Not for any military purpose," he replied. "For what?" "For a newspaper engraving." "Umph!" Some soldiers resented the special privileges of the newspapermen, but most of the veterans realized the reporters and artists were only doing their job in the best way they knew.[9]

Inherent in the artists' efforts to curry the favor of the army was the danger that they would illustrate the war mainly from the viewpoint of the officers. The traditional images of war already overemphasized the role of the officers, but circumstances worked to throw the artists continually into the company of the officers. Their desire for information and passes required them to cultivate officers. Their need to move rapidly meant that they rode on horseback with officers rather than walk in the dust and mud with the foot soldiers. During campaigns they centered their activities around headquarters to be certain nothing escaped their attention. Many of them were also flattered to be on familiar speaking terms with colonels and generals. Crane and Davis and several of the younger artists were skilled name-droppers, mentioning Grant or Logan or McPherson in their letters as casually as they named places on a map. More mature artists like Alf Waud, Henri Lovie, and Winslow Homer did not feel the need for this glory by association. The officers' perspective was perfectly legitimate if it was balanced with illustrations of the soldiers' war. But some of the sketchers were never aware of their bias.

The army did restrict the artists on several occasions. But usually this was because the army did not distinguish the artists from the reporters, and considered them all members of the same fraternity. The sketchers and scribblers lived and worked together; artists seldom campaigned with other artists but rather in the company of a reporter. But while they had much in common with the reporters, sketching was never as highly competitive as news reporting, and there was no reason for one artist to violate military secrecy in order to scoop another artist. Unlike the reporters, artists never stole official orders or reports. But because they worked together, overzealous army officers sometimes included artists in their proscriptions of reporters.[10]

In the summer of 1862 General Henry Halleck ordered every newspaperman with the army in Tennessee to leave the lines. Alex Simplot, however, sneaked back through the lines and rejoined the army by posing as a sutler. Frank Leslie directed one of his artists to prepare a cartoon showing Halleck's soldiers harassing reporters and artists but ignoring Confederate spies who pilfered Halleck's muster rolls and secret plans. Most of the field generals, however, would not endanger good public relations with general expulsion orders. Usually they expelled only the specific offender, hoping he would serve as an example for the rest.[11]

The chief inquisitor of the journalists was William T. Sherman. He did not conceal his contempt for the "buzzards of the press who hang in scent about our camps . . . filling our transports . . . reporting our progress . . . inciting jealousy and discontent, and doing infinite mischief." He thought reporters were dangerous and insidious enemies of the Federal cause because they betrayed secret military information and because their exaggerated reports of sickness and casualties caused "frantic despair at home." He was just as hostile to the artists. He disliked the "awful likeness" of his brother, the senator from Ohio, that appeared in *Harper's Weekly*, and he refused to pose for artists who wanted his portrait. In late 1861, W. R. McComas, one of Leslie's artists in the West, asked Sherman for permission to accompany his army. Sherman refused. "You fellows make the best spies that can be bought," he told McComas. "Jeff Davis owes more to you newspapermen than to his army." McComas retorted that he had never had his loyalty questioned, and that every commander he had followed had been satisfied with his behavior. When he asked if he could visit just the camps in order to relieve the anxiety of the people at home, Sherman again was adamant: "The people . . . feel such an interest that they sit by their fires, not knowing or caring about the wants of their soldiers. I wish no more discussion, sir. I have given my decision. If I allow you, I must allow all." Leslie rushed to the defense of his Special. In an angry editorial, he denounced the "pompous fools and martinets" who obstructed the work of the artists with absurd restrictions.[12]

Eventually Sherman was more friendly to the artists. Perhaps he decided to follow the example of Grant, who always welcomed artists, telling one of them: "We are the men who make history, but you are the men who perpetuate it." During Sherman's campaign through Georgia and the Carolinas, he accepted Theo Davis and William Waud as unofficial members of his staff. Sherman was an amateur artist himself, and on one occasion when he was watching them work, he suggested in jest that they send Harper just one big picture for all South Carolina: "one big pine tree, one log cabin, and one nigger."[13]

Only once did the army use its full power of censorship against one of the illustrated newspapers. On April 26, 1862, *Harper's Weekly* published two "bird's eye" pictorial maps from the Peninsula. An officer of the Topographical Engineers drew the pictures, and Harper later claimed that the commanding general of the Corps had approved them. The first view of Great Bethel showed an area already occupied by the Federal army. But the second map of Yorktown appeared during McClellan's siege of Yorktown, and it showed details of the fortifications, the location and size of the artillery, the position and identity of the combat and reserve units, and even the exact location of McClellan's headquarters.[14]

The publication of these pictures caused immediate consternation in New York and Washington. On May 3, *The New York Times* claimed that two days after this issue of the *Weekly* reached the Peninsula, the Confederates shelled McClellan out of his camp. The War Department immediately suspended the sale of the *Weekly,* and Secretary Stanton telegraphed the Harpers that they were guilty of "giving aid and comfort to the enemy." He demanded that one of the brothers come to Washington at once. Fletcher Harper was furious. He threatened to hold every officer who interfered with the *Weekly* responsible for his actions in the courts, and he sarcastically suggested that overzealous officers give more attention to suppressing the rebellion and less to suppressing loyal northern newspapers. When he reached Washington, he found Stanton in a belligerent mood, but he refused to concede that the *Weekly* had betrayed any useful information to the enemy. Undoubtedly he reminded Stanton that the *Weekly* had given strong and unqualified support to the administration, and that there could be no doubt of its loyalty. Stanton saw the point of Harper's argument. He was well aware that McClellan's slow progress on the Peninsula was unpopular, and he was not willing to lose Harper's goodwill. He revoked the suspension, and before Harper left his office he even thanked him for his support of the administration. Harper in turn agreed that some censorship was necessary to control newspapers of doubtful loyalty.[15]

The suspension of the *Weekly* did not pass unnoticed. Leggett informed his readers he was deferring the publication of several sketches on the advice of army censors, and he assured his subscribers that the illustrations he did print were not of any value to the enemy. Arthur Lumley also took the warning to heart. In a letter accompanying a sketch of an army signal station, he explained that he did not dare disclose the new signal code, "for to do so might introduce me to [the federal prison at] Fort Lafayette."[16]

The majority of the sketch artists spent most of their time in only one theater of the war. Alfred Waud sketched the entire war in Virginia; Lumley and Forbes were there for three years. Alex Simplot never was far from the western rivers he had known since boyhood. There were exceptions of course. Henri Lovie sketched in the East—in western Virginia and at Fredericksburg—as well as in the West. William Waud was in the West with Farragut, on the Peninsula with both McClellan and Grant, and in the Deep South with Sherman. Theo Davis was probably the most widely traveled. He saw action on the Potomac front and on the Carolina coast, sketched the battle of the *Monitor* and *Merrimac,* was with Grant at Vicksburg and Chattanooga, and ended the war accompanying Sherman through Georgia and the Carolinas. General John A. Logan thought Davis saw more of the war than any other man.[17]

To acquire mobility, the sketch artists burdened themselves with a minimum of baggage. Their clothing was entirely utilitarian: tough shoes or jack boots for protection, coats and trousers of a strong fabric that they could wear for weeks and even months without a change, and a wide-brimmed hat to shade their eyes and sketch pads from the sun. Alf Waud wore a holstered pistol, but most of the artists did not carry weapons. A large portfolio suspended from a strap over the shoulder contained paper, pencils, crayons, charcoal, ink, pens, brushes, and a few water colors. For battle skteching they ordinarily made pencil drawings, but for camp scenes they often preferred crayon and charcoal. They used ink and water colors for the more detailed illustrations they submitted to their publishers. A pair of powerful field glasses, a sure-footed horse, a rolled blanket, saddlebags with a change of clothing, a few rations, and extra drawing supplies completed their essential equipment.[18]

Experienced field artists practiced a similar economy when working. During every campaign, they studied the topography of each area, noting the foliage, terrain, architecture, and outstanding landmarks which would provide background for their illustrations. They familiarized themselves with the men in the army, their uniforms, and their equipment. When sketching a battle they temporarily cleared their minds of all these details to give their full attention to the rapidly changing scene before them. Skilled artists developed an extremely quick shorthand. A sweeping line or two indicated the horizon or a ridge of hills in the background. A pencil smudge suggested the main clusterings of trees and underbrush. A wavering circle was sufficient to show shells exploding in the air, a clustering of short lines enough to indicate where other shells scattered earth and dirt. Entire battalions and regiments in formation appeared only as a row of short lines like a picket fence. Ordinarily they did only one or two of the figures in some detail to remind themselves of a particular posture, a wounded man begging for relief or the stance of the commanding general as he surveyed the field. Rather than take the time to sketch every detail, they wrote brief notes on the margins for the engravers. Using a shorthand such as this, an experienced artist could make a working sketch in only a minute or two.[19]

Every artist faced two major obstacles when sketching a battle—lack of time and lack of visibility. The shorthand outline was their main method of saving time. They also worked on horseback whenever possible, making a sketch from one place, then dashing to another to make a second sketch with a slightly different perspective. They avoided getting too close to the impenetrable mass of swirling battle smoke and fighting men, and if possible they posted themselves a hundred yards or so behind the lines, preferably on elevated ridges where they had freedom of movement and did not have to worry too much about the fire of the enemy. But every battle was unique in this respect; Antietam and Gettysburg were easy to sketch, Shiloh and the battles on the Peninsula extremely difficult. Alf Waud wrote Harper from the Peninsula that it was impossible to get an extended view from any one place, and Charles Page, a *Tribune* correspondent, told his editor he could not give a complete account of the fighting at White Oak Swamp when "not one-tenth of the field was in view from any one point of vision." Arthur Lumley not only made several ascensions with balloonist Lowe, but he also spent many hours on roof tops and in church steeples trying to get the "Big View." By the end of the war, practically every sketch artist considered himself an expert tree scaler and mountain climber.[20]

The artists soon realized to their advantage that one battle was often very much like another. Most of the war illustrations were made by artists "on the spot," but sometimes they arrived too late to witness personally all the action, and then they had to improvise. By examining the field and with the help of men who were participants, they produced quite accurate illustrations. They knew the appearance of the army, and had seen the men fighting on other occasions; all they really needed were the particulars. Lovie's sketches of the fights at Lexington and Fort Donelson were based on his own inspection of the area supplemented by Franc Wilkie's descriptions of the battles. In both cases, soldiers testified to their accuracy. And re-creating a battle by means such as these was a far cry from Fletcher Harper telling his New York staff artists to illustrate the battle of Shiloh purely on the basis of newspaper accounts.[21]

But all the talent of the field artists went for nought if their sketches did not receive skillful handling in New York. Engravers re-drew every field sketch on wood, cut away the uninked sections, and then made a metal impression to use on the presses. The fidelity with which the printed woodcut reproduced the detail of the original sketch depended entirely upon the expertness of the engravers. Good engravers improved poor field sketches and careless engravers ruined excellent field sketches. Frank Leslie understood this better than any of the other publishers. He was a former engraver himself, and despite his many other duties, he personally supervised the preparation of each illustration. Every one of his field artists knew he could rely on Leslie's engravers to transform his sketches into polished illustrations.

The engraving for *Harper's Weekly* was at first abominably bad. Illustrations in the *Weekly* were monotonous, lacking in detail, and often marred by bad perspective. When Alf Waud submitted an admittedly hurried sketch of a bayonet charge at the battle of Fair Oaks, Harper's engravers reproduced it as an illustration showing nearly five hundred men in a perfect line, each man a mirror replica of the man on either side, every man running with the same leg forward, each bayonet poised at exactly the same height. When that particular issue of the *Weekly* reached the Army of the Potomac, the soldiers greeted it with shouts of derision. Harper's other artists were equally disgusted with the shabby appearance of their illustrations, but there was little they could do until Harper demanded better work. Most of Harper's engravers never got closer to the war than the east bank of the Hudson River, but they did not hesitate to "improve" the composition and appearance of sketches made by artists right on the scene. They moved and eliminated figures and added others. Alex Simplot knew western rivers better than any New York artist, yet they repeatedly added a log or a snag to his river sketches, apparently for no better reason than to indicate the direction of the current. They also made caricatures of the field artists' portraits of the Confederates to assist Harper's various propaganda campaigns. Without exception their alterations failed to improve upon the original sketches.[22]

Poor engraving, however, was the least painful of the sketch artists' hazards. Most of them suffered casualties of one sort or another in the field. James R. O'Neill, one of Leslie's part-time artists, was killed. Another of his artists, C. E. F. Hillen, was severely wounded during Sherman's campaign against Atlanta. Theo Davis was twice wounded, and although he recovered each time, his war injuries plagued him for the rest of his life. Others were captured. In 1863, Confederate troops captured the unfortunate Hillen, and during the advance to Gettysburg, Lee's cavalry made a prisoner of still another of Leslie's artists, George Law. Only the help of some Union sympathizers saved Henri Lovie from being jailed in Kentucky by a group of drunken Confederate vigilantes. But unless the artists were in uniform, the Confederates usually released them without delay. On one occasion, Alf Waud's captors even posed for him before they sent him back to the Union lines.[23]

Illness and exhaustion took an even greater toll. Edwin Forbes was sick from exposure after the battle of Cedar Mountain. Alex Simplot gave up field sketching because he could not throw off a bad case of chronic diarrhea. The older artists suffered more than the younger men. The Waud brothers repeatedly took long furloughs to recover from sunstroke, various "fevers," or just sheer exhaustion. After Shiloh, Lovie was "played out." He wrote Leslie that "riding from 10 to 15 miles daily, through mud and underbrush, and then working until midnight by the dim light on an attenuated tallow 'dip,' are among the least of my *desagremens* and sorrows." He begged a furlough: "I am deranged about the stomach, ragged, unkempt, and unshorn, and need the cojoined skill and services of the apothecary, the tailor and the barber, and above all the attentions of home. . . ." Though he gave up sketching during Grant's campaign against Vicksburg, two hard years in the field contributed to his early death while still a young man.[24]

There were many personal tragedies. Alf Waud buried a friend who had been his companion on many campaigns. Tom Nast spent a night in the Harrisburg jail when he should have been sketching the battle of Gettysburg. Artists worked on the space-rate system of payment, and nothing was more disheartening than to lose sketches. F. C. H. Bonwill of *Leslie's* lost several month's sketches during the Red River expedition, and in 1864 another of

Leslie's artists, Joseph Becker, lost his portfolio during a battle near the Rappahannock River.[25]

The problems that most concerned the sketch artists involved maintaining good relations with the army and overcoming obstacles to making good sketches. Essentially, they considered themselves reporters who worked with pictures rather than words. They did not consider it part of their task to pass judgment. They wanted to portray the war as honestly and frankly as possible, but again that was a job of reporting and not of interpreting. Each artist had his opinions on the soundness of army strategy, the tactical skill of the generals he observed, and the quality of leadership—or lack of it—throughout the army as a whole. But these were private opinions, and they did not find expression in their sketches. Their pictures portrayed appearances, not competency. Each artist learned quite early that qualitative evaluation of the war was a subject that their publishers had reserved for themselves and for their editorial artists.

VII

The Enemy

The work of the sketch artists in establishing new images would have been much easier if they had had a monopoly of war pictures. But from the very beginning of the war, several groups of artists competed for the mind of the public. While the field artists experienced warfare at first hand and tried to illustrate it in terms of a new realism, other artists were working at cross-purposes to them by interpreting the war from a purely patriotic point of view. The printmakers consistently used the images of the Heroic War in their battle pictures long after the field artists had abandoned them. At the same time, editorial artists and cartoonists drew pictures to support the main themes of northern propaganda. The publishers of the illustrated weeklies encouraged both the new images of their field artists and the patriotic images of their cartoonists. Yet this was perfectly consistent with the fact that the Civil War was both a military conflict and a complex political and social upheaval.

The objective of the editorial artists was to create a disciplined mass support of the war and an unfavorable image of the Confederate enemy. They knew that in the long run the success or failure of the war effort depended upon the sentiment of the home front. Creating a complete personality for The Enemy was relatively easy because after Bull Run the public *wanted* to believe the worst about the Confederates. Artists appealed to the Puritanism in the American character by interpreting the war as a battle between the forces of light and the forces of darkness. For several decades the abolitionists and their political and journalistic allies had been arguing that southerners were the personification of all evil. The artists now presented evidence that the Confederates waged war with vicious and unnecessary brutality. Northerners became outraged. But they were also comforted in the knowledge that they were sacrificing for a righteous cause.

Prior to the war, northern images of southerners were little influenced by pictures. The publishers of the illustrated weeklies and many of the commercial lithographers served a national market which included the South, and they were not inclined to publish pictures that were critical of southerners. Currier and Ives made it a rule not to publish prints about either slavery or abolition. Frank Leslie and Fletcher Harper were politically neutral. Instead of illustrating the slave trade and slave auctions, they offered their readers innocuous illustrated tours through the South, such as those "Porte Crayon" wrote and illustrated for Harper. The printmakers published sentimental pictures of southern scenes designed to please everybody and offend no one. Pictures such as these, however, had some influence. Franc Wilkie believed that many northern boys who joined the army in 1861 were "romantic dreamers who caught glimpses in the distance of dark-eyed women with raven hair . . . who enjoyed in anticipation the languid delights of the orange groves, the flowering hedges, the beauty of the magnolia blossoms, and the genial air of the 'sunny South.' "[1]

But the publishers could not avoid controversy altogether. They had to illustrate the Kansas Wars and John Brown's raid against Harper's Ferry and his subsequent trial and execution, and hope their pictures would not anger too many subscribers. They were not always fortunate. When in 1860 Leggett published several pictures showing Alabamans tarring and feathering a northern woman who was teaching Negroes, the indignant and sometimes obscene letters of protest from southerners were indicative of the furor Leslie and Harper wanted to avoid. Many northerners were also displeased with Leslie's and Harper's timidity. Harper's refusal to commit the *Weekly* to the Republican viewpoint, or any viewpoint for that matter, led Horace Greeley of the *New York Tribune* to refer to it as a "Weakly Journal of Civilization."[2]

Consequently, sources other than pictures shaped the images of the South. Northerners read stories in their newspapers and magazines that denounced southerners. Anti-slavery orators harangued their audiences about the iniquities of slavery and its influence in warping the southern character. Harriet Beecher Stowe's *Uncle Tom's Cabin* (sometimes illustrated) and Hinton Helper's *Impending Crisis* described a life of brutality and squalor among the slaves and poor whites. These critics presented an apparently logical argument—southerners hated northern institutions, particularly its free labor system; slavery made southerners into cruel and tyrannical masters who had no respect for human dignity; thus, southerners threatened the democratic ideals of the North. At first critics made some distinction between good and bad southerners, but as the crisis approached they argued that slavery had produced in the South an entirely new race of degenerates.[3]

Southerners were even more dependent upon sources other than pictures for their images of the North. Prior to the war the great majority of pictures distributed in the South came from northern publishers, and while some of these pictures catered to southern interests, they were never numerous enough to have a significant impact. But both southerners and northerners interpreted what pictures were available in accordance with their own preconceptions. In portraits showing the gaunt face and burning eyes of John Brown, northerners saw a dedicated and deeply-religious crusader for freedom, while southerners saw only fanatical anti-southern hatred. Southern editors and orators described the North as a dismal land of crowded city slums and dank factories, where immigrants and other ignorant men embraced the teachings of abolitionist demagogues. More and more southerners came to believe that the North's primary desire was to destroy slavery and thus undermine "the southern way of life."[4]

There were men in both sections who knew how erroneous these stereotyped ideas were. But lack of sympathetic communication between the sections produced an isolation which nurtured suspicion. The majority of people preferred to believe anything that bolstered their own sense of superiority.

The beginning of the war brought many changes in the attitudes of the public and the picture publishers. Northerners and southerners closed their minds to moderation and demanded pictures more appropriate to the mood of the times. Having lost their southern market, the publishers were anxious to retain the goodwill of that which remained. The lithographers and engravers issued hundreds of new prints calculated to appeal to the surge of patriotism that swept over the North. Stationers prepared new patriotic designs for their pictorial envelopes. The publishers of the illustrated weeklies followed suit. Leslie was for some time unenthusiastic about the war. He tried to flatter northerners without permanently alienating his reserve of goodwill in the South. As late as a year after the beginning of the war, he was still offering to save back copies for his southern subscribers. But Harper abandoned his earlier caution—and his allegiance to the Democratic party—and pledged the loyal support of the *Weekly*. Leggett followed Harper's example.[5]

Their main problem was to translate war hatred into pictorial forms. For many years cartoonists had used caricature in political campaign pictures; during the war they used this same technique against the Confederacy. The scrawny figure of Jefferson Davis, for instance, became the cartoon symbol representing the physical and moral degeneration of the South. But most cartoons were so blatant and exaggerated that they defied credulity. The publishers needed a more subtle way to attack the enemy.[6]

News pictures and photographs were one possibility. Ordinarily the sketch artists and field photographers did not think of themselves as propagandists, even though many of their pictures had a powerful patriotic impact. For the most part, they made their pictures as honestly as possible, and avoided caricature and exaggeration. But they could control neither the re-drawing of their sketches nor the captioning of them. Many field artists were surprised to discover that their sketches of a minor skirmish on the picket line became, with the proper captions and some exaggeration by the engravers, illustrations showing how the enemy "murdered" or "assassinated" Federal soldiers. Leslie did not permit his engravers to distort his artists' original presentation of a subject, but he did employ flamboyant captions. Harper exaggerated his news pictures to support the *Weekly's* patriotic programs, and before the end of the first year of the war, many of his news pictures served more of an editorial than a news-reporting purpose. Photographs were not easily susceptible to tampering, but they still served the purposes of propaganda. Brady's photographs of emaciated Federal soldiers released from southern prisons made a tremendous impression upon the public.[7]

The most effective type of propaganda picture was the editorial illustration. It had a practically unlimited utilization, from symbols such as the flag or the eagle and portraits of George Washington and the heroes of the Revolution to harsh caricatures of home-front laggards and brutal illustrations of battlefield atrocities. It was adaptable to every kind of picture medium: broadsides, lithographed prints, stationery, recruiting posters, humor magazines, and illustrated newspapers. The great majority of the Civil War editorial illustrations was trash, discarded and forgotten within a day or two of publication. But in the hands of an artist like Thomas Nast, it was an extremely potent force for creating patriotic images.[8]

Nast came to the United States while still a young boy, and in his late teens he went to work for Frank Leslie. He was a short stocky boy who tried to grow a mustache and beard to lend maturity to his round young face. When Leslie reduced his salary to less than four dollars a week, and then defaulted on it several times—once because he had taken all the money from the till to buy a yacht—Nast transferred to the *Illustrated News*. In 1860 he sketched a championship boxing match in England and then the Garibaldian Wars in Italy. He returned to the United States in the spring of 1861, did a superb series of illustrations of Lincoln's inauguration, and after the start of the war, drew editorial cartoons for Leggett and prepared Alf Waud's field sketches for the engravers. But he was not satisfied with the *News*. In early 1862 he rejoined Leslie for several months and then transferred to *Harper's Weekly*.[9]

The partnership of Nast and Harper dominated illustrated journalism for the next thirty years. In later years they were not always in complete agreement, but during the Civil War they interpreted the issues of the conflict in perfect harmony. Both men saw in the *Weekly* a medium for indoctrinating more than a half-million readers in their duty to God and the nation. Harper contributed publishing and editorial skill, and Nast contributed ideas in pictorial form. They understood and appreciated each other's talent; together they raised editorial cartooning to its greatest heights.[10]

Nast's success was based both upon his ability to project his own convictions and upon his skill as a cartoonist. His editorial pictures were harsh and uncompromising. He did not think of them as works of art but rather as blunt weapons. Though he had a subtle and discriminating mind, he also possessed the faith of a crusader in American democracy. He refused to temper his treatment of the Confederates with compromises or amused tolerance. He believed that the editorial artist must take a positive and aggressive stand on every issue; in his hands the cartoon became an instrument of moralistic idealism and savage attack.[11]

Paradoxically enough, a Christmas illustration provided the first indication of Nast's potential influence. Late in 1862 he drew a picture showing a young war wife praying for her soldier husband, who in another scene warmed himself by a campfire as he looked at photographs of his family. "Christmas Eve 1862" struck a chord that no other war picture had touched to that time. Colonel John Beatty of the Third Ohio Volunteers wrote in his diary: "The picture . . . will bring tears to the eyes of many a poor fellow shivering over the campfire in this winter season. The children in the crib, the stockings in which Santa Claus deposits his treasures, recall the pleasantest night of the year." Letters of thanks came into the Harper office from all over the North. Another colonel cried when he unfolded the illustration by his own campfire: "It was only a picture, but I couldn't help it." This spontaneous public reaction proved the huge influence of the sentimental picture. Harper immediately encouraged Nast to expand his output of editorial illustrations in support of the *Weekly's* various patriotic campaigns.[12]

Most of these campaigns depended upon the artists creating a brutal image of The Enemy. If northerners were convinced that the enemy committed atrocities, then they would be more inclined to support the war effort by sacrificing their money and men. If they believed that this was a war of "Civilization against Barbarism, Light against Darkness, Right against Wrong," then they might also adopt such controversial proposals as the use of Negro troops and the emancipation of the slaves. The battle of Bull Run provided the first reports of enemy atrocities, and many later skirmishes and battles added more proof to the indictment. Using this evidence, the artists created an image of The Enemy by developing several associated themes— enemy mistreatment of prisoners, enemy barbarism on the battlefield, enemy abuse of southern Unionists, and the inhumane ferocity of enemy guerrilla troops in the West.[13]

Perhaps the greatest misfortune arising from Confederate victories in the early years of the war was that the South accumulated more prisoners-of-war than it could properly care for. In the absence of a system of exchange, the Confederate prison camps were soon overcrowded and plagued with serious problems of health and discipline. The prisoners attributed their suffering not to shortages of personnel and supply, but to the supposed brutality of their keepers. When they escaped or were released, they returned home with lurid tales of horror.

As early as the winter of 1861–62, Leslie and Harper published pictures by men who had escaped from Libby prison in Richmond. Harper's pictures showed the cold rooms of the former tobacco warehouse, where prisoners decorated their walls with such patriotic mottos as "United We Stand, Divided We Fall" and "The Union Must and Shall be Preserved." The artist tried to create the setting of the Christian martyrs in Roman dungeons; a single ray of sunlight penetrated the darkness from a small window, and the prisoners turned their eyes toward Heaven for deliverance. The illustrations in *Leslie's* showed the Confederate jailers exhibiting their prisoners to gape-mouthed spectators, a "revolting and incredible" practice which Leslie thought was comparable only to the Chinese practice of public execution.[14]

Nast based several editorial illustrations on the prisons upon the escapees' accounts. One picture of Belle Isle prison in Richmond showed a group of miserable men huddled on the wet ground of their squalid camp, unable to defend themselves when their guards kicked them and then laughed at their agony. He recalled the horrors of slave drives with another illustration showing brutish Confederate soldiers driving a column of chained prisoners through a small southern town. The guards prodded the prisoners with sabers and bayonets, and the townspeople jeered, shook their fists, and thumbed their noses. Nast also inserted a plea for emancipation by showing a few slaves along the road sympathizing with the prisoners; one Negro woman even offering a prisoner a loaf of bread.[15]

A chill of horror gripped northerners when they saw pictures of the men released from Confederate prisons. All of them were sick; many resembled living skeletons. Here was proof to dispel the most skeptical disbelievers. In October of 1863 the artist for the *Illustrated News* who sketched the arrival at Annapolis of some exchanged prisoners, reported that only a third of them were expected to survive. A cartoon in the same issue showed Jefferson Davis gloating and rubbing his hands as he inspected some prisoners in Libby: "I think this little lot is about ready for exchange." The following June, another group arrived at Annapolis, and Harper and Leslie published copies of the photographs taken at the time. Pictures of prisoners who had lost their hands and feet from malnutrition testified to the "inhumane treatment" which had reduced them to a pitiful state of near-death.[16]

By 1864 conditions within the prison camps of both belligerents were frightful. Illness and disease reached epidemic proportions and dozens of men died every day. Photographers on each side portrayed the huddled prisoners, the inadequate shelters, the death lines, and particularly the muddied filth at such northern camps as Elmira in New York, Douglas near Chicago, and the southern camp at Andersonville in Georgia. But these photographs were not available either to the public or to the publishers on the other side until after the war. In the absence of this evidence, each side remained confident that only the enemy abused its prisoners. Harper's artists fostered this illusion with a series of illustrations portraying the clean spaciousness of the northern camps, the genuine concern of the camp administrators for their prisoners' health, and the model behavior of the guards. Southern artists countered with pictures contrasting the "fine treatment" shown northern prisoners at Belle Isle with the noxious conditions in northern prisons. An artist for the *Southern Illustrated News* showed northern prisoners playing cards in front of a row of clean white tents, while a second picture portrayed a southern prisoner languishing in solitary confinement in a dark Ohio penitentiary.[17]

Northerners were fascinated with this evidence of southern malignity. A Congressional investigating committee encouraged the public to inspect carefully the photographs showing the condition of returned prisoners. On Broadway in New York a few enterprising book dealers displayed illustrations and photographs of prisoners to attract attention to the other items in their windows. When a reader complained to George William Curtis, Harper's political editor, that prison atrocity pictures made his children shudder, Curtis replied that he would have been amazed if they did not: "Such pictures are for the parents to ponder. This is the spirit which inspires the rebellion."[18]

Northerners also were convinced that the Confederates planned to loot the North. Editorial artists encouraged this idea by portraying Confederate troops ravaging the wealth of the countryside through which they passed. But like the words "murder" and "assassination," the word "loot" applied only to the enemy; there was another word to describe Federal troops doing the same thing. Sketch artists frequently submitted a picture of the enemy *looting* livestock and crops from loyal Union farms, and then several weeks later they submitted another sketch showing Federal soldiers *foraging* livestock and crops from disloyal Confederate farms. But many northerners looked upon foraging as righteous punishment for traitors. Henri Lovie sketched a Federal foraging party in Missouri seizing the livestock of a female rebel, who he claimed swore more ferociously than any of the rough soldiers who stalked and stumbled around her farmyard grabbing her chickens, geese, and pigs. He thought she was so hard in her manner that he found it impossible to pity her, and when she turned to him and asked, "Are the devils there going to kill all my goslings?" he could not help laughing in her face.[19]

The "drunken and ignorant hordes" that composed the rank and file of the Confederate army supposedly delighted in wantonly destroying property. Pictures of the enemy rabble running rampant through Union homes and stores, destroying furnishings, stealing valuables, ripping and stripping and burning, and usually finding some liquor to feed their courage, appeared frequently in the illustrated press. But the artists again made a careful distinction between the needless looting of the enemy and the psychological warfare of Sherman's bummers in Georgia and Sheridan's ravaging of the Shenandoah Valley in Virginia.[20]

Pictures of Confederate desecration of Union wounded and dead suggested that the enemy had discarded all the restraints of civilized men. Illustrations from the first battle of Bull Run had shown Confederates bombarding army field hospitals, and later illustrations tried to prove that they frequently bayoneted wounded soldiers. Northerners were particularly infuriated when they saw pictures showing Confederates stripping dead Federal soldiers of their shoes, clothing, and weapons. Leslie and Leggett printed several sketches by soldiers who claimed to have witnessed such atrocities. One of Nast's first editorial illustrations for *Harper's Weekly* showed enemy scavengers at work after the second battle of Bull Run. In a scene that reminded his readers of a Holloween specter dance, he showed the enemy ghouls with their camp followers stripping the Union corpses. Expressions of fiendish cruelty and stupidity twisted their faces. Then for contrast, Nast showed the anguish of several northern women who had come to the field to look for the bodies of their sons and husbands.[21]

Southerners did not deny that their troops sometimes took clothes, shoes, and weapons from northern warehouses and even from the Yankee dead to replenish their own worn-out and irreplaceable equipment. But they did not think this was desecration. In 1864 the *Southern Punch,* the Confederacy's short-lived humor magazine, published a picture entitled "An Appeal to the Mothers and Daughters of the South," showing three barefoot veterans of the Confederate army in Tennessee warming their frozen feet in front of a fire. Apparently the mothers and daughters responded by sending a new supply of shoes. But as early as 1862 the Yankees were the main source of new uniforms and shoes, and even then most southern soldiers had a ragged trampish appearance. Late in the war, a sketch in the *Southern Illustrated News* of a fully-uniformed and well-shod Confederate picket was greeted with some bitterness by the veterans, most of whom had not seen such a resplendent creature since the first year of the war.[22]

In the war of atrocities, southern artists answered every pictorial accusation from the North with pictures of their own. Illustrations and cartoons in the *Southern Illustrated News* and the *Southern Punch* portrayed the Yankees as mercenary abolitionists, fanatic with hatred and lust as they committed unspeakable atrocities against innocent southerners. When northern sketch artists made working plans of Confederate torpedoes and land mines as examples of the "infernal machines" which the "dastardly" foe had invented, southern artists retorted with sketches of a poisoned artillery shell designed by the Yankee to spread disease and death. Without a doubt the *bête noire* of the southern illustrated press was General Benjamin Butler, the Union commander in New Orleans who issued an order that Federal officers and troops were to treat any lady of New Orleans who insulted them as a woman of the street. Every southerner considered this directive an outrage against southern womanhood, and Confederate artists portrayed Butler as the "vilest of scum," a hyena that robbed graves, a beast of a man who preyed upon southern honor and chastity.[23]

Northern artists also tried to prove that the Confederates abused helpless civilians. According to them, one group that bore the brunt of Confederate ferocity were the men and women living in the South who held their loyalty to the Union above their loyalty to the South. Fletcher Harper cherished the hope that these southern unionists would undermine the Confederacy from within. In early 1862 one of his staff artists pictured unionists cheering Federal gunboats on the Tennessee River, and another illustration showed some east Tennessee unionists taking the oath to the flag at a secret meeting. But it soon became apparent that the southern unionists' main contribution was to serve as martyrs. Many had to flee their homes. Nast dramatically illustrated the dangers that faced one group that tried to survive in the Louisiana swamps. If one believed the artists, the enemy frequently used savage bloodhounds to hunt down and kill these refugees. A typical *Harper's* illustration showed two trapped unionists about to be torn to death by a pack of hounds.[24]

But even these pictures were mild compared to the pictures of Confederate guerrilla warfare in the West. Northerners anticipated atrocities in the West; the bloody legend of Indian warfare was full of tales of torture. During the Civil War they were not surprised to see pictures of the massacre of

Federal troops in the Southwest by the Indian allies of the Confederacy. Moreover, in the mid-Fifties, newspaper reporters had added to the legend with extravagant stories about the atrocities of the border wars in Kansas and Missouri. After 1861, however, there were no special artists assigned to this region, and consequently most of the guerrilla pictures were done by editorial artists. Their imaginations produced the most sensational atrocity pictures of the war.[25]

Artists like Nast were seldom satisfied unless they could include in one picture examples of every kind of human depravity. In the summer of 1862 Nast illustrated John Hunt Morgan's raid into Kentucky. He ignored the fact that Morgan's raiders struck primarily at railroads, bridges, and telegraph lines. On the contrary, he contended that Morgan's men were interested only in loot and lust; wherever Morgan's men attacked, "shrieks of agony have gone up to Heaven from outraged matrons and maidens, butchered children, and sacked households." After seeing the evidence, Nast expected his readers to come to the conclusion that such "God-forsaken wretches can not be found anywhere in the world out of the Feejee Islands and the Southern Slave States."[26]

Later that summer Nast did a purely imaginary picture of a Confederate raid on an unsuspecting western town. He showed drunken guerrillas wrecking a train, gutting a factory, burning huge stores of wares, and firing a church—including the American flag that flew from its steeple. Again he emphasized the atrocities against non-belligerents. Three of the raiders tied a man to a stake and used him as a target. Others shot a Negro, dangled a baby upside down by its feet, and fired a pistol at the feet of a small boy to make him dance to avoid the bullets. Near a man hanging from a flagpole, two guerrillas dragged away a young woman as they whispered their intentions to each other, while a third seized a mother who held her infant in her arms. Another raider bayoneted a helpless man while his companions broke open trunks and boxes in their search for loot. And out in the street, either bayoneted or shot, a little dog lay bleeding to death.[27]

Nast's pictures dictated a standard for the other editorial artists. Even Frank Leslie gave free rein to his staff artists when they illustrated Charles Quantrill's sack of Lawrence, Kansas. With Nast leading the way, a pictorial stereotype of the southern soldier took form. In picture after picture, he created a composite character for the southerner. He was a dirty creature clothed in rags; his body was thin and grotesque with oversized hands and feet; his face was sharp and drawn from dissipation, his eyes bright with hate, his mouth twisted into a lustful sneer. To give an oriental cast to the features, Nast added thinning hair and stringy chin-whiskers. This caricature was specific as well as general; Jefferson Davis was the prototype, and the obvious conclusion was that every southerner was a minion of the evil genius of the rebellion. Nor did Nast ignore southern women. He seized upon reports that many of them smoked to prove that they lacked the grace and daintiness of femininity. As gross unkempt viragos, they were perfect partners for their slightly effeminate sons and husbands.[28]

The editorial artists had varying success in convincing their readers that their image of The Enemy was valid. They were least effective among the troops. Soldiers joined the army with oaths of vengeance against the Confederates, only to discover when they fraternized with them across the picket line that they were not like the artists had portrayed them. They also quickly learned to respect them as fighters. Edwin Forbes was impressed with the southerners' "dashing bravery," and he thought that most Federal soldiers regarded them with a "wholesome respect, even a reasonable fear." Theodore Lyman, a staff officer with General George Meade, wrote his family: "Instead of being exasperated at the Southerners by fighting against them, I have a great deal more respect for them than ever I had in peace-time." Furthermore, most Union soldiers eventually realized that the Confederates believed in their cause. Lyman told his family, "There is no shadow of doubt that the body of Southerners are as honestly, as earnestly and as religiously interested in this war as the body of Northerners."[29]

But the primary target of the editorial artists were the folks at home, and among them their efforts were much more successful. This was apparent from the readiness of many northerners to believe that Confederates used Union bones and skulls as ornaments. The illustrated weeklies published pictures showing how southern women fashioned baby rattles from the ribs of a Yankee drummer boy, made flower pots and drinking cups from Union skulls, and strung teeth and finger bones to make necklaces and bracelets. Newspaper reporters and some soldiers claimed to have seen these objects; many clergymen and people as prominent as Senator Charles Summer of Massachusetts and Nathaniel Hawthorne corroborated the evidence. Edward Dicey, correspondent for an English newspaper, reported that many northerners hardened their attitude toward the enemy after exposure to atrocity stories and pictures. At first he personally believed that the atrocities were exaggerated, but in time he too came to believe in them. He was also sure that the "belief in the truth of these narratives was universal in the North, and produced painful and personal bitterness towards the South."[30]

If this was true, then the patriotic artists had been eminently successful in creating an image of The Enemy. Atrocity pictures helped to indoctrinate the northern mind to a full and unqualified support of the war. They also permitted the editorial artists to mobilize public opinion on the Home Front behind some of the basic political and social objectives of the northern crusade.

VIII

The Home Front

The image of The Enemy was fundamental to the efforts of editorial artists to inform northerners on the home front about their wartime obligations. When they drew pictures showing how Confederates desecrated the bodies of Federal soldiers, mistreated Union prisoners, and waged war against women and children, they also hoped to channel the resulting anger into attitudes and activities that would contribute directly to winning the war. They were convinced that an aroused and dedicated populace was essential to victory. They insisted that women maintain morale and that men either serve in the army or in some way contribute substantially to the war effort. They mobilized public opinion against war profiteers, inefficient administrators, and self-seeking leaders. They attacked critics of the war. In their enthusiasm, they created on the home front a war within a war, complete with its own enemies and its own image of the ideal citizen-soldier.

Northerners were ready for another crusade. For more than a quarter of a century they had participated in one crusade after another—dress and diet reform, temperance and prohibition, feminism and abolitionism—and they reacted instinctively to the language and symbols of reform. Sentimentality and a fondness for the melodramatic provided an emotional basis for reform; puritanism contributed the moral foundation. They liked brisk slogans that dramatized the issues. Rather than struggle with the complex causes of social problems, they preferred simple explanations that promised easy solutions. Conformity was mandatory. Every man must make his choice between the forces of good and the forces of evil. The non-conformist, the doubter, and people who vacillated were potentially dangerous. Like the sinners, they too had to be reformed. When the cause was national survival, every man had to perform his patriotic duty whether he wanted to or not.[1]

During the weeks between Sumter and Bull Run, there was no need to stimulate patriotism. Patriots stuck postage stamps in their hat brims, and women wore Union bonnets of alternate layers of red, white, and blue bunting. They flocked to rallies and applauded orators, and from a hundred wharfs and railroad stations they cheered the departure of the volunteers. Teen-agers wrote essays and debated the issues of the war. Children dressed in make-believe uniforms, marched with broom sticks, and re-fought every battle in their parlors and backyards. The youngsters even copied the thought pattern of their parents; in New York City a little boy accompanying his mother on a charitable errand through a dingy alley into a squalid tenement house, looked around and asked, "Mamma, isn't this South Carolina?"[2]

One of the lessons of these weeks was that patriotism was as profitable as it was popular. Every kind of picture sold well. Decorated stationery enjoyed a new vogue as soldiers eagerly puchased envelopes and lettersheets with their regimental insignia, and men and women on the home front used stationery decorated with flags, cartoons, and patriotic mottos. Portraits and prints sold by the thousands. Twenty-two year old Lester Frank Ward, later the nation's foremost sociologist, was so delighted with his purchase of "Abraham Lincoln," "The Soldier's Dream," "The Brave Wife," "The Young Cavalier," and "Little Jennie" that he gave several of them to his family and friends. Artists recalled the unity of the Founding Fathers, and they drew pictures showing the "Spirit of 1776," "Columbia," and the eagle hovering over the volunteers. Every northerner knew that history blessed the cause of the Union.[3]

Fletcher Harper and some of the other publishers believed that pictures could also shape the patriotic impulses into certain modes of behavior. After the disaster at Bull Run, they became concerned about the morale of the home front. To sustain popular support of the war, some of them began to interpret patriotism as a duty and an obligation. Anthony Trollope, an Englishman who toured the United States in 1861–62, described the tyranny of wartime patriotism. He found that northerners could not remain tranquil without arousing adverse criticism. Woman were embarrassed if they had not sent a son, husband, or brother to the army. Men who were not in uniform had to show how they were helping to win the war. Fear of social ostracism tended to press every citizen into a mold of conformity. Patriots thought this was highly desirable. Harper was perfectly willing to use pictures to silence critics, to demand effective leadership from the government, and with the glare of adverse publicity to drive young men into the army. But all the other publishers would not follow his lead. They agreed that the primary purpose of the war was to maintain the Federal Union, but beyond that there were serious differences of opinion. They could not agree on the specific personalities or policies of the Lincoln administration, and each one had his own opinions about the various generals and their management of particular campaigns. Issues such as conscription, the enforcement of loyalty, emancipation, and the creation of Negro regiments, aroused the bitterest controversy. The result was internal feuding within the industry.[4]

There was no unanimity in Washington or within either the Republican or Democratic parties, and it was hardly to be expected that the picture publishers would present a united front. Some publishers did not feel that they had any responsibility to shape public opinion; they made pictures for anybody who had the money to pay for them. Several northern printers of patriotics—decorated stationery—even printed issues for sale in the Confederacy. Large print houses such as Currier and Ives remained strictly neutral on all political issues. *Vanity Fair*,[5] the most spritely of the northern humor magazines, consistently opposed the Republican party and was sometimes bitingly critical of the government. Frank Leslie skillfully shuffled his various editorial positions with disarming ease. Several changes of publishers and editors at the offices of the *Illustrated News* resulted in complete somersaults of policy.[6]

Only *Harper's Weekly* consistently equated patriotism with support of the Lincoln administration. This was Harper's decision, but he was strongly influenced to it by George William Curtis, the *Weekly's* political editor who was also a practicing politician within the Republican party. They reserved the right to criticize individuals in the government—including the President —and to disagree with specific policies, but never to the extent of undermining faith in the government as a whole. The *Weekly's* policy was more than just a masthead proclamation. Harper used news articles, news pictures, human interest stories, serialized novels, and especially editorial cartoons to support the policies of the editorial page. Having defined patriotism and loyalty to his own satisfaction, he then turned the wrath of the *Weekly* against anyone who criticized the administration.[7]

Harper's campaign against Horace Greeley was an example of one loyal publisher attacking another for personal as well as political reasons. Cartoonists generally delighted in ridiculing Greeley, but mainly because the outspoken editor of the *New York Tribune* was a man whose personality and appearance invited caricature. Harper was seeking vengeance. Before the war Greeley had condemned the *Weekly* for its lack of editorial courage, and Harper never forgave him. He struck back after the debacle at Bull Run. Greeley had spearheaded the cry "Forward to Richmond," and with the wisdom of hindsight, Harper decided to make Greeley the scapegoat. John McLenan, a veteran cartoonist on the *Weekly* staff, portrayed the irrepressible Greeley as a buffoon general telling General Scott how to manage the war. Another cartoon showed him brandishing a club labeled *"Tribune"* as he ranted and shouted atop Lincoln's desk demanding the dismissal of the cabinet. The third of the McLenan cartoons portrayed Greeley as a lunatic in an asylum, lunging against his chains and insanely shouting that he was a "general, a nigger, and even, ha ha, a newspaper editor."[8]

The Greeley cartoons were indicative of the fault-finding nature of the early war cartoons. Editorial artists attempted to affix the responsibility for defeat on individuals rather than on an antiquated army and an unprepared public. Inevitably cabinet officers assumed a good share of the blame. Cartoonists associated Lincoln's first Secretary of War, Simon Cameron, with beef contractors, munitions makers, and other profiteers who supplied the army with shoddy. Cameron escaped to the relative obscurity of a ministership at St. Petersburg. His successor, Edwin M. Stanton, appeared to be oblivious to cartoon criticism. His suppression of *Harper's Weekly* certainly earned him a watchful respect among publishers and artists. Occasional cartoons in the *Illustrated News* implied that his timidity was responsible for Federal defeats,[9] and all the illustrated weeklies criticized him for the disasterous repulse at Fredericksburg. But Stanton and the War Department were not the subject of as much editorial abuse as might have been expected.[10]

Consequently the main assaults fell on the Secretaries of State and Navy. They were attractive to the cartoonists for several reasons. Both faced difficult problems; Secretary of State William Seward in countering the Confederate sympathies of European governments, and Navy Secretary Gideon Welles in maintaining an effective blockade of the Confederacy. To solve these problems, both Secretaries became involved with Great Britain, and much of the criticism of their toadying to John Bull was an obvious appeal to the strong anti-British sentiment in the North. Cartoonists particularly attacked

Seward in November and December of 1861 during the *Trent* affair, when two Confederate agents were taken off a British ship and then later released to quell British protests at this violation of neutrality. But fully as important was the fact that Seward and Welles lent themselves to caricature. Seward's sharp-beaked nose was a cartoonist's delight, and undoubtedly he would have been the subject of many more cartoons if Welles had not been an even better subject. Welles' wild white hair and flowing beard almost demanded that the cartoonists portray him as Rip Van Winkle or Father Neptune. In any case, they presented him as a doddering and incapable old man. The Rip Van Winkle personality supported the contention that he dozed when he should have been alert. Several *Harper's* cartoons pictured him asleep while John Bull smuggled out southern cotton and tobacco. One of Leslie's artists showed a recruiting officer accepting a four-year-old into the Navy because he would be full grown before "old Welles wakes up." Other cartoonists argued that Welles failed to provide the Navy with enough ships. Currier and Ives issued several cartoon prints showing Confederate blockade runners escaping from the entire Union Navy—two leaking wash tubs! [11]

Artists and publishers were not so foolish as to rely on criticism alone. Ordinarily they were as free with approval as with disapproval. Hundreds of cartoons praised Lincoln for his calm and decisive leadership, complimented generals for successful campaigns, and honored the volunteers in every imaginable way. On the home front, they applauded men and women for their devotion to the cause. Nor was criticism confined to northerners. Cartoonists gave much more attention to Jefferson Davis and to the British and French governments because of their aid and sympathy to the Confederacy. Nevertheless, Harper and several of the other publishers continued to use cartoons and editorial illustrations to indoctrinate the public. During the first two years of the war, when victories were scarce and morale dipped low, they believed they had to tell men and women in the North exactly what was expected of them. [12]

The double standard restricted the participation of women. War was a masculine affair, and as much as possible, women and children were to be shielded from its cruelty. Ordinarily it was a rare sight to see women anywhere near the army. They sometimes were spectators at army reviews, officers' wives occasionally visited their husbands in camp, and when the war brought the armies north to Antietam and Gettysburg, they provided the troops with food and refreshment. There were other exceptions. Alf Waud sent Leggett a sketch of a pretty young woman who sold cider, apples, pies, cakes, and tobacco to the men in the Army of the Potomac. He reported that the soldiers treated her with perfect respect and kindness, but nevertheless she wore a pistol in a holster strapped around her waist, proving she was well aware of the "rough nature of her vocation." Winslow Homer also sketched a woman washing clothes in an army camp. But most of the volunteers felt this was work best left to Negro women. Their own women could do the washing at home.[13]

There was less resistance to women working with the Medical Corps. Even so, male attendants monopolized the field hospitals, and women nurses were usually assigned to the permanent hospitals where their main function was to comfort convalescent soldiers. Homer and Nast and several other artists praised their work, showing them at the bedsides of the wounded heroes, reading and writing letters for them, and in other ways given them some feminine attention. There was an implied suggestion in each of these sketches that other women might well spend more time on errands of mercy in the hospitals.[14]

Women were expected to help the Union only in ways that did not compromise their femininity. Middle-class mores reigned supreme. Every artist assumed that women were sensitive and delicate. Publishers were hesitant at first to print horror pictures because they believed they were too frightening for women and children. Artists assured the men in the army that the darlings they had left at the picket gate were not being tarnished by the war. Every woman was a princess, and while her knight was away slaying dragons, she kept herself pure and lovely. Women might work for the war, but they were not expected to perspire while they did so. Consequently the artists totally ignored the thousands of women who worked in factories and on farms producing weapons and food for the armies.

Artists showed women how they could serve in ways that were genteel. In June of 1861 Winslow Homer illustrated one appropriate activity—a group of ladies in a parlor sewing havelocks for the volunteers. Other artists duplicated this scene many times, substituting socks, shirts, cakes, and cookies for havelocks. Charitable and service organizations provided other opportunities. The United States Sanitary Commission encouraged women to help provide for the health and welfare of the heroes. Women raised funds for the

Commission by sponsoring society dances and benefit performances, and they helped maintain the private hospitals and other services the Commission provided for the men in the service. In 1863 and 1864, several of the large Atlantic seaboard cities held Sanitary Fairs, and the illustrated weeklies portrayed these gala events, showing how women sold war momentos to raise funds. Nothing could be more respectable than the church bazaar gone to war.[15]

But this concern for feminine respectability was something of a shell. While women were severely restricted in their physical contributions, they were encouraged to exert every possible social and emotional pressure in support of the war. It was a man's war, but if the men lagged in their enthusiasm, the artists expected the women to renew their courage.

Men on the home front had even sterner obligations. Artists and publishers tried to maintain a constant flow of manpower into the army. They sketched the recruiting posts in New York's City Hall Park, where handsome soldiers extolled the advantages of their own regiments. Artists made extra money by drawing strident scenes on recruiting posters showing a "fierce-looking trooper" at a charge or a Union soldier "exterminating" the enemy. Many a prospective volunteer was intrigued by the large pointing hands on these posters. Colonel Camille Ferri-Pisani, who toured the eastern United States in the summer of 1861, remembered seeing "poor famished Irishmen devour these seductive advertisements . . . fascinated . . . by those diabolical hands" pointing to a description of the food and rations. Nevertheless, the Irishmen and many others resisted the entreaties of the recruiters.[16]

Lincoln's initial call for seventy-five thousand volunteers was over-subscribed. But the defeat at Bull Run occurred when the men who had enlisted in April for three months were nearing the end of their terms. They were anxious to get home, and throughout July and August they left the army by the thousands. Other young men who had not yet enlisted were now less inclined to do so. Harper was shocked; defeat called for greater not less exertion, for an expansion rather than dismemberment of the army, for more enlistments—particularly the re-enlistment of the three-month volunteers. He immediately used the influence of the *Weekly* to stimulate enlistments. He stepped up the production of atrocity pictures, and he instructed his editorial artists to shame every young man who failed to serve his country.

His first targets were the three-month volunteers. Several of his cartoonists suggested that men who would not re-enlist deserved no welcome upon their home-coming. McLenan showed a "Daughter of Columbia"—the wife of a returning three-month volunteer—repelling the embrace of her husband: "Get away! No husband of mine would be here while the country needs his help!" Other artists implied that the volunteers who left the army were deserters. One cartoon showed the men of the Fourth Pennsylvania and of Varian's New York Field Battery deserting the field with gleeful shouts that they're off for home because their three months are up, hurrah! But picking out particular regiments put Harper in an untenable position. Leslie and Leggett and most of the printmakers would not support this type of criticism. Moreover, Harper soon learned that he was needlessly damaging reputations. Most of the soldiers of the Fourth Pennsylvania and Varian's Battery were not deserters, and they were understandably angry at the slur against their units. Josh Billings recalled that many men—including the "most worthy and loyal of citizens"—did not re-enlist for entirely adequate reasons, and they resented the implication that they were cowards. Harper shifted to a positive tack. One cartoon showed a young son offering to help his father take off his boots. But his father—a three-month volunteer home on leave—replied that he'll leave them on as he is only going to have a cup of tea and then he'll be off again.[17]

Harper also tried to encourage *new* enlistments, and in this campaign he was supported by the other publishers. Artists enlisted the support of women. One of their primary appeals was that every man who enlisted was sure to win his lady's heart. A patriotic envelope typical of many had pictures of the flag and a young woman together with the motto: "Our hearts are with the Heroes, Who defend our glorious Flag." A cartoon in *Vanity Fair* showed a wife telling her husband that she would take his place behind the counter so he could enlist. Other artists used the same theme in a more pointed way. *Vanity Fair* showed a parlormaid rebuffing an over-amorous cook: "Don't bother me! Why ain't you away soldiering with the rest, you great hulking fellow? Kisses is for them that comes back!" Another cartoon showed Arabella and Augustus listening to a hero tell about the fight at Bull Run, and Arabella, "who adores the defenders of our Union," tells Augustus: "Oh, how I do wish you were a major—or captain—or—or something 'nice.' " In this and other cartoons, the artists implied that men who stayed at home were effeminate. McLenan pictured a woman holding her husband on her lap:

"He shouldn't go to the horrid war, away from his 'wifey, tifey,' and spoil his pretty mustache, so he shouldn't, sweet little boy. He shall have a petticoat and a broom, and stay at home."[18]

Yet young men continued to stay at home. Early in 1862 Edward Dicey saw very few indications in New York City of any great enthusiasm for the war. In contrast to an earlier visit, the bookshop windows were bare of war prints. He then went west, but found the situation there just the same. Many state governments began conscripting men for the army. Frank Leslie supported conscription in the interest of justice. He believed that many men of the middle and upper classes had failed to do much to crush the rebellion, and that so far the war had been a poor man's fight. Artists ridiculed the "swells" who attempted to dodge the draft. A provision in the Militia Act of 1862 allowing a draftee to hire a substitute elicited a number of cartoons portraying men who took advantage of this loophole as effeminate cowards. Cartoonists called upon the women to tell their boys friends who found substitutes that they, the women, had found substitutes for them.[19]

But artists and publishers who interpreted the question of military service only in terms of courage vs. cowardice grossly oversimplified the problem. Fletcher Harper was especially blind to any viewpoint other than his own. He apparently could not see that in many instances the opposition to military service stemmed from more general grievances. Too many people saw too much evidence of political and business profiteering. Resentment was particularly strong among workingmen who foresaw an influx of southern Negroes threatening their jobs, and who also felt that the substitute clause of the draft discriminated against them. In many areas Democratic politicians quietly and unofficially provided leadership for the opposition. When the Congress passed a national conscription act in 1863, hostility to the draft had crystalized. In New York City it virtually exploded.

On Sunday, July 12, 1863, the names of the first Gotham conscripts appeared in the New York newspapers. By the following morning the East Side was seething with anger. Small bands of sullen men and women gathered in the streets. The Irish were out in force, but they were not the only ones. All of them were furious with the huge impersonal operations of the draft, and they were ready to vent their rage on anyone who represented authority. They moved inexorably toward Third Avenue and draft headquarters. There agitators spurred them on, and they poured into the building to burn the hated conscription records, and then set fire to the building itself. Once ignited, the riot quickly spread to most of the East Side. Rioters broke into and looted stores, particularly liquor stores. Fired with liquid courage, some marched to the armory on Second Avenue and seized rifles and ammunition, while others disarmed soldiers in their barracks. Many seized clubs and paving stones for weapons. Now numbering in the thousands, the mob began attacking anyone and everything associated with the war, particularly army troops, abolitionists, and Negroes. For more than three days, New York lived in terror.[20]

Frank Leslie sent seven of his office artists into the streets. Trying to remain as inconspicuous as possible, they mingled with the spectators as they made their sketches. They showed the mob breaking into clothing stores and throwing the loot out into the streets where women rioters fought among themselves for the best pickings. Others sketched the brawling hand-to-hand battles between rioters and police. They also showed how troops were forced to shoot and bayonet rioters. The regiments in the city at the start of the riots were both desperate and angry; artists showed how the bodies of several army officers had been mutilated. There were also horrible atrocities committed against Negroes. The rioters behaved as if Negroes were responsible for all their troubles, and they turned against them with a mad hate. Leggett's artists showed them plundering and burning a Negro orphan asylum, and at another place they sketched the body of a lynched Negro hanging from a tree as several rioters set it aflame with torches.[21]

There was fear of a direct attack against the *Harper's* office. The mob was incensed against newspapers that supported the draft—the metropolitan police saved Greeley's *Tribune* from burning only after a vicious fight with the rioters—and rumors were rife that the rioters planned to burn the Harpers' Building. Fletcher Harper and his brothers immediately barricaded the entrances and distributed weapons to some of their employees. George William Curtis also heard that the mob planned to burn his home on Staten Island. He quickly evacuated his family to the country, and then joined a neighborhood defense unit. But the mob never reached either Staten Island or the Harpers' building.[22]

The assignment to sketch the riots for the *Weekly* went to Thomas Nast. He had just returned from Pennsylvania where he had missed the battle of Gettysburg, and he was in no mood for another failure. Dressed in a natty suit, spats, straw hat, and carrying a cane, he joined the crowds that were watching the mob. He worked his way uptown to make sure his wife and daughter were safe. At Second Avenue and 34th Street, he saw rioters throw a rope around the neck of an army officer and beat him with rocks and clubs as they dragged him along the street. He sketched the looting of Brooks Brothers and other near-by tailors' shops. At Fifth Avenue and 43rd Street, he witnessed the mass assault on the Colored Orphan Asylum, and sketched the rioters as they chased and beat the Negro children who fled from the burning building. At one point, a "fearful looking desperado" tried to rob him at gunpoint, but with a touch of bravado, Nast called out to some nearby rioters: "Boys, here's a fellow wants to draft me; are we going to stand for that?" and then slipped away in the brawl that followed. During the next two days, he was again in the streets, sketching the attack on the *Tribune* office and a lynching in Clarkson Street. At one corner on the far East Side, he sketched the body of a sergeant lying in the gutter, the neighborhood youngsters lifting its arms and letting them fall with a dead thud. Their mothers were busy chatting on nearby stoops, apparently not at all concerned about their children's unusual plaything.[23]

The artists did not hesitate to affix the responsibility for the riots. Every one of them was convinced that only the worst elements of the city's population had taken part, and by the "worst elements" they meant the Irish. Their pictures were actually caricatures, showing besotted Irishmen in a bacchanalian orgy, burning, killing, and plundering in the streets of New York to the delight of their shrieking wives and squat-faced offspring. Several pictures also showed Democratic leaders and supposed Confederate agents haranguing the mobs and urging them on to more violence. The implication was obvious. For the moment at least, traitors on the home front—"Copperheads"—posed an even greater threat than the Confederate army.[24]

Heretofore, the picture publishers had paid only passing attention to the Copperheads, who they thought were only a small group of disloyal Democrats. Clement Vallandigham of Ohio was the symbol of the movement, but the cartoonists had treated him as a noisy and harmless buffoon. In the spring of 1863 they were amused when the government exiled Vallandigham to the South; one of Leslie's cartoonists portrayed Vallandigham as a birdie in a badminton game between Lincoln and Jefferson Davis.[25]

But the widespread and violent resistance to the draft in New York was also embarrassing to the publishers. Only several weeks prior to the riots, their cartoonists had criticized Pennsylvanians for failing to succor the Union troops marching to Gettysburg. Now New Yorkers had actually turned against the army. The riots indicated that the campaign for conformity on the home front had not been completely successful. Fletcher Harper must have thought about this as he directed the building of barricades. There was also some criticism of the cartoon warfare. A writer for *The Nation* argued that many of the "forlornly absurd pictures" were malicious examples of journalistic license. He believed that the "nondescript abominations" failed to make valid criticism or show mature judgment. They did not stimulate real patriotism, and they made Federal statesmen appear "quite as ridiculous" as the Confederates. Northern cartoonists, he concluded, has done "a sorry job" of their satire.[26]

Yet even the critics admitted that the cartoons pleased the crowd. By 1863 the public preferred *Harper's Weekly* because it most vigorously supported the war. Leslie provided better news pictures, but his circulation steadily declined. Apparently when people purchased an illustrated newspaper, editorial policy was more important than the quality of the pictures. Northerners also continued to buy cartoon prints irrespective of their quality, requiring only that they preached patriotism as the most admirable of all virtues. Although sales rose and fell in response to the success or failure of the armies, the printmakers prospered. Patriotism remained profitable.

Editorial artists argued that the morale of the army depended upon the material and moral support of the home front. But the converse of this argument was also true: the success of the home front campaigns hinged upon the progress of the war. The July draft riots reflected a general disillusionment with the war. Propaganda could not stem the decline in morale that inevitably accompanied repeated defeats in the field, and slogans and rallies were not adequate substitutes for victories. By the early summer of 1863, it was abundantly clear that the home front and the war front were mutually dependent.

Oddly enough, the riots occurred several weeks after northern armies won two great victories at Vicksburg and Gettysburg. However, these triumphs soon had a huge impact on the home front. Perhaps the nation was at last on the road to reunion. Harper even abandoned his campaigns to stimulate enlistments, and basked in the warm glow of the victories. Momentarily, the home front crusade retired into hibernation. But the techniques and themes editorial artists had developed were ready for use if the need again rose.

IX

Vicksburg and Gettysburg

The first week of July 1863 was a time of triumph for the Union. Even the draft riots in New York two weeks later did not tarnish the victories. In the West, Ulysses S. Grant captured Vicksburg, opened the Mississippi for the Union, and cut the Confederacy in two. This was an odd campaign for the westerners, more like the war of attrition they associated with the Army of the Potomac, but they proved they could handle a pick and shovel as well as anyone. The easterners also fought a campaign that reversed the usual patterns. At Gettysburg they fought on the defensive for a change, and when the battle was over they saw Lee's battered veterans in retreat. Westerners were fighting like easterners and easterners like westerners, and it demonstrated that the differences were not as real as they had once been. When Grant came east early the next year, the union of the armies was complete.

The Vicksburg campaign was the grand climax of the Western River War, but only a few of the Bohemians who had followed the westerners from Springfield to Shiloh were present for the final victory. Alex Simplot and Henri Lovie were soon to retire from the war. After Shiloh, Simplot had sketched Henry Halleck's campaign against Corinth. But in June he went home to Dubuque to rest and recuperate. In November he campaigned with Grant's army in Tennessee but produced few sketches. About the time of Shiloh, he contracted a chronic case of diarrhea which he could not cure, and early in 1863 he left the army for the last time.[1]

Simplot's retirement was a blessing in disguise for Fletcher Harper. As long as Harper relied on Simplot, the *Weekly's* coverage of the western war suffered. At Donelson and Shiloh he showed a remarkable skill for arriving on the scene long after the battle was over. Even when he was present, his sketches lacked tension and excitement. He much preferred to draw the paraphernalia of war—ships, forts, and guns—rather than the men themselves. His portraits

112

of the westerners were conventional and uninteresting; he seldom showed men who ached, swore, and sweated. It was ironic that the artist who so seldom sketched the daily miseries of the army had to leave the army as a victim of one of its most common complaints.

Harper's replacement for Simplot was Theodore R. Davis, an effervescent young man around whom many legends grew. Franc Wilkie was responsible for the story that during the Vicksburg campaign Davis frequently changed clothes with dead Confederates in full sight of the enemy, "simply for the novelty of the change."[2] The story is doubtful, but there was no doubt that Davis enjoyed his work. Most of the generals from McDowell to Grant knew and liked this slender sandy-haired young man with the gregarious manner and quick smile. Though only twenty-three, he had nearly six years' experience as a sketch artist. He was a fast worker, interested in every aspect of army life, and usually he submitted his sketches with a letter full of his own personal adventures. He was not as mature as Alf Waud, but he was the most productive of all of Harper's artists. His appointment to Grant's army immediately injected new life into the *Weekly's* western illustrations.[3]

Henri Lovie spent a long furlough with his family in Cincinnati after his great effort at Shiloh, but even at home he could not escape the war. In July and September 1862 he sketched several campaigns across the Ohio River in northern Kentucky. During December he was with the Army of the Potomac sketching the battle at Fredericksburg, and early in 1863 he campaigned in central Tennessee. Late in February, he rejoined Grant's army at Young's Point opposite Vicksburg.[4]

For several days before Lovie arrived at Vicksburg, heavy thunderstorms had soaked the region, leaving a "vast watery solitude" and a gloomy mist to envelop the army. Oilcloth figures sloshed through the mud and huddled in their tents. Then on the third day the weather cleared up "gloriously," and for the first time Lovie could see some of the problems involved in taking Vicksburg. Assault up the face of the bluffs upon which the city was located would have been suicidal. Enemy batteries on the bluffs threatened disaster to any attempt to run down the river in order to move on Vicksburg from the south. The Yazoo Delta, a sluggish lowland of swamps and bayous, was an impenetrable barrier for any army approaching Vicksburg from the north. Yet somehow Vicksburg had to be taken. It was the key to the last stretch of the river not yet in the possession of the Union, and until it was captured, it was a gateway through which the wealth of the western Confederacy poured into the old South.[5]

So far the Confederates had repulsed every assault against Vicksburg. Admiral David Porter was not able to reduce it with bombardment from the river. When Grant advanced out of Tennessee with an army, Confederate raiders destroyed his unprotected supply depots and forced him to withdraw. The Yazoo Delta stopped several combined army-navy expeditions. Lovie accompanied one of these and sketched its failure. One of his illustrations showed a small river steamer snagged between two huge trees, heavy black smoke billowing from its stacks as if in agony, the crew straining to free it with windlasses and leverage poles. Theo Davis and Lieutenant George W. Bailey, the officer who supplied Leggett with illustrations from Grant's army, accompanied other expeditions into the bayous and added their evidence to Lovie's. These failures convinced Grant that the route to Vicksburg did not lie through the swamps.[6]

There was another possibility. For some time the Engineers had been digging a canal across Young's Point to create a by-pass to a point south of Vicksburg. Lovie assured Leslie that "the canal will be a success . . . [and] we will certainly be able to run our largest boats through the cut-off in less than two weeks." But his sketches did not support this confidence. They showed Negro work crews poling equipment on rafts along a shallow flooded ditch that was no more capable of floating steamboats than the flooded forest land on both sides of the river. Moreover Grant had no faith in the canal; he kept the men digging merely to keep them busy.[7]

Lovie tried to dispel some of the concern about the apparent *impasse* of the army at Vicksburg. He expressed "great faith" in Grant's "stubborn perserverance" and the eventual success of the campaign. He also reassured Leslie's readers that despite reports about the unhealthy conditions along the river, there was less sickness than had been claimed. The hospital arrangements for the army were the best he had seen, and he promised to sketch them "as soon as more pressing matters are taken care of." It was this promise that took him upriver to the army recuperation center at Lake Providence. It was a lovely spot when he arrived; spring was budding the trees and shrubs, and thousands of songbirds filled the evergreen groves. Soldiers boated and fished on the lake, shot ducks and geese, played football, and just relaxed on the grass. Lovie promised to sketch the scene. But then something occurred that made these and other sketches entirely unnecessary.[8]

Ever since he rejoined the army he saw men become rich by buying cotton in the South and selling it in the North. The army swarmed with speculators; even several of the Bohemians had become unexpectedly wealthy. For a tired war artist who never had enough money to do all the things he wanted for his family, the temptation was too strong. At Lake Providence the opportunity came to buy into a share of cotton, and Lovie seized it. Several weeks later he was, by his standards, a rich man. Jubilantly he rushed home to Cincinnati, bought his parents the farm in Germany they had always wanted, and retired from the war.[9]

Leslie never found another artist who could adequately take Lovie's place, nor one who could compete on equal terms with Theo Davis. He had several other artists in the West—W. R. McComas, J. M. McLaughlin, and Frank Schell—but they were busy sketching campaigns elsewhere. Finally in May he assigned another of the Philadelphia Schells, Fred B. Schell,[10] to the army at Vicksburg. But before Schell arrived, the stalemated campaign suddenly exploded into action, and for several weeks Davis had the field to himself.

Grant gambled on a bold plan. Midway in April he marched his army down the Louisiana side of the river to a point south of Vicksburg. Then on the night of the 16th Porter's fleet dashed past the Vicksburg batteries. Davis was with the army, and so missed one of the more spectacular actions of the river war. Leslie's staff artists recreated the scene from newspaper descriptions, showing the fleet silhouetted against the burning buildings on the opposite shore, the night sky crisscrossed by the sparking shells from the Vicksburg batteries. The flotilla got past Vicksburg with surprisingly little damage, and during the next two weeks it ferried Grant's army across the river to the Mississippi shore.[11]

Early in May the westerners pushed off toward the state capital at Jackson some sixty miles away. They passed through a rich countryside where the roads were colored with flowers clinging to the rail fences marking the edges of plantation fields. For a hungry army that had cut itself off from the North and had to forage for its supplies, it was also a countryside rich in crops and livestock. But Davis was more interested in sketching the skirmishing and fighting along the route of the advance. Gunfire was a stimulant to him, and he began to flood Harper with sketches. He pictured the capital at Jackson in flames, and wrote Harper, "I could not help but think of the sketches that I have sent to you of the devastation of the rebels on the Baltimore and Ohio railroad, and the raid of Stuart into Chambersburg. At the moment we seem to have beaten the rebels at this their favorite game."[12]

On May 18 and after several days of stiff fighting, Grant reached Vicksburg. Flush from recent victories at Champion's Hill and Black River Bridge, the westerners were confident they could take Vicksburg by storm. Fred Schell made his first sketch of the campaign during the second of two futile assaults, showing a few of the attacking troops reaching the top of the fortifications, jabbing with their bayonets and using their rifles as clubs as they desperately tried to hold their position. It was not enough. They laid aside their weapons and reached for shovels and picks. In the days that followed they dug their own system of trenches parallel to the Confederate entrenchments. By the end of May they had closed the ring around Vicksburg. Porter's fleet held the river, and each night the gunboats dropped down to throw shells into the city. Grant brought siege guns in from the North to pommel Vicksburg during the day. Both armies settled down to a war of attrition.[13]

The westerners continued to dig. Davis and Schell showed how trenches slanted diagonally forward from the main system of fortifications and then branched out into a second inner ring. The network resembled a giant spider web with Vicksburg trapped at the center. It was hard hot work measured by the shovelfuls, but Davis reported that the men worked steadily and "with a comprehension of plan that is surprising. . . . Each hour's labor of our gallant men makes such a change in the scene that it must be a busy pencil that keeps before the readers of *Harper's Weekly* the workings of this regular siege." The rays of the sun beat down from cloudless skies and bounced back into the men's eyes. "Oh! could I but portray the heat!" Davis lamented, "the pencil cannot." Yet he did show men who stripped off their shirts and tied sweatbands around their brows as they worked, and many of his illustrations were filled with great splotches of glaring white emptiness where men looked like dark shadows, as if Davis had been squinting his eyes while he sketched.[14]

The trenches were also where many of the westerners lived and slept. Some of the main trenches were two levels deep, the upper step for the artillery and sharpshooters, the lower level for living quarters. Here the men cooked and ate their food, washed their clothes and hung them to dry, and cleaned and stacked their guns. They relaxed in shade patches under bough-woven canopies, leaning against a dirt wall with their caps pulled over their faces. They built huts and shelters with whatever material was available. Discarded pork barrels were a godsend for tables and stools, and two or three stacked on end made an excellent chimney. There was abundant cane in the area for roofing and flooring and to make dry springy beds. Some men dug shallow caves in the hillsides and lined them with cane. Davis spent many nights in one of these caves and reported that they were "excellent shelters."[15]

Some subjects Davis and Schell did not portray, either because they did not seem important at the time or because they were subjects best left alone. They ignored the medical and sanitation problems of trench warfare, the disease-breeding mud and the stagnant scum-covered water that collected in the trenches after a thunderstorm. They neglected the teamsters upon whom the entire army depended, even for its drinking water. Fraternization with the Confederates was common enough throughout the siege, but because fraternization did not suit the popular images of The Enemy, they chose to ignore it. But in most other respects, they were thorough and complete.[16]

Fighting in the forward trenches and rifle pits was particularly hazardous when Confederate sharpshooters were sometimes only several dozen yards away. It was also dangerous for the artists to sketch from those advance positions, but they took the chance. Davis reported that his sketchbook bore "indisputable evidence that sketching in plain view of sharp-eyed rebels must be rapid enough." The shovelmen devised ways to protect themselves. Some used sap rollers, two barrels bound end to end with saplings and filled with dirt, and by keeping these between themselves and the enemy, they could dig with some safety. For the sharpshooters there was the additional challenge of enticing the Confederate defenders to expose themselves and then to make the kill without getting shot in return. Davis illustrated this war of wits with several sketches showing how marksmen put their caps atop the entrenchments to draw the fire of enemy snipers, who thus exposed themselves for just the instant Federal sharpshooters needed to pull the trigger.[17]

Perhaps such devices were not sporting, but chivalry had long since died on the western front. Each man was waging his own battle for survival in the rifle pits, even though he might fraternize during the evening with the men he had been trying to kill during the day. Most of the men in the forward lines respected the skill and courage of the defenders, and Davis and Schell shared this respect. They did not caricature the enemy, and they did not create atrocity pictures even though they had innumerable opportunities to do so. Late in June, the Federals exploded a mine under a sector of the enemy lines and pushed several regiments forward to rush through the gap in the defenses. To their horror, many of the men fell into their own mine crater. Schell sketched the Confederates rolling grenades down on the trapped men, who desperately tried to throw them back before they exploded. Ordinarily this would have been the occasion for an atrocity picture illustrating the inhumanity of the enemy, but Schell's presentation was matter-of-fact and without rancor. Davis even found some humor in the mine fiasco; he sent Harper a sketch of Abraham, a Negro Confederate cook who had been blown clear across into the Union lines: "De Lord, Massa, 'tink neber should light—yah! I went up 'bout free mile." And when Davis showed him his portrait: "Yah, yah! de Lord, dis chile shore—Massa give me a quarter?"[18]

By the end of June the Confederate garrison was nearing the end of its resistance. Sniping and bombardment from the Federal trenches by day and from the fleet at night had taken their toll of life and property. The food supply was dangerously low, and many people in Vicksburg were eating mule meat and rat flesh. General John C. Pemberton knew that he and his men were trapped; they could not break through Grant's lines, they could not expect relief from the outside, and they could not hold out much longer. He asked for terms. On the afternoon of July 3 he passed through the lines to meet with Grant. " 'Twas very hot," Davis noticed, as he sat on a grassy slope near the oak tree under which the two generals were talking. Charles A. Dana, the War Department's special representative with the army, and John Rawlings, Grant's chief of staff, stood behind Davis to shield his sketchbook from the sun. He showed both men seated as they discussed terms, Grant resting his chin in his hand, Pemberton's dejection apparent from the way his hands hung limply over his knees. Davis reported that they talked for about ninety minutes and then parted with a friendly handshake.[19]

The following day there was surprisingly little jubilation during the surrender. Davis and Schell sketched the stacking of Confederate weapons, the victors sitting quietly atop their trenches watching the enemy file by. Even considering the anniversary, there was no celebrating; "not a cheer went up, not a remark was made that would give pain." The westerners were fully aware of what they had accomplished—for the first time since 1861 the Mississippi was open from St. Paul to New Orleans—but most of them were too exhausted to care. That afternoon Schell sketched a second meeting between Grant and Pemberton, Grant standing with his hands folded behind his back and puffing easily on a cigar. Schell then sketched the Federal army as it paraded into Vicksburg along a shell-scarred street. The Negroes were frankly jubilant, but the marching men were as quiet and sober as the citizens of Vicksburg who turned out to see their conquerors.[20]

The victory at Vicksburg made a national hero of a man whose true appearance was virtually unknown. The sketches Schell and Davis made at the time of the surrender were almost the first field portraits northerners had seen of Grant.[21] Certainly this was not due to lack of contact with Grant, nor to any antagonism on his part against artists; on the contrary, he was interested in their work. But all the veteran western artists who knew and admired Grant had neglected to include him in their sketches. Lovie had campaigned with him from Missouri to Vicksburg; Simplot was a classmate of Rawlings, and early in 1862 he renewed their acquaintanceship in order to meet Grant. But neither had sketched him. Davis first met Grant in 1862, and by the time of the Vicksburg campaign they were close friends. He was an eating and sleeping member of Grant's staff on the march to Vicksburg, and he helped create an informal image of the general by reporting to Harper that Grant's headquarters were "less pretentious than those of his corps-commanders" and his mess was "unnecessarily inferior as to viands and equipment." Yet he waited until the surrender of Vicksburg before he included Grant in any of his sketches.[22]

Photographic portraits added confusion to ignorance. Until 1863 the only available portrait was one made early in the war at Cairo, when Grant temporarily wore his beard much longer than his usual short clip. By the time he first attracted national attention, his wife Jessie had him clip his beard, but the portrait publishers were unaware of this, and they blithely continued to produce portraits of a long-bearded Grant. To confuse matters even more, a beef contractor named William Grant, who bore a remarkable resemblance to the long-bearded general, had also had a portrait made at Cairo that was mistakenly submitted to the illustrated weeklies as a second Ulysses S. Grant portrait. For two years Leslie and Leggett used both portraits interchangeably, while Harper relied entirely upon the portrait of the beef contractor. Davis reported that westerners who knew Grant by sight thought the mix-up of portraits was a magnificent joke. The printmakers were dependent upon the photographers and the illustrated newspapers for their likenesses of Grant, and in perfect innocence they published magnificent lithographs of Grant galloping into battle with his full beard flowing in the wind. The original error kept compounding itself. As late as the autumn of 1863, Grant's appearance was so little known by his own men that an enterprising if dishonest photographer did a good business in Chattanooga selling them fraudulent Grant portraits.[23]

Grant had a new portrait made at Vicksburg, but it did little to dispel the prevalent image of Grant. Sylvanus Cadwallader of the *New York Herald* thought that none of Grant's portraits were true to life. Any picture that showed him "standing perfectly erect, with coat buttoned to the throat, posing as a military martinet, would seem unreal to those who saw him oftenest in periods of relaxation. . . ." When posing for a picture, he was "constrained and unnatural . . . too stiff and austere in appearance to do himself justice." His early portraits always showed him impeccably uniformed, but his friends knew that he "was inclined to carelessness in dress and attitude." When in 1864 Grant came east to assume a new command, Mathew Brady had to ask for a portrait of him so he could recognize him at the train depot, and the short rumpled man that stepped off the train bore little resemblance to the portraits of "The Hero of Vicksburg." That summer Brady saw Grant again before Petersburg, and he photographed him in unsuspecting moments around headquarters, a cigar clenched in his teeth, his coat wrinkled and unbuttoned because he preferred it that way. But until that time, the public lived under the illusion that Grant was the very model of a modern major general.[24]

Vicksburg was a campaign of attrition for an army that had previously specialized in quick movement; Gettysburg was a campaign and battle much better suited to the experience of the westerners, but it was the Army of the Potomac that fought and won it. Late in June Lee crossed the Potomac. General George Gordon Meade kept his own troops between Lee and Washington as both armies fell back across Maryland. On July 1 advance units of Lee's army skirmished with Meade's men on the outskirts of Gettysburg just across the Maryland line in Pennsylvania. The skirmish quickly developed into a battle as both commanders committed more and more troops to the fight, until finally some 160,000 men were engaged in what was certainly one of the decisive battles of the war.

Lee's invasion caught the Artists' Corps of the Army of the Potomac off guard. Arthur Lumley was temporarily out of action, and Leggett had to find someone to take his place. Harper and Leslie were also short-handed. Ordinarily Theo Davis and Frank Schell would have been present for Gettysburg, but they were in the West. Harper could count only on Alf Waud, and Waud was in a depressed mood; just a few days earlier he had buried his old friend, L. W. Buckingham of the *New York Herald,* who had been killed while trying to escape a guerrilla ambush. Waud still had Buckingham's personal belongings as he rode north. Leslie's artist, Edwin Forbes, had followed the cavalry on a wild ride to Aldie, far from the route of the main army. Then he stopped over in Baltimore before he rejoined Meade. Consequently he arrived at Gettysburg only after the three-day battle was two-thirds over.[25]

Prior to the war, Forbes had been studying for a career in oil painting, but like many other impecunious art students, he became a field artist for Leslie.[26] In many ways he was well qualified for his work. He had a lively curiosity, great sensitivity, and he was an extremely skilled artist. Battle experience in the Shenandoah Valley and at Second Manassas, Antietam, Fredericksburg, and Chancellorsville qualified him as a veteran. There was only one flaw. He recalled: "I fully expected when I started for the front to accompany troops into the battle and seat myself complacently on a convenient hillside and sketch exciting incidents at my leisure." But his first battle experience in June of 1862 at Cross Keys showed him "how greatly reality differed from imagination." As he galloped forward, he discovered that he could not get within a half-mile of the battle without exposing himself to the fire of the enemy. Suddenly he realized that "to be a spectator was nearly as dangerous as being a participant," and he quite frankly admitted that his desire to witness a battle at close range "underwent great change. I concluded to wait for a more convenient opportunity." He rode back to an elevated ridge, and there seated on Kitty, his sure-footed little mare, he sketched the battle through his binoculars. In the following months he sketched the most important battles of the eastern war in the same way, through his binoculars at a safe distance, and always he was ready to touch his spurs to Kitty's flanks when a stray shell whistled in his direction. His sketches did not suffer because of his caution; indeed they were full of the details of close-in-fighting. But under no conditions would he chance the dangers himself.[27]

His determination not to expose himself was due to more than a desire to avoid personal injury. He simply did not want to see the hurt and pain of war. Casualties always disconcerted him. At Cross Keys it was the sight of the "desperately wounded who were being carried to the rear" that made him turn around and ride back. He spent one black rainy night huddled under a wagon with a wounded veteran who wondered whether his sweetheart would still have him when she saw his scarred face, and in the morning Forbes slipped away early so he would not have to see the man's face. He seldom included views of wounded or dead men in his sketches. He much preferred the quiet backwaters of the war, and his happiest days were those spent on the picket line. The undisturbed loveliness of a quiet countryside always attracted him, and he liked to ride with the cavalry through the calm valleys and across the misty ridges of the Shenandoah. But the war could not always be that enjoyable, and as he rode toward Gettysburg, he was approaching the climax of his personal dilemma.[28]

In the meantime, the publishers dispatched staff artists to Pennsylvania to supplement the work of the field artists. They might as well have saved themselves the effort. George Law, an occasional contributor to *Leslie's,* barely had time to dispatch two sketches of the Confederate army in Chambersburg before he was captured. Albert Berghaus, another of *Leslie's* staff artists, made only one sketch of the enemy burning a railroad bridge near Wrightsville. Thomas Nast sketched the preparations in Philadelphia to meet the invasion, and then hurried on to Harrisburg, only to find himself under arrest. One of his in-laws had been arrested for wearing a Confederate flag, and the local authorities would not allow Nast to leave town until after the battle. Upon his release he moved toward Gettysburg, meeting wounded men returning from the battle, and he sketched a small skirmish near Carlisle, but that was the extent of his contribution to the *Weekly.*[29] Frank Bellew was the only "extra" to reach Gettysburg. An Irishman born in India and a resident of New York City since the mid-Fifties, Bellew never claimed to be anything more than one of the best cartoonists in the profession. Readers of *Leslie's, Harper's Weekly,* the *Illustrated News,* and *Vanity Fair* loved his work. Leaving the pubs and taverns near Park Row to go to war was an implausible experience for him, but he agreed to sketch Lee's invasion for the *Illustrated News.* He sketched the citizens of Harrisburg digging entrenchments, and then rode on to Gettysburg. During the three days of fighting, he made several good sketches, including one of the desperate Confederate assaults on the third day. Yet despite his success, he did not try field sketching again for another ten months. Perhaps this was because four or five days on horseback left him with a very painful case of saddle boils.[30]

For a while the photographers outnumbered the artists. Brady was at Gettysburg with Timothy O'Sullivan, one of his best operators, and they were joined by a former associate now working for himself, Alexander Gardner. They spent long hours each day waiting until the fighting was over so they could take their cameras out onto the field. While they waited, they photographed landmarks, artillery batteries, and groups of tired exhausted soldiers.[31]

As the only experienced field artist at Gettysburg until the afternoon of the second day, Alf Waud had a unique opportunity to make one of the outstanding pictorial scoops of the war, and he did not let the chance slip by. Brady photographed him during the battle, sitting on a huge boulder, jack-booted and full-bearded, a dark wide-brimmed hat shading the sketch pad resting on his knees. On the afternoon of the first day he sketched the massed Federal artillery pouring shell across the several hundred yards of open fields against the enemy positions. The artillerists worked furiously, ramming the charges home, and then snapping into position to await the order to fire. Squads of supporting infantrymen crouched behind clumps of rocks and brush and reloaded their muskets. Puffs of powder hung in the air over the field. In this and several other pictures Waud showed the vast extent of the battlefield at Gettysburg. When the firing stopped late that afternoon, Meade's army occupied a long hooked line from Culp's Hill on the right flank along Cemetery Ridge to two hills on the left flank known as Big and Little Round Top. Lee's army held a parallel position a quarter mile away along Seminary Ridge.[32]

Waud's friend and benefactor, General Gouverneur K. Warren, commanded the Federal left, and there Waud resumed work on the afternoon of the second. He made several sketches from a signal station on Little Round Top, showing Warren scanning the field through binoculars as he listened to a report from a scout. A second sketch showed two lines of Warren's men taking cover behind a low stone wall and firing rapidly at two onrushing waves of Confederate infantry. Several artillery pieces supported the Federal infantry. For a closer view Waud moved forward cautiously to sketch the ferocious struggle in the Devil's Den at the foot of the slopes. By evening, the

Confederate assaults had been broken, and he rushed along the length of the line to sketch a late attack against the Federal right. He spent the morning of July 3 well behind the lines sketching the reserves as they advanced up the long rear slopes of Cemetery Ridge to take their positions. In the early afternoon he joined them in the Union center where the main Confederate attack was expected. In several magnificent sketches he pictured the repulse of the Louisiana Tiger Brigade and then the frantic assault of Pickett's Brigade. With their failure, Lee regrouped his army and prepared for the long retreat. Waud added the final details to his sketches and rushed them off to New York. He could well be proud of them. They ranked with Lovie's Shiloh sketches as one of the outstanding picture-reports of the war.[33]

When Forbes arrived at Gettysburg late on the afternoon of the second, he rushed to the Little Round Top and sketched the scene as it might have appeared several hours earlier. What he showed from behind a battery were the lines of advancing Confederate infantrymen still in strict formation and some several hundred yards distant, and while his re-creation was good, it lacked the immediacy of Waud's illustration of the same scene. He then moved to the right flank to do the battle there, but when he discovered that enemy skirmishers were still active in the area, he made a quick withdrawal. As he told Leslie in a note that night, the fighting around the cemetery was "too hot" for him to risk a sketch, but he planned to go back the next morning.[34]

But as he ate his breakfast the following morning and talked with some of the men about what they might expect before the day was over, he became concerned. Everyone was discussing the artillery bombardments of the previous two days and agreeing that it had been the heaviest fire of the war—a virtual fury of shells that pinned men to the ground. For the first time he realized that the only place from which he could sketch the battle was Cemetery Ridge. As he pondered his problem, the bombardment began, slowly at first and then building in intensity to a deafening roar, and when the men with whom he had been talking moved up to their positions along the ridge, he found he could not force himself to join them. All morning he hung back far behind the lines, listening to the rumbling thunder of the guns, scanning the Union lines through his glasses, and "wondering at the discipline and coolness of the men under the fire they were taking." He tried to keep busy by sketching wagon trains and reserve troops pushing by him toward the front. Even a pause in the cannonading at high noon did not reassure him; he was still convinced that it would be folly to venture up onto Cemetery Ridge. Throughout the afternoon wounded men stumbled past him, and he learned from them that Pickett's Brigade was making a desperate assault against the Union center. But still he did not budge. It was as if his body was frozen. No matter what was happening, he could not force himself to go forward into that hell of ball and shell.[35]

The silence on the morning of the fourth told Forbes it was safe to move up into the area of the battle. On the ridge he sketched exhausted men resting behind the cordwood breastworks that had protected them on the preceding day. And then on the far side he saw a scene that convinced him he had been wise to stay away. "The sight was ghastly," he wrote, "everything bore the mark of death and destruction . . . the whole slope was massed with dead horses . . . the earth was torn and plowed by the terrible artillery fire, and under fences and in corners, and anywhere that slight shelter offered, the dead lay in dozens. . . ." These were the scenes Brady immortalized—clusters of bodies twisted into grotesque poses, hands still clenching cold weapons, eyes staring sightlessly, mouths pulled open in the stiffness of death. He and O'Sullivan had been busy all morning making pictures; Harper soon published nearly a dozen of their best. Even Forbes could not avoid the bodies: "It was difficult to tread without stepping on them." That day and the next he visited all the places where the fighting had raged—Little Round Top and the Devil's Den, the slopes of Cemetery Ridge and Culp's Hill—and he made furious sketches of battles he had not witnessed over ground that was now still and cold. By the evening of the fifth, he had completed seven sketches and a map of the field to send to Leslie. He then joined the slow pursuit after Lee. At Frederick in Maryland, he was stranded. "I shall go on if possible tomorrow morning," he wrote Leslie; "my horse is lame." It had been raining for several days, and he was cold and miserable.[36]

July was the turning point of the war for Frank Leslie. On the 25th he issued a supplementary issue with Schell's sketches from Vicksburg, Forbes' Gettysburg sketches, and the sketches his staff artists had made of the New York draft riots. But despite this bold exterior he was seriously worried. In the East, Forbes had proved unreliable; in the West, Leslie had lost the advantage over Harper the moment Henri Lovie left the army. There were other reasons for concern. His policy of partisan neutrality had proved quite successful—

among non-partisans; but by 1863 there were few such individuals left in the North. Circulation was declining, and for the first time since 1855, *Leslie's* was in second place among the illustrated weeklies.

But if there was concern at *Leslie's,* there was desperation at the offices of the *Illustrated News.* Arthur Lumley missed Gettysburg, and although he remained with the army for several more months, he submitted only occasional sketches. When he retired, Leggett was left without a single full-time sketch artist at the front. Circulation skidded, and eventually a new management resorted to desperation measures to save the paper.

At *Harper's* there was jubilation. Fletcher Harper's two years of building was showing results. His artists were setting the pace. Nast's editorial pictures were without serious competition. Theo Davis, soon to be joined by William Waud, gave the *Weekly* undisputed supremacy in the West. Competition remained intense in the East, but after Gettysburg Alf Waud was undoubtedly the top sketch artist with the Army of the Potomac. Advertising picked up, and circulation remained steady at 120,000 copies a week. After July 16, when Federal troops restored order in riot-torn New York, Harper relaxed. The future was bright.

X

At Ease

Pictures illustrating the campaigns at Vicksburg and Gettysburg and the horror of the New York draft riots indicated that the images of warfare had undergone extensive revision. Gone was the crusading fervor of the Heroic War. In the first two years of the war, editorial artists created the image of The Enemy, showed northerners how to be ideal citizen-soldiers, questioned the strategy of Fremont and McClellan, denounced Burnside's tactics at Fredericksburg and praised Grant's campaigns at Henry and Donelson, and criticized or approved the military and political decisions of Lincoln and his cabinet. But gradually they shifted from a negative to a positive approach, relied less on attacking specific individuals, and instead concentrated on rallying public opinion to some of the controversial wartime issues—emancipation, use of Negro troops, and the political control of the war. After 1863 the role of the editorial artists declined with the mounting tide of Federal victories, except for brief flurries of activity during the presidential campaign of 1864 and in the bitter aftermath of Lincoln's assassination.

At the same time, sketch artists had been developing a new artistic concept of war. The eastern artists who achieved full maturity at Gettysburg and the western artists who campaigned with Grant and Sherman in the Ohio and Mississippi valleys were dissatisfied with the conventional images. No longer were they entranced with the men on horseback, the generals with plumed hats, and the momentary heroes. They had also learned that war involved much more than combat with the enemy, and that soldiers were not automatons but individual men with a magnificent variety of appearances and attitudes. Gradually they began to illustrate the war from the viewpoint of the men in the ranks. The result was a new composite panorama of army life, composed of distinct images of Billy Yank when he was at ease, when he was under fire, and when he was on the march.

127

At the beginning of the war the publishers were convinced that their subscribers and regular purchasers wanted combat pictures. Their general assumption was that crusading armies spent every moment in the frenzied pursuit of victory. Frank Leslie persistently maintained that his aim was "not to give the results of artistic studies of imaginery scenes, so as to display the genius of the artist, but to mirror life as it passes, portraying the scenes of great events of public interest." He sent his artists to the front to sketch the *war,* and that was to take precedence over every other subject. As late as 1864 he published one of Forbes' sketches showing several soldiers looking at a peep show, but he explained to his readers that because the army had gone into winter quarters, there were no longer any stirring views of an heroic nature to publish.[1]

But many officers and soldiers with the armies were not so certain that combat was the beginning and the end of army life. Major James A. Connolly was thoroughly disenchanted with the images of the combat army. "In your last letter," he wrote his wife, "you seem to think that I don't give you enough description of battles, armies, scenery, etc. If you were as tired of battles and armies as I am you wouldn't care to spend much time on them for they are very unpleasant things to be in and one does not like to reproduce memories of unpleasant things."[2] Alert sketch artists soon realized that fighting and skirmishing accounted for only a small part of each soldier's time. For every ten hours of battle, a soldier usually spent ten weeks in the camps or on bivouac. Although the combat hours were crucial, a number of the artists concluded that their portrayal of the war was incomplete so long as they illustrated only the fighting army. Winslow Homer in particular was convinced that the true personality and character of the soldiers was to be found in their postures and expressions when they were off duty and at ease.

Homer was a commercial artist only because he needed the income. Recognition of his talent as a painter came late, and in the meantime he supported himself by drawing pretty girls on sheet music covers and painting gay pastoral pictures for the illustrated weeklies. He served an apprenticeship with J. H. Bufford, a Boston lithographer, and in 1858 went to New York to study and exhibit at the National Academy of Design. As a part-time artist and engraver for *Harper's Weekly,* he earned sixty dollars a page—the best rate of any artist on *Harper's* staff. Temperamentally, he fitted the stereotype of the artist: gregarious and happy one moment, morose and withdrawn the next.

Mathew Brady.
(*Brady-Handy Collection, Library of Congress*)

Thomas Nast.
(*Brady-Handy Collection, Library of Congress*)

Fletcher Harper.
(*Brady-Handy Collection, Library of Congress*)

Alfred R. Waud (standing, right), December, 1863.
(Prints and Photographs Division, Library of Congress)

Floating Battery in Action against Fort Sumter, April 12, 1861, from a sketch by an officer; *Leslie's,* April 27, 1861. *(Courtesy of Henry E. Huntington Library)*

...alry Charge at Fairfax Court House, May 31, 1861; *Harper's Weekly,* June 15, 1861.

(Prints and Photographs Division, Library of Congress)

...ttle of Bull Run, July 21, 1861, by Arthur Lumley; *Leslie's,* August 3, 1861.

(Courtesy of Henry E. Hungtington Library)

Death of General Lyon at Wilson's Creek, August 10, 1861, by Henri Lovie; *Leslie's* August 24, 18
(Prints and Photographs Division, Library of Congr

Home Front Indifference, probably by Frank Bellew; *New York Illustrated News,* July 18, 1863.

(Prints and Photographs Division, Library of Congress)

FANCY PORTRAIT OF THE VIRGINIA GENTLEMAN WHO OBJECTED TO THE OCCUPATION OF ALEXANDRIA BY ELLSWORTH'S ZOUAVES, BECAUSE THEY ARE NOT "FIRST FAMILIES." See page 91.

First Family Virginian, by Thomas Nast; *New York Illustrated News,* June 15, 1861.

(Prints and Photographs Division, Library of Congress)

Union Prisoners in Richmond, Virginia; *Harper's Weekly,* January 18, 1862.
(*Prints and Photographs Division, Library of Congress*)

Retreat of Dresser's Battery at Shiloh, April 6, 1862, by Henri Lovie; *Leslie's,* May 17, 1862, Supplement.

(*Prints and Photographs Division, Library of Congress*)

lay in Camp—Soldiers Playing "Foot-Ball," by Winslow Homer; *Harper's*
kly, July 15, 1865.

k of Fredericksburg, by Arthur Lumley—a sketch his publisher was *not* willing to print.

Sappers at Work during the Siege of Vicksburg, by Theodore R. Davis; *Harper's Weekly*, July 11, 1863.

(Prints and Photographs Division, Library of Congress)

Longstreet's Attack at Gettysburg, by Alfred R. Waud; *Harper's Weekly*, August 8, 1863.

(Prints and Photographs Division, Library of Congress)

Union Soldiers, by Winslow Homer.

(Courtesy of the Cooper Union Museum)

Union Soldier, by Edwin Forbes.

Union Soldier, by Edwin Forbes.

(Prints and Photographs Division, Library of Congress)

Lincoln and Miscegenation; a print issued by Bromley and Co. of New York, 1864.
(Prints and Photographs Division, Library of Congress)

The Brave Wife; a print issued by Currier & Ives.
(Prints and Photographs Division, Library of Congress)

Straggler, by Alfred R. Waud; *Harper's Weekly,* March 28, 1863.
(*Prints and Photographs Division, Library of Congress*)

Escaping Brush Fires in the Wilderness, by Alfred R. Waud; *Harper's Weekly,* June 4, 1864.
(*Prints and Photographs Division, Library of Congress*)

Bomb-proof Rifle Pit at Petersburg, October, 1864, by A. W. Warren; *Harper's Weekly,*
November 5, 1864.

(*Prints and Photographs Division, Library of Congress*)

Burial Detail at Petersburg, 1864, by E. F. Mullen; *Leslie's,* September 3, 1864.
(*Prints and Photographs Division, Library of Congress*)

Compromise with the South, by Thomas Nast; *Harper's Weekly,* September 3, 1864.
(*Prints and Photographs Division, Library of Congress*)

Sheridan's March up the Shenandoah, a sketch by Alfred R. Waud.

(*Prints and Photographs Division, Library of Congress*)

Friends calling at his Washington Square quarters never knew whether he would grab their hands in greeting or slam the door in their faces. Despite Harper's urging, he refused to work full time for the *Weekly*. "I had a taste of freedom," he recalled. "The slavery of Bufford's was too fresh in my recollection to let me care to bind myself again. From the time that I took my nose off that lithographic stone, I have had no master, and never shall have any."[3]

But Harper did persuade Homer to accompany the Army of the Potomac during the Peninsula campaign, and later he followed Grant in the Wilderness. During the spring of 1862 he became a familiar figure around McClellan's camp, a slightly-balding young man of twenty-six with a heavy beard and handle-bar mustaches. The men liked to watch him work as he sat atop a barrel with a large paper pad balanced across the knees, sketching rapidly with bold sharp strokes and then smudging with his thumb for shadow and depth. He scribbled a half dozen or more quick studies on a single page, then flipped the sheet over and made some more. No subject was too insignificant, no detail too small to escape his attention, and he filled his notebooks with studies of such things as the folds and creases of an officer's boots and the way a veteran slammed home his ramrod.[4]

Many of his published illustrations from the Peninsula were battle pictures, because at the time that was what Harper wanted. But even the majority of these were studies of personnel rather than pictures of a particular skirmish. He cared not one whit for the battle itself, only for the men. He particularly liked the superb posture of cavalry troopers as they sat their horses, their shoulders and elbows thrown back to balance the forward thrust of their bodies. "Sharpshooter" was a graceful study of a Union rifleman perched in the branches of a tree. Privates, corporals, and contraband Negro laborers around the camps posed readily for him. Some of his favorite portraits were of teen-age boys who tried to hide their age by wearing their caps low over their brows. "Surgeon at Work" was one of the first pictures to give attention to the army doctors. "Thanksgiving," "Winter Quarters," "News from the War," a study of the arrival of newspapers in camp, and "Pay Day" were based upon his working sketches. On his own time he painted several water colors of army life and published a series of lithographs entitled *Campaign Sketches*. In 1863 he exhibited "The Last Goose at Yorktown," showing a skirmish between two hungry soldiers and a very wary goose, and "Home Sweet Home," a study of homesick soldiers. Harper noticed with some pride that the latter painting was sold by the second day of the show. Nevertheless, two years passed before he could persuade Homer to accompany the army once again.[5]

Homer's interest in the ordinary appearance of the soldiers put him well in advance of the other artists. But from the very beginning of the war, Mathew Brady shared Homer's interests. Many of Brady's camp portraits were magnificent studies of a relaxed army—a soldier gazing pensively into a bubbling pot of stew, a general propped against a tree, a Negro contraband asleep under a wagon. Yet the notion persisted that aimless activity was intolerable. Officers explained that routine duties kept the men in trim condition, but the men themselves had more pungent explanations for this busy-work. Consequently the first images of the army at ease were a compromise between the way the soldiers actually passed their non-combat hours and the way people on the home front thought they ought to be spending that time. Sketches from the camps in 1861 portrayed beehives of martial activity; picket duty appeared to be an endless series of skirmishes. But as Alf Waud, Arthur Lumley, Edwin Forbes, and some of the other veterans of the Army of the Potomac recognized the fallacies in these sketches, they began to follow the lead of Homer and Brady.[6]

Army reviews were one form of activity that some people thought served a useful purpose. During the period of the McClellan command, they were a standard part of army routine. When Lincoln visited the Army of the Potomac late in 1861, McClellan ordered one of the most impressive of the grand reviews. Lumley and Alf Waud showed the President and the General taking the salute from the soldiers. A host of spectators, including many of the pretty wives of the officers, enjoyed the spectacle. A band provided the beat for a seemingly endless line of infantrymen in close formation, artillerists riding their gun carriages and caissons, and cavalrymen holding a tight rein on their mounts. Waud's giant sketch showed some ten thousand troops assembled on one field; Leggett claimed it was the "largest wood engraving ever made in the United States."[7]

Yet reviews had only a limited popularity. Many westerners never participated in a review until they marched down Pennsylvania Avenue with Sherman's army at the end of the war. They never appealed to the men in the ranks. Sam Nichols, a veteran with the Massachusetts Volunteers, thought it was "terribly fatiguing to go through with the ceremony—worse even than a day's march of thirty miles." By 1864 the army called a review only to honor a visit of the President or to welcome the arrival of a new commanding general. Nichols' first thought when he heard that Grant was to lead the Army of the Potomac was, "This army will probably be reviewed, another scene for the artists of the illustrated press." Yet by that time even the sketch artists had lost their enthusiasm for reviews.[8]

Picket duty had a greater and more lasting attraction. Edwin Forbes found the picket line "strangely fascinating." The first few times he went out to sketch the men on patrol, he was apprehensive of ambush, but he noticed that the pickets themselves were not at all concerned. Thereafter he looked forward to the hours he spent on the line, sharing meals with the men, and afterward relaxing around a fire and listening to their talk. On the picket line he escaped from the tensions of the camps and battlefields; there the war seemed remote and sometimes unimportant. As well as he could he tried to convey these impressions in his sketches, showing the pickets patrolling the line and then returning to their huts to pull on their pipes as they watched their suppers cook.[9]

Winter on the line allowed the artists to portray scenes of solitary loneliness such as were available nowhere else in the army. The pickets built makeshift mud and bough huts against the cold winds and drifting snow, but even at best these provided shelter only after the men were off duty. Until then, they faced the elements in regulation-issue coats and cloaks. Lumley sent Leggett a sketch of a scene he and the other artists saw many times—a picket standing duty in a March snowstorm, leaning in frozen stiffness on his rifle, his coat pulled tight around his neck, his head bent under the cold.[10]

Union and Confederate pickets were often within shouting distance of each other, and they exchanged a good-natured banter across the lines. "It seemed scarcely possible." Forbes wrote, "that within so short a distance were men who at a moment's notice might engage in deadly conflict and yet the men who do such deadly work are free from actual malice." Artists testified to the informal friendships that sprang up between enemy pickets, and showed how they exchanged newspapers, tobacco, and coffee. During these exchanges it was mutually understood that neither would take the other prisoner. Alf Waud sketched one exchange where an uninitiated officer appeared and took the Confederate picket prisoner, much to the disgust of his own men who argued that the picket should have been allowed to return to his own lines.[11]

Fraternization with the enemy was not ordinarily punished, but other violators of military law sometimes suffered unusually harsh penalties. Early in the war Leslie published a sketch of a soldier tied to a tree in such a way that all his weight rested on his toes and pulled against his arms tied high behind his back; Leslie's disapproval was expressed in the accompanying caption: "Way in which bad officers make bad soldiers worse." But rather than shock the people at home with pictures showing corporal punishment, the sketch artists illustrated the sometimes-bizarre methods by which the army ridiculed and humiliated minor offenders. The first time Forbes saw the army make an example of two thieves, he was awakened from an afternoon siesta by the drummers and fifers playing the "Rogue's March." Jumping to his feet, he saw a great crowd of soldiers running toward the center of the camp, and seizing his sketchbook, he joined them. The officers in charge stripped the insignia from the two thieves, shaved their heads, hung placards labeled "Thief" around their necks, and then ordered them drummed out of camp. Forbes told Leslie that the scene was "one of great merriment among the regiments, and will undoubtedly have a salutary effect in the way of an example. A soldier, with true soldierly pride about him, would scarcely prefer such an indignity to being shot." The punishment for drunkards was similar; after being shaved and decorated with placards labeled "I got drunk" or "Too fond of whiskey," they often had to march around the camp in a whiskey barrel. According to a writer in *Harper's Weekly,* such treatment should have taught every drunkard "the virtue of temperance for the rest of his life."[12]

Death by firing squad was reserved for murderers, deserters, and spies. Waud, Lumley, and Forbes illustrated at least three military executions. While sketching the execution of five deserters, Forbes was impressed by how hard the army worked to achieve a dramatic effect. A muted band played the "Dead March" as the entire corps drew up in a three-sided square to watch the approach of the condemned men. After a few words with a chaplain, they were blindfolded and seated on their coffins next to open graves. The music stopped, and then the rifles of the firing squad cracked the silence. Each regiment filed past the corpses, "an awful and solemn duty," one soldier recalled, "yet necessary for the safety of the forces." Even so, Forbes reported that the execution of the deserters "did not deter two men of the same company to which the deserters belonged from slipping away on the very night of the execution; and they were never captured."[13]

Some aspects of camp life required the artists to use a good deal of discretion. They approached the problems of sickness and sanitation with caution. One tough old veteran complained, undoubtedly in jest, that the newspapermen were not at all interested in the skill with which the army dug sinks. The few illustrations showing soldiers gambling were mainly the work of western artists. When Henri Lovie sketched the westerners playing poker, roulette, and chuck-a-luck, Leslie described the scene as "camp life in one of its worst phases." But he added: "Morality must not be too exacting . . . make great allowances for brave men, whose hearts are with their far off homes, and who require occasional excitement to carry them through their labors." Soldiers everywhere consumed tremendous amounts of beer and hard liquor when they could get it, and drunkenness was not uncommon. But except for pictures showing the punishment of drunkards, the artists might have been sketching a camp meeting of the Temperance League. They also ignored fist fights and brawls and the men's penchant for practical jokes. It was a well-behaved army—if one believed the illustrations.[14]

Sketch artists and photographers generally portrayed the camps as sanctuaries where the men relaxed from the tensions of the war. Most of the artists thought of themselves as intermediaries between the men in the service and their families and friends at home, and they were perfectly willing to paint a bright and cheerful picture. And under most circumstances camp life *was* rather pleasant. Walt Whitman wrote his mother from a camp near Culpepper: "There is more fun around here than you would think. . . ."[15]

One of the surest ways to reassure servicemen's families about the welfare of their boys was to show their living quarters. Summer shelter consisted primarily of tents embellished with bough and branch canopies, hammocks, pine-needle mattresses, and scrap-timber tables and stools. Winter quarters were much more elaborate. Late in 1864 Joseph Becker was with the Army of the James when the men built their winter quarters. He told Leslie he could hardly believe "the alacrity with which our brave boys, most of whom have been accustomed to all the luxuries of a city life," cut and notched logs and gathered all the other materials they needed. A few laid board floors, but most were satisfied with hard-packed dirt. Then they raised the walls and carefully chinked each crack with clay or mud. Many soldiers finished their cabins with a roof of tightly-woven boughs packed with mud, but others undertook the tedious work of splitting logs with axes and wedges to make shingles. The

133

pride of every cabin was its chimney. Andrew McCullum did a series of illustrations for Leslie on chimney architecture. The most common material was green timber lined with clay and mud. A few made a sort of narrow teepee from fence rails. Pork barrels and oyster cans with the ends knocked out and stacked end to end made the best chimneys. With the building of a sandbox stove, they were ready to move in.[16]

Anxious to add to their own creature comforts, many soldiers spent the winter improving the interiors of their cabins. They insulated and decorated their cabins by lining the inside walls with tree bark. They built bunks for their sleeping rolls and usually a table and several stools. Their equipment and extra clothes hung from wall pegs. Portraits and pictures completed the interior decorations. All of this work required a good deal of effort on their own time after completing their regular duties, but they considered it worthwhile. "It is amazing," Becker wrote Leslie, "to see with what an air of satisfaction they look around them when their work is completed, and they sit down to take their first smoke in their new habitation. Truly, every man is a Robinson Crusoe. . . ."[17]

Forbes spent the winter of 1863–64 at Rappahannock Station and Culpepper Court House in cabins similar to those of the men, except he had a removable canvas roof which gave him better light by which to work. He was glad to be away from the pressure of combat and to be free to sketch the men at ease. That winter he wandered through the camps sketching whatever caught his fancy—contrabands shaving enlisted men in homemade barber chairs, infantrymen lounging on their bunks reading letters from home or rushing to greet the newspaper carriers with papers telling of the war in other theaters. He showed men washing their clothes in cold winter streams and squatting on their haunches whittling on a stick as they waited for their coffee to boil. He liked nothing better than spending an evening in front of a fire, smoking his pipe, and talking with the men. Sometimes he set up his easel and painted water colors from the notes in his sketchbook. For the most part, he worked to please himself. But he sent many of his sketches to New York, and somewhat to his surprise Leslie published most of them.[18]

By 1864 Leslie and the other publishers were printing many at-ease sketches, but their choice of subjects was sometimes puzzling. Artists never hesitated to sketch men marching in the mud, but illustrations of muddy camps and rain-soaked tents were rare. They made innumerable sketches of foraging parties bringing in livestock and grain and vegetables, but very few of men returning with firewood. They were fascinated by pickets cooking their meals over small fires, but they thought perspiring cooks working over huge pots of stew were merely prosaic. Nor were they particularly interested in what the troops thought about their food. Only Thomas Nast portrayed the grumbling and sarcastic comments to the cooks that were common enough in the mess lines.[19]

It was the same with recreation. Many soldiers spent their off-duty hours between supper and taps and on Sunday afternoons quietly and by themselves, but the artists were primarily interested in the vigorous group activities. They ignored the singing and dramatic clubs, but not the riotous stag dances. They passed by the chance to illustrate religious meetings, which were not well attended anyway, but they did sketch the elaborate costume parties that attracted many of the officers' wives. They were delighted with competitive contests, and sports: barrel rolling, three-legged races, greased-pig chases, wrestling, boxing, and sharpshooting. Baseball and soccer football were the most popular team sports. Homer was only one of many artists who sketched a football game, showing a few men kicking the ball, but most of the players in his illustration were having much more fun swinging their fists and jabbing with their elbows. It was undoubtedly the closest any artist ever came to illustrating a general brawl.[20]

The artists reassured the folks at home that their soldiers celebrated the holidays in the traditional manner. In 1864 J. E. Taylor and Joseph Becker did a complete report on Thanksgiving in the Army of the Potomac, illustrating the elaborate preparations required to bring in and distribute the huge supplies of food. A final sketch in their series showed the happy results— a half-dozen men seated around a table directing the work of the man who carved the turkey. Earlier in the war, Homer did a series on Thanksgiving when the army made less effort to provide the necessities. Many of the men got their Thanksgiving treats through the mails, and Homer showed that most of them were pleased with their pies and cookies, but he could not resist including the startled expression on one man's face when he opened his package and found a raw fish.[21]

Christmas with the army was a time for sentiment and homesickness. "It is Christmas Eve," one soldier wrote in his diary in 1864, "and I am alone. Dan and Milt have gone to town. Griff is on guard. Nobody to interrupt my quiet meditations, and I can but think of the many happy hearts that now beat in my Northern home, of those surrounded by friends and relatives and the influence of home." This was the mood Thomas Nast created each year when he showed Christmas with the troops as he believed the readers of the *Weekly* imagined it to be. His effort for 1861 showed a dozen soldiers representing Young America, "proud and erect, undismayed by intestine conflict or foreign dangers," with their cups raised in a toast for "The Union Forever." A year later he showed Santa Claus in one of the camps distributing useless toys to the men, who received them with expressions of childish wonder on their faces. And what should Santa find at the bottom of his pack but a goodly supply of the latest issue of *Harper's Weekly*.[22]

The field artists knew that Christmas in the army was often a day much like other days except for gift boxes from home with mufflers and stockings, cookies and candies, and maybe a cake. Perhaps there was also a better-than-usual meal that evening. In 1861 the Army of the Potomac celebrated the first Christmas of the war with a costume party—Arthur Lumley sketched it for Leslie—but by 1863 and 1864 many men were so far away from the supply depots that whatever celebration they had was of their own making. An artist for the *Illustrated News* showed how Federal pickets toasted the good health of their Confederate counterparts across the line. Forbes was especially lonely one Christmas day until a friend invited him to a holiday dinner on the picket line. Some miles away from camp he found his hosts preparing the meal in a crude shelter thrown up against a fence. He could scarcely believe what he saw when they set the dinner on the table: rabbit stew, fricasseed chicken, griddle cakes with honey, and coffee. It was the most enjoyable feast he had had in months.[23]

Many soldiers were avid readers, but they found it extremely difficult to get interesting reading matter. They were often indignant with the religious tracts and church publications they found in the reading rooms of the United States Christian Commission: "We are not a lot of little children with minds too narrow to contemplate anything deeper than these small 'stories with a moral.'" The Sanitary Commission offered back issues of the daily and illustrated newspapers to their own regiments, but these groups could satisfy the demand of only a small part of the army. Some men subscribed to newspapers, but inevitable delays in the mails and frequent changes of address often meant that their papers reached them many weeks late. Most of the troops had to pay the prices demanded by sutlers and newsboys. Along the Potomac, five-cent newspapers often brought the distributor a 250 per cent profit, and magazines like *Harper's Monthly* sold for twice their ordinary price. In some armies the shortages were acute. At one time Sherman ordered newspapers reserved for men who had seen combat, and sometimes only officers could afford the prices. This latter situation led one disgusted private to plead: "Gentlemen of the Star fraternity . . . for God's sake do us the favor to let us read your old papers when you get through with them, if you can possibly work yourself up to so generous a pitch."[24]

Illustrated newspapers were in even shorter supply than the dailies. As late as March of 1865, only two thousand copies of *Harper's Weekly* and *Leslie's* reached the Army of the Potomac each week. This was scarcely sufficient to meet the requirements of men who "devour papers with a rapidity that would astonish them that have less leisure time." When Leggett received reports from soldiers that they could not get copies of the *Illustrated News,* he complained that there was "very unfair management somewhere." Prices were often inflated by the demand; in early 1862 *Leslie's* was selling in Nashville at twenty-five cents to one dollar a copy. Forbes, Waud, and Homer sketched the arrival in camp of newsboys with huge packs of illustrated newspapers thrown over their saddles, and showed the chaos that followed as the men fought to buy one of the rare copies. Robert Ferguson, an English traveler, arrived at the Army of the Potomac on a mail boat carrying a consignment of *Harper's* and *Leslie's,* and he watched a regiment line up to receive their copies. "A curious sight it was to see," he wrote, "a tearing up of envelopes . . . a general rustle of opening leaves, and in a moment every man as if it had been part of his drill, was down upon the ground with the same big picture before him."[25]

Soldiers were critical readers who delighted in finding inaccuracies in the illustrations. They roared with laughter at sketches showing officers who wore their swords on the wrong hip, cavalry troops who mounted from the off-side, and infantrymen who marched into battle at the regulation hundred and ten steps a minute but nevertheless kept pace with their colonels on horseback. They thought Alf Waud's sketch showing a regiment marching into battle at shoulder arms was hilarious. On the other hand, Henry N. Blake, a captain in the Massachusetts Volunteers, was incensed when one of the illustrated newspapers made a hero of an officer he knew from personal experience to be an unmitigated coward. And veterans were frankly contemptuous of illustrations portraying major generals who exposed themselves to gunfire at the head of their men, when they all knew that field generals stationed themselves well behind the lines where they could direct the rapid deployment of their army. Pictures such as these lent credence to the cartoon in *Vanity Fair* showing "Our Artist" using toy soldiers as models for a sketch made "on the spot."[26]

Cavalrymen groaned in despair at some of the pictures showing them in action. At the beginning of the war, the illustrated newspapers were filled with pictures of "savage-looking troopers, mounted on fierce war studs, dashing at terrible speed at the head of malicious columns into the enemy's country." What especially amazed the troops was how, in the pictures, they could ride at a full gallop and fire their rifles with one hand and wave their sabers with the other. But the artists solved the problem by conveniently draping the reins over the pommel. And how they handled those flashing sabers! Nast showed one trooper who rammed his saber through the body of an enemy cavalryman so hard that six inches of the blade protruded from his back.[27]

Soldiers were not the only critics. A correspondent in the *Indianapolis Journal* wrote from Vicksburg that the "exaggerated pictures in the illustrated papers usually provoke our merriment," and a reporter for the *Cincinnati Daily Times* thought that many of the battle illustrations were "little better than a substantial farce." McClellan once remarked that artists' sketches of fieldworks were more likely to confound than aid the enemy. In 1864 the Executive Committee of the New York Historical Society reported that "the illustrated newspapers are full of sketches purporting to be pictures of important scenes, but the testimony of parties engaged shows that these representations, when they are not taken from photographs, are not always reliable." Leslie thought the charge of the Society was "grossly unjust." But he did not hesitate to accuse *Harper's Weekly* of faking a sketch of the battle of Chickamauga, and all the publishers accused each other of creating many of their battle illustrations in their New York art rooms.[28]

Nevertheless, soldiers also applauded the work of the artists. An officer at Port Royal asked his brother to send him every copy of *Leslie's:* "His map of this place is very correct; we went by it altogether on our last reconnaissance, and found it entirely correct." John C. Gray, stationed in South Carolina, had high praise for several portraits in *Harper's Weekly.* Private Oliver Willcox

Norton of the Pennsylvania Volunteers wrote his sister that the latest issue of the *Weekly* was "one of the choicest numbers I have ever seen. 'The Picket' is a gem of a woodcut . . . lifelike and true. . . . Keep it to show me when I come home." But the surest praise of all was the simple fact that every issue of the illustrated newspapers that reached the army was sold out within a matter of minutes. Hospital officials and women who worked among the convalescents also testified to the popularity of the illustrated weeklies. Repeatedly they asked the public to save their old issues for the hospitals, indicating a shortage there as well as among the front-line troops.[29]

Pictures of the army at ease were not as controversial as combat illustrations, and as a result they seldom elicited direct testimonials. But the artists portrayed many of the incidents and scenes that soldiers described in their letters and diaries. Jenkin Jones, a Wisconsin artilleryman, wished he were an artist so he could sketch the "grand and sublime sight" of the army bivouacking in the field with hundreds of campfires illuminating the hillsides—a scene Forbes sketched in an illustration entitled "Going into Bivouac at Night." Many men described picket duty in phrases that would have served as captions for illustrations, and the same was also true for sketches of camp quarters, holiday celebrations, regimental sports, and even punishments and executions. Because soldiers and sketchers described the same subject so closely, the lack of criticism was a testimonial of approval.[30]

Despite the tradition that cloaked war in images of vigorous warriors and the early disinclination of publishers to accept non-combat sketches, the artists persisted in sketching the army at ease. And in the long run, the war worked in their favor. By 1864 the artists were also establishing new images of the army under fire and on the march, and as these further undermined the old images of a crusading army, they increased general interest in what the soldiers did when they were off duty.

XI

Under Fire

During the winter of 1863–64, artists who had been portraying the army at ease had also been preparing to take the field once again. Long months in the winter camps along the Potomac had given them an intimate familiarity with the attitudes and appearances of the men who would soon be thrown into the bloodiest fighting of the war. This was an experienced and confident army that the artists had been sketching at ease—men who knew their work and performed it with easy skill. Yet nobody knew what was ahead, except that the fate of the Army of the Potomac was in the hands of a general new to the East. Early in March, Ulysses S. Grant arrived in Washington to take command of all the Union armies. Lincoln hoped that at last he had found a general who wanted to fight.

Grant was still an unknown quantity. Few people even knew what he looked like. Veterans sent for copies of the illustrated newspapers with Grant's portrait, but they were not much help. Edwin Forbes sketched the first meeting of Grant and Meade, but he showed Grant in an unnatural Napoleonic pose. Mathew Brady scarcely recognized the general when he met him upon his arrival in Washington, and as they rode from the railroad station to Williard's, he invited Grant to come to his studio the following day for a sitting. When they reached the hotel, not many of the officers in the lobby paid any attention to the short rumpled man in blue until somebody told them who he was.[1]

The next afternoon Grant went to the White House to accept his commission as major general. One of Harper's artists recorded the scene, but his portrait did not add any glory to Harper's engraves. Then in the company of War Secretary Stanton, Grant kept his appointment at Brady's studio. Brady posed the general and then noticing that the light had faded since he had last checked it, he sent one of his associates up to the roof to draw the shades back from the skylight. The assistant was so nervous he put his foot

140

through the skylight, sending a shower of glass down into the room below. Some of the large splinters missed Grant's head by only a few inches. Brady was horrified, Stanton blanched, but according to Brady, Grant hardly flinched at all. The sitting went on. As they were leaving, Stanton took Brady to one side and suggested they had better not mention what had occurred because the public might get the idea that someone had made an attempt on the new commander's life.[2]

An hour later Grant left Washington to join the army, and Brady had his portraits. One was particularly apt and characteristic—Grant standing with one hand resting on his lapel and the other jammed into his pants pocket. The only thing missing was his cigar. Several weeks later, Brady and Tim O'Sullivan and a second team of operators left the capital in two of the whatisit wagons. They spent most of April in the camps recording the army's preparations for the spring campaign.[3]

Alf Waud had also recently rejoined the army. He had been ill during the winter, and in December when a photographer made two portraits of him, he looked much older than when Brady had last photographed him at Gettysburg. Even so, he was still an extremely handsome and vigorous man. A month later, George Augustus Sala saw Waud galloping back and forth on a large brown horse, "blue-eyed, fair-bearded, strapping and stalwart, full of loud, cheery laughs and comic songs, armed to the teeth, jack-booted, gauntleted, slouch-hatted, yet clad in the shooting jacket of a civilian." In Sala's opinion, Waud knew more about the "several campaigns, the rights and wrongs of the several fights, the merits and demerits of the commanders, than two out of three wearers of generals' shoulder straps." He reported that Waud had been offered a commission on many occasions, but had declined each time. Three years of attendance on the army had given him an air of assurance that was apparent in the slight swagger of his walk and the ease with which he gave advice. He was in the prime of his life, an intelligent and mature man looking forward to another typical campaign along the Potomac. Grant would surprise him.[4]

Edwin Forbes also was on hand to take the field again. The past several months in winter quarters had been the most satisfying of his war experience. His time had been his own to spend in the camps and on the picket line sketching the side of army life he so much preferred. But as Grant ordered the army forward to the Rapidan River, Forbes had no idea how radically different this campaign would be from all the previous ones he had sketched.

Leslie also dispatched a second artist to the army. In 1859 Joseph Becker was seventeen when he started to work for Leslie as an errand boy. With the beginning of the war he wanted to join Lovie, Schell, Lumley, and Forbes in the field. Leslie told him to practice sketching, and then helped him improve his work—as he had helped Nast many years earlier—by severely critcizing every sketch. By the spring of 1864, Leslie had sent out artist after artist, but had had "considerable ill-luck" with them, and finally he gave Becker his first field assignment. He was concerned that Becker, a "slender delicate fellow" who had always been in poor health, could not withstand the physical strain of field life, and as he was leaving Leslie told him, "Joseph, I don't expect to ever see you alive again." Yet Becker flourished in the field and became hearty and robust, and he was probably the only sketch artist who did not suffer permanent damage to his health as a result of the war.[5]

On May 4, 1864 Grant sent his army across the Rapidan into Confederate Virginia. Ostensibly his target was Richmond, but his primary objective was to force Lee into battle, knowing that his own superiority of numbers and resources gave him a distinct advantage. Forbes, Waud, and Brady recorded the scene at the crossing as the long lines of wagons and men approached the river, filed across on pontoon bridges, and regrouped on the south side. Immediately ahead was the Wilderness, fifteen miles of tangled tinder-dry underbrush and ragged second growth so thick in many places that a man could not see more than fifty feet in any direction. It was familiar terrain to some of Grant's veterans; fifteen months earlier they had fought the battle of Chancellorsville a few miles away. Along the route of the advance, Brady photographed the bleached bones and skulls of the unburied dead from that battle. Grant hoped to slip through the Wilderness without a fight, but Lee had picked this as the ideal place to face Grant on terms favorable to the Army of Northern Virginia.[6]

The Battle of the Wilderness (May 5–6) was as wild and disorganized as its name. The armies became hopelessly entangled, regiments were separated from their commands, and small pockets of men fought on without the slightest idea of how the battle was going only a few yards away. A private from a Wisconsin regiment was captured and was being taken to the rear by a Confederate soldier when both men suddenly found themselves in the midst of the Union lines. Grant and Lee could not coordinate the movement of their armies, and even the divisional commanders seldom knew where all their regiments were at any one moment. After inconclusive fighting on the 5th, both armies mounted major attacks on the following day, only to have them falter when the troops came under cross fire from the enemy and sometimes even from their own men. Late that afternoon, fires broke out in the dry under-brush. The battle ebbed to a close.[7]

At no time could the artists sketch more than scattered and isolated sections of the battle, yet considering the obstacles, their illustrations were surprisingly complete. Forbes made several sketches from a hill near the Wilderness Tavern, and then moved in closer to sketch one of the skirmishes in the woods. This was Becker's first experience under fire, and he remained close to Grant and his staff, showing them dispatching couriers and signaling orders to send the infantry reserves up in support. Waud pictured a battery of artillery firing across one of the few open spaces in the Wilderness, and he showed some Union soldiers running in a large group of prisoners, but he did his best work deep in the woods. He made one excellent close-up study of Wadsworth's division advancing in rough formation through the trees, the men firing, ramming in a new charge, and firing again. Late on the following day, he and Forbes portrayed the nightmare of the wounded when the brush fires began. Waud showed men with crippled legs watching in horror as the flames crept toward them and licked at their clothing. They cried out for help and beat at the flames with their hands and tried to pull themselves along on their elbows. Friends lifted them into makeshift blanket stretchers and rushed them to the rear. But many others could not make themselves heard above the roar of the flames.[8]

Grant sent the wounded back to the field hospitals, and then ordered additional supplies of ammunition forward to the front. That was the first hint that a new policy was in order. The men learned about it when he sent them south toward Spottsylvania, and a thrill of excitement ran through the ranks. No retreat! Forbes was on the road when Grant and his staff pushed through, and he showed the men giving him a roar of approval. Some of them were so exhausted they lay by the roadside, and others hung from the shoulders of their comrades, but they cheered and raised their caps as he passed by. Few had any illusions about what lay ahead.[9]

Grant reached Spottsylvania Court House on the evening of the 8th, but

Lee's army had gotten there first and was entrenched abreast the route of the advance. The fighting there from May 9 to 12 was fully as furious as in the Wilderness. Forbes and Becker sketched the frantic charges of the Union brigades, the men taking shelter behind trees and fences and then rushing across the open spaces fronting on the Confederate defenses. The slaughter was immense. On the 10th and the 12th, brigades of picked men assaulted the "Bloody Angle" salient in the center of the Confederate lines, where thousands of men on both sides died in some of the fiercest hand-to-hand fighting of the war. Waud was at the salient for a few moments on the 12th. A heavy rain pelted down and turned the earth to mud. The men who had just seized the salient squatted in the trench behind an embankment, resting and waiting for a counter-assault. Wounded and dying men lay in the mud, and minnie balls exploded overhead in tight white puffs. In the nearby forest, trees cracked and splintered after four days of artillery fire, stood like crippled sentinels.[10]

After Spottsylvania, Grant made another flanking movement toward Richmond to force Lee out of his entrenchments. He had sworn to "fight it out on this line . . . if it takes all summer," and Lee was holding him to the promise. The two armies followed parallel routes as they approached Richmond, Lee keeping his own forces between Grant and the capital, Grant leapfrogging his corps one over the others with masterly skill. By the first of June they had reached Cold Harbor. Veterans of the Wilderness and Spottsylvania looked at Lee's entrenchments and asked themselves whether the rebels won because they could fight or because they could dig. But the Union troops were also becoming proficient pick and shovel men. Forbes sketched the breastworks they threw up at Cold Harbor—a ditch and a log-backed embankment—and showed how each man jammed his rifle into the ground by the bayonet close to where he was working. Waud sketched mortar crews firing shells and grenades into the rebel lines. The men pitched their pup tents and built small fires over which they heated their rations and warmed pots of raw coffee. On the evening of June 2, they learned that at daybreak they were going to make a direct assault against Lee's entrenchments. Many of them printed their names and addresses on slips of paper and pinned them on the backs of their shirts to identify their bodies. Few of them expected to come back.[11]

The first hour of fighting the next morning was the most costly sixty minutes of the war—seven thousand Union casualties. Most of the Union brigades did not even reach the Confederate lines, and those that did were soon hurled back. One Federal division seized the positions on its front for several desperate moments, and Waud made a superb sketch of the men frantically turning captured field pieces on the Confederates who fell back to a second line of defenses. Others disarmed prisoners or helped friends who had been shot down in the assault. But the fire from the Confederate secondary lines thinned their ranks, and Confederate counter-attacks forced them back. Grant called the battle off at noon. Years later he admitted that if he had it to do again, he would never have ordered the frontal assaults at Cold Harbor.[12]

The Wilderness, Spottsylvania, and Cold Harbor introduced northerners to a new style of warfare against which they instinctively recoiled. A month of fighting had brought Grant within sight of Richmond, but Lee's army was still intact. McClellan had once been as close and then failed to take the city. Many people wondered if even the capture of Richmond could compensate for the appalling losses. More than fifty thousand men had fallen. Grant believed he could withstand losses like these for a while because there were always more northerners to fill the ranks, and because in proportion to its original strength, the Army of Northern Virginia had taken even heavier casualties. But many people saw only the number of total casualties. Serious doubts arose whether Grant was a competent general or a mere butcher leading his men to slaughter. His kind of grinding warfare did not evoke much enthusiasm among people still thinking in terms of the traditional battle images; it was horribly costly, and it was not particularly heroic. Grant's quiet self-assurance and casual bearing appealed to his own troops, but he did not inspire widespread confidence on the home front.

Brady and the sketch artists were also aware that they were witnessing something new in warfare. To see Grant repulsed and then plunge on into Virginia to fight and be repulsed again and again was not the way campaigns had been conducted in the past. Yet they soon understood how Grant intended to use his superior resources to wear down Lee's resistance. Their photographs and sketches provided the details. Fletcher Harper warned his readers not to expect a quick end to the campaign. Grant was facing an army, he said, that fought with "valor and tenacity" and was prepared to contest every inch of ground. Northerners would have to gird themselves for a very long and costly campaign.[13]

Waud, Forbes, and Becker illustrated some of the most notable features of the new battle images. Examples of battle fatigue and complete physical exhaustion appeared in most of their sketches. When the men marched they cared little about ranks, formations, or cadenced steps, but concentrated solely on dragging one foot ahead of the other. They frequently drifted off to the side of the road and leaned against a tree and rested for a few minutes before going on. Some of them dragged their rifles by the muzzle with the butt of the stock tracing a narrow furrow in the dust behind them. Waud several times sketched them during a halt, resting with a slump-shouldered stance or leaning on their rifles, their exhaustion apparent in the sightless expressions on their faces.[14]

Grant's veterans seldom passed up an opportunity to rest. Becker's sketch of the reserves at Spottsylvania showed hundreds of busy men at work, except for four soldiers skulking behind a fence-rail breastwork—an unusual inclusion for a freshman artist. Both Waud and Forbes sketched scenes where soldiers were supposed to be digging entrenchments but instead were playing cards, talking, and sleeping with their heads on their arms. Winslow Homer showed three ranks of men sleeping in the Wilderness. One or two men were awake, smoking and watching the sentries pace back and forth, and several others talked quietly among themselves, but most of them were sprawled on the ground with their heads resting on haversacks, blankets pulled tight under their chins, their rifles clenched between their knees.[15]

More striking were photographs and sketches of the wounded. It was a rare illustration from this series of battles that did not show stretcher-bearers carrying wounded men to the rear. In many instances the soldiers themselves had to evacuate a wounded companion in whatever way they could devise at the moment. Waud showed how they lifted him into a blanket or draped his arms and legs over two rifles. Forbes sketched one of the field hospitals at Spottsylvania, and earlier he showed some of the wounded from the Wilderness being ferried across the Rappahannock to the hospitals near Fredericksburg. Brady photographed them waiting there to be treated, a few sitting upright with their arms in makeshift slings, but others lying on the ground too badly hurt to move. Many died even after reaching the hospitals, and as Brady showed in several photographs, it was often some time before they were buried in unfinished pine coffins. Meanwhile, the bodies were laid out in rows and covered with blankets. Sometimes the corpses were barefooted;

if their shoes were new, they could be put to better use by men who were still alive.[16]

Brady and O'Sullivan also photographed the battle dead at Spottsylvania, and later they photographed a mass burial at the Bloody Angle. The bodies lay stacked three and four deep in the rain-soaked trenches, and Union soldiers covered them with the same dirt Confederates had shoveled out when they dug the entrenchments several days earlier. Two weeks later at Cold Harbor, Forbes sketch a "Bucktail's Last Shot"—a Pennsylvania volunteer still in firing position behind a rail fence with a bullet in his forehead. Brady had pictured similar scenes at Antietam and Gettysburg as had Henri Lovie at Shiloh and Arthur Lumley at Fredericksburg and Chancellorsville. But these pictures had appeared as exceptions to the usual battle illustrations. By the time of Cold Harbor, pictures of northern casualties and corpses appeared with frightening regularity.[17]

Moveover, officers, men, and artists were no longer interested in the standard martial postures that had seemed so grand at the beginning of the war. They still performed many of the same maneuvers, but with a restraint and lack of enthusiasm that would have seemed almost unpatriotic two years earlier. At Spottsylvania, Waud had all the ingredients for a heroic sketch when General Gouverneur Warren tried to rally a Maryland brigade that had been repulsed in one of the first assaults. Warren was mounted on a white horse and he held a shot-torn flag. Waud showed the Marylanders gathered about the general, several of them cheering and waving their caps, but most of them stood and listened quietly, and the expressions on their faces showed they were not eager to make another assault.[18]

The old images suffered other casualties. The first few minutes at Cold Harbor shattered and destroyed forever the illusion that assaulting regiments could withstand concentrated rifle and artillery fire without taking tremendous casualties. Bayonet fighting had been a favorite subject for the artists because, like cavalry troopers fighting with sabers, it seemed to be the ultimate challenge to the individual soldier. But it had never been as common as they had indicated in their sketches. In nine out of ten infantry assaults, either the attacking wave broke and washed back before it reached its objective, or the defending troops saw inevitable defeat only fifty feet away and hastily retreated from the field. The battles from the Wilderness to Cold Harbor involved more than the usual amount of hand-to-hand fighting, yet the sketch

147

artists did not produce the usual number of heroic bayonet pictures. Instead they showed a melee of struggling men clubbing with their rifle butts and wrestling each other to the ground. Traditional images would then have shown the men cheering lustily as a young flag-bearer planted the colors in the breastworks. But as Waud showed at the Bloody Angle and at Cold Harbor, when assaulting troops took a position, they either fell down in exhaustion or took care of their own wounds and those of their comrades. If the flag was there, that was fine, but they were not particularly concerned one way or the other.[19]

The new images also indicated that Grant and his army were not especially artist-conscious. Earlier in the war, many officers and soldiers performed as if artists, photographers, and reporters were recording their every move for all the world to see. McClellan, for instance, never let himself be caught in an unguarded moment; even when he went to look at the picket lines he made a spectacle of the inspection. Grant, on the other hand, seemed unaware that he was the symbol of the new army. Brady made photographs of Grant in the field that would have horrified McClellan and some of the other picture-conscious generals. One portrait showed him leaning against a tree, only two buttons holding his vest together, his trousers hanging shapelessly from his hips, a worried frown crossing his face. His indifference was also characteristic of his men. They were no longer fascinated by Brady and his cameras, and they took for granted the presence of the sketch artists. Veteran troops were not interested in providing heroic poses. On the other hand, they did appreciate sketch artists who portrayed the new warfare realistically. At the end of the Cold Harbor campaign, young Oliver Wendell Holmes asked his parents to keep "some daily [newspaper] record of this campaign & also a pictorial [*Harper's*]. Waud is quite a truthful draughtsman."[20]

After Cold Harbor, Grant changed his tactics without altering his basic strategy. Having failed to take Richmond from the north, he swung his army across the James River to try the southern approach. By June 16 he had established his base at City Point and was assaulting the Confederate defenses around Petersburg, the railroad center some twenty-odd miles directly south of the capital. When direct attacks failed with more heavy losses, he ordered his army into a siege. For the many northerners who had hoped that Wilderness, Spottsylvania, and Cold Harbor were only temporary aberrations, the siege of Petersburg was a grievous and painful disappointment.

The first few weeks were a welcome change for men who had been marching and fighting since early May. There was continued hard fighting, but at
times the front was relatively quiet. Forbes sketched a squad of men at ease,
sleeping on the sun-warmed ground, catching up on their newspaper reading,
and watching their coffee boil over a low fire. William Waud, now a special
artist for *Harper's Weekly*, made several large panoramic illustrations of
the extensive network of Union and Confederate trenches and the spires and
stacks of Petersburg as seen through a light summer haze—pictures reminiscent of the Big Views of '62. Another sketch showed the officers of one headquarters group reclining in camp chairs under a bough-covered arbor: "One
of the most delightful places within the lines," Waud wrote Harper. "The birds
build their nests in the trees overhead, and the squirrels play around the
quarters as if they were not within reach of whistling bullets and bursting
shells."[21]

But these camps in the sheltered forests behind the lines bore little resemblance to the surroundings of the combat troops. They were constantly at
work digging trenches eight and ten feet deep, reenforcing them with heavy
logs and timbers to withstand the pounding of the daily bombardments, and
filling sandbags to place at head level to catch bullets from Confederate
snipers. Pup tents and bough-covered arbors were poor shelter against enemy
mortar shells, and so they built "bomb-proofs"—strong dug-out shelters
lined with logs and roofed with several feet of dirt. These were safe, but they
required constant repairs, and they made the men feel like burrowing animals
living in the confined heat and darkness of their holes, showered with dirt and
rocks every time a shell exploded nearby. The open air of the trenches was
not much better. Dry dust churned and eddied after each step until it was
caked on their clothing and baked into their skin. Frequent summer thunder-
showers turned the dust to mud, and rain water collected along the bottom of
the trenches in filthy stagnant pools. Then the heavy autumn rains came and
filled the trenches until the men were standing in water to their knees and
waists. And always there were the enemy mortar shells to smash the bomb-
proofs and tear up the trenches, and enemy snipers who snatched away a
man's life if he lifted his head too high. All this Brady and the artists tried to
portray.[22]

Hopes for a quick breakthrough to end the trench warfare soon evaporated.
Grant's troops made many costly assaults, but with little success. Then atten-

tion turned to a mine being planted under the Confederate lines. Throughout July the Engineers dug a tunnel to a magazine where they planted eight thousand pounds of explosives. By the early morning of July 30 the fuse was ready, and the assaulting troops crouched in the forward trenches awaiting the orders to spring forward. Alf Waud and two new sketchers Leslie sent to Petersburg, Andrew McCullum and E. F. Mullen, were poised to record the moment of the explosion. "With a muffled roar it came," Waud told Harper, "and . . . upwards shot masses of earth, momentarily illuminated from beneath by the lurid flare. For a few seconds huge blocks of earth and other debris, mingled with dust, were seen in a column perhaps a hundred and fifty feet in height, and then the heavy volume of smoke, which spread out in billowy waves on every side, enveloped all like a shadowy pall. . . ." They sketched the soldiers jumping out of their entrenchments and rushing forward into the smoke and settling dust toward the huge crater left by the explosion. For the first few minutes all seemed to go well. But the Confederates were not nearly as hurt and disorganized by the explosion as had been anticipated, and their guns began to tear apart the attacking lines. Many of the soldiers who reached the edge of the crater slipped and stumbled into it, and then were picked off as they tried to claw their way out. A few reached the Confederate trenches only to be shot and to die there. The rest faltered and then fell back to their own lines—four thousand casualties weaker than when they had started. Grant condemned the entire project as a "stupendous failure."[23]

E. F. Mullen gave Leslie's readers some idea of the gruesome aftermath. One of his illustrations showed the Confederate earthworks littered with rocks and debris and the bodies of dozens of horribly-mutilated soldiers. During a truce on the following day, he followed the burial crews to the edge of the crater. His sketch there showed Confederate soldiers standing like "malevolent spirits towering to an unnatural height against the sky" as they watched the crews dig narrow trenches and bury the dead soldiers who lay on the ground with hundreds of flies flicking about their faces. It was one of the most grisly illustrations of the war.[24]

Still the casualties mounted. Confederate snipers picked off hundreds of Union soldiers, and artillery and mortar crews added their toll. Probing assaults to test the enemy defenses always ended in a painful loss of blood and life. William Waud sketched a small search party with lanterns moving cautiously through the woods at night looking for men wounded in a battle several hours earlier. Sickness was rampant in the filthy trenches, and tired and weakened men collapsed from exhaustion. Forbes stumbled on a soldier he thought was dead, and started to sketch him. Suddenly he was startled to see the eyelids tremble and slowly open. "He looked at me in a dreamy fashion," Forbes remembered, "then drowsily closed his eyes again as if too exhausted to interest himself in anything, and remained motionless. I finished my sketch and left him in the care of those who would look after him." Most of the men Brady photographed lying face down in the trench mud were beyond caring.[25]

Scenes like these appearing week after week throughout the autumn of 1864 made it apparent that there was little chance of breaking Lee's defenses before the spring. Attention shifted to cavalry raids against depots and railroad lines, and to Sherman in Georgia and Sheridan in the Shenandoah Valley. McCullum and Mullen and Harper's A. W. Warren stayed on, but by August Forbes, Becker, and the Wauds had all abandoned the Petersburg trenches. Forbes took the first extensive furlough he had had since joining the army early in 1862. Becker returned for short stays, and he worked other fronts when Petersburg was quiet. Alf Waud moved on to the Shenandoah to follow Sheridan. William Waud joined Benjamin Butler's Army of the James to sketch the digging of the Dutch Gap canal. Someone undoubtedly reminded Butler that another army at Vicksburg had failed in a similar undertaking, but Butler was not the kind who took advice and he had to fail for himself. Periodically Waud returned to Petersburg to check on the progress of the siege. But he complained in a letter to Alf that it was "mighty difficult to make pictures that don't look like old blocks. . . . I have made no sketches for the last month—for the simple reason of there being nothing to sketch although I have spent my time gyraling from left to right of the army in anticipation of the grand move always about to be made."[26]

There were no grand moves in the immediate offing. Grant extended his lines to tighten his grip on Petersburg, and his troops continued to pound the enemy. He had seized the initiative when he first crossed the Rapidan, and it seemed clear he would keep it until he had ground Lee into submission. But trench warfare was as costly a way to defeat Lee as assaulting his army in the field. And either way, victory was much more expensive than defeat had ever been in the old war. This was perhaps the most striking and frightening facet of the new battle images that emerged from Virginia between May and October of 1864.

Nor could traditionists derive any comfort from pictures from the other active fronts. Artists and photographers in the Shenandoah and Georgia were preparing illustrations of the Army on the March that only further supported the brutal images of the New War.

XII

On the March

Grant's campaign from the Wilderness to Petersburg introduced northerners to the war of attrition. Beginning in May 1864, Grant maintained a constant and unrelenting pressure against the Army of Northern Virginia, wearing down the strength of Lee's combat troops, destroying their sources of supply, and undermining their will to resist. Infantrymen dug entrenchments and sniped, skirmished, and assaulted the enemy. Artillerists subjected Confederate defenses to a constant bombardment. Cavalrymen—those dashing warriors who had earlier thrilled northerners with their slashing saber fights—now destroyed enemy communications and supply lines—something of a comedown when the troops dismounted and helped win the war with picks and shovels.[1] The New War was hard and costly; officers showed the wear and tear along with their men, and many swivel-chair generals who had demanded a ruthless offensive whimpered at the price. But in the army itself, the men saw the first glimmerings of the final victory.

The experience of Grant's veterans was not unique. A few days after Grant crossed the Rapidan, Sherman left Chattanooga to begin a plunge into the Deep South that eventually carried him to Savannah and then northward into the Carolinas. The ferocious battles before Atlanta exposed Sherman's westerners to the New War as surely as if they had been fighting alongside the Army of the Potomac. At the same time, Nathaniel Banks was supposed to attack Mobile, Franz Sigel was to advance in the Shenandoah, and Benjamin Butler was to move against Richmond. They failed, but other commanders were more successful. Admiral David Farragut seized Mobile from the sea. In September and October, Philip Sheridan led Sigel's discouraged veterans to a series of stunning victories. Butler's men saw action in the Petersburg trenches. Front-line troops everywhere were undergoing similar experiences —fighting the terrain, the rain, and the mud, assaulting entrenched positions,

153

suffering casualties, and then marching without rest to another battle. The scope of the war had expanded to an extent that would have seemed impossible two years earlier. Battles involving 150,000 men were unusual as late as Gettysburg, but by the following summer they were common occurrences. In 1861 northerners thrilled to a march of one hundred miles; in 1864 they watched 60,000 men march five or six times as far. Battle lines were four or five miles in length, camping armies sprawled over many acres, and marching columns reached back to the horizon.

Under these circumstances, sketch artists abandoned the futile attempt to portray everything they saw, and instead sketched episodes and incidents that were representative of the larger scene. Alf Waud, Henri Lovie, Arthur Lumley, and Mathew Brady used this technique in earlier campaigns; Waud brought it to perfection in the Wilderness and at Spottsylvania and Cold Harbor. A skillful use of detail was essential: Lovie showing dry tree branches cracking to the ground during the artillery barrages at Shiloh, Waud illustrating the terror of men caught in the brush fires of the Wilderness, Brady's incomparable portraits of the battle dead at Gettysburg, and Frank Schell's and E. F. Mullen's sketches of burial squads at Antietam and Petersburg. This method had also proved useful for picturing camp life. Many of the best of Homer's, Forbes', Waud's, and Lumley's at-ease sketches were quick studies of scenes that could have taken place anywhere.[2]

The episodic technique was especially useful to portray the army on the march. But at the beginning of the war, the artists preferred the "Big View" of the marching army. Waud, Forbes, Lovie, and Simplot submitted sketches from Virginia and Missouri that showed men marching rigidly in columns abreast to the beat of a cadenced step. Cavalry guarded the flanks of the column, wagon trains followed in the rear, and scouts and skirmishers ranged far ahead of the van. Each man carried a full pack with a tightly-rolled blanket on top, a haversack with several day's rations, a canteen, and the other standard accouterments. All were apparently familiar with the regulations; every rifle rested at the same angle on the right shoulder. The army was on parade, and in terms of the heroic images, it was a magnificent sight. Samuel Sturgis, who led part of Fremont's army in Missouri, liked to ride to a high point on the prairie and look back at the line of marching men. On one occasion during the advance to Springfield, he offered to halt the entire column so Simplot could sketch the scene.[3]

Beginning in the winter of 1861–62, artists and photographers created more realistic marching pictures. They showed the rigors of the march, and gradually their sketches accurately portrayed the real appearance of men in the field. But only in the last year of the war did they show how armies on the march waged their own war of attrition by methodically destroying the substance and morale that nourished Confederate combat troops.

Nothing contributed as much to the new images as the weather. In August of 1861 Frank Schell sketched a Massachusetts regiment caught in a drenching rainstorm, the men pushing their wagons through a quagmire of mud while others huddled against a rail fence and held straw and hay over their heads to keep the water off. Rain plagued McClellan's advance on the Peninsula; Lumley and Brady made many pictures of the Engineers struggling to conquer the mud. Henry Mosler showed how snow brought the Army of the Ohio to a virtual standstill. Some people on the home front could not understand how heavy weather could wreak such havoc with the movement of crusading armies, but it was no mystery to the men in the ranks. William Bircher explained that "rain, snow and hail . . . knocked all the enthusiasm out of trying to be a hero. . . ."[4]

Men in every theater of the war praised and damned the qualities of their particular mud. Alonzo Quint, the chaplain of the Second Massachusetts, told the readers of the *Congregationalist* that Virginia mud "is not like New England mud. It is more like mortar, and deep beyond your imagination." As if to illustrate Quint's description, Alf Waud sent Harper four sketches showing infantrymen sloshing through a foot of mud, cavalry horses rearing and plunging in frantic lunges, teamsters hitching a dozen horses to a single wagon and prying the wheels free with fence rails, and men living in camps surrounded by a virtual sea of mud from which there was no escape.[5]

Henri Lovie thought no mud surpassed what the westerners encountered on the advance from Shiloh to Corinth. "I have had considerable experience of mud," he told Leslie, "but in all my rides, or rather wallowings, I have seldom experienced such difficulty in getting my horse along, and I only succeeded by driving my spurs so vehemently into his poor sides, that he made those desperate plunges which carried us through. . . ." Four miles from Corinth he made one of the best mud sketches of the war. Wagons, mounted officers, and infantrymen were snared in the mire. Teamsters threw supplies from their wagons to lighten the load, and lashed their frantic teams in the struggle to inch ahead. Foot soldiers avoided the most trampled sections of the road and picked their way with careful deliberation through the grasping muck. He showed mud choked between the spokes of the wagon wheels and clinging like taffy to the rims, and also how the horses strained to free their hooves from the mud with what must have been a wet sucking sound.[6]

That winter Lovie compared eastern mud with western when he sketched Burnside's advance to Fredericksburg. Together with Lumley and Waud, he showed why winter campaigning was so difficult. Waud sketched a column of men leaning into the wind of a heavy rainstorm that lashed their clothing and soaked their bodies. Lumley portrayed the oath-filled struggle between teamsters and their horses as they thrashed and wallowed in the quagmire along the Rappahannock. Lovie showed a dead horse lying abandoned in its traces alongside a road gashed with the frozen wheel ruts of wagons that had already passed by.[7]

By the late winter of 1862–63, "Rappahannock Mud" was a byword for inactivity in the Army of the Potomac. Cartoonists used the idea with some success. A cartoon in *Leslie's* showed Jefferson Davis seated comfortably in a tree while Lincoln, ensnared in the mud, complained that if it wasn't for the mud he would soon fetch him out of there. One of Harper's cartoonists showed a soldier commiserating with a dispatch-carrier about how hard it is to walk on the roads hereabouts; the courier—sunk to his waist in the mud—retorts that he ain't walking, he's Hooker's orderly, and he had a fine smart horse under him.[8]

Second on the soldiers' list of marching grievances was dust. In the hot summers of the South, the earth baked and then flaked. It swirled up when disturbed and settled in their hair and beards and all over their faces. It imbedded itself in their shirts, pants, and socks. It eddied in the air when they bivouacked and added grit to their rations, and it muddied the water at the streams where they filled their canteens. But it was at its worst when thousands of feet churned it into huge dense clouds that hung in the air in the wake of the columns. The men welcomed the light summer showers that cooled the air, settled the dust, and seemed to add a spring to the turf. Forbes noticed that marching men did a washing whenever they had a chance, giving their clothes "a lick and a promise" in a cold water stream, and then tying their socks, shirts, and bandana handkerchiefs to their rifles to dry in the breeze. Most of the artists also sketched men splashing and washing in a river or rushing down to a small stream to refill their canteens. Nast's large illustration entitled "The Halt" showed soldiers clustering around a water pump in a farmyard, filling their canteens and taking water to their horses and teams. Several men soaked their feet in buckets of water, and others splashed it over their heads and let it drip deliciously down their necks.[9]

Deterioration of uniforms also contributed to the appearance of veteran marching troops. Romanticists euphemistically described the color of Federal uniforms as a "soft butternut brown." But the true color of a well-worn uniform was sallow yellow. Sunlight and hard washings on river rocks quickly faded the original blue dye. Nature then recolored the fabric with field dust, road grime, swamp water, and clay mud. The men added smears of gunpowder, grass stains, and meal grease. Branches and shrubs tore the cloth, and the smoke from green-wood fires contributed a unique fragrance. Many soldiers also found that their shoddy uniforms and equipment wore out much too quickly. Pants, shirts, and coats came apart at the seams, socks rotted when they became damp, blankets shredded and disintegrated after a few weeks' use, and knapsacks, belts, and other accouterments could not withstand the rough use the men gave them. Cartoonists castigated contractors who provided the men with shoddy, but field artists provided even more striking evidence. Early in the summer of 1862, Forbes sketched several tatterdemalions from the Federal Army of Virginia. They were exhausted from fatigue and weak with wounds, and their slouched postures and tired faces told a story of misery. But most pathetic of all was their ragged appearance—their uniforms were torn and shredded, their hats limp and shapeless, and several of them marched barefoot.[10]

Shoes containing as much cardboard as leather seldom lasted for more than a month or two. Men who could not get new shoes then had no choice but to march barefoot. Forbes remembered seeing barefoot soldiers gingerly picking their way over sharp places in the road, trying to ignore the "inconsiderate" laughs of a few of their comrades when they made a misstep and winced with pain. William Waud showed how they wrapped rags around their shoes to hold them together for a few more miles. The tragedy of marching barefoot, as many soldiers testified, was that even when they got new shoes, they could not wear them because their feet were so tender and swollen. This condition provided field artists with many sketches of footsore soldiers soaking their feet in water. It also explained why men in both armies stripped new shoes from dead soldiers, but the well-shod editorial artists in New York who created the atrocity illustrations never appreciated the circumstances.[11]

A haphazard uniform and grit-lined face were soon marks of distinction among veteran troops. Major James Connolly claimed he was "proud of the rags" he wore. "It doesn't make any difference in the field," he told his wife, "for a fine uniform does not make a soldier." Theodore Lyman came to the same conclusion as he watched Grant's veterans march from Cold Harbor to Petersburg: "The more they serve," he wrote, "the less they look like soldiers and the more they resemble day-laborers who have bought second-hand military clothes. I have so come to associate good troops with dusty, faded suits, that I look with suspicion on anyone who has a stray bit of lace or other martial finery."[12]

By 1863 the men no longer cared how they looked while marching. Gone were the pomp and pageantry of the grand procession. In 1861 a tightly-disciplined march had been useful in training raw troops, but strict formations and parade-ground procedures only hindered experienced soldiers. So they threw away most of the regulations. They still marched in ranks, but the officers did not try to keep them "dressed up." One veteran of Sherman's army explained that the cadenced step was completely impractical in the field, "good enough for a mile or so, or on dress parade," but "intolerable if kept up for any length of time or any great distance." Instead, they marched in rout steps, each soldier picking his own way and swinging along in easy loose strides. They carried their rifles on whichever shoulder was most comfortable at the moment. They rolled their blankets lengthwise, folded the roll in half, and carried it over one shoulder. Perhaps their appearance was shabby, but nobody questioned their ability to march with amazing proficiency.[13]

Marching also provided pleasures to compensate for the hardships. Sometimes the marches were easy, and after bivouacking, those who had the energy and the inclination engaged in horseplay and other fun. During Sherman's march from Atlanta to Savannah, Theo Davis had a riotously good time. When he was not in his tent working over his sketches by candlelight, he was singing with some of the officers of Sherman's staff or pitting his strength against theirs in a jumping match. At Milledgeville he joined with the reporters in "repealing" Georgia's ordinance of secession at a mock session of the legislature. Almost single-handedly, he kept alive the traditions of the old Bohemian Brigade.[14]

The war also gave many men their first opportunity to travel. They were delighted with the mountains of Tennessee and western Virginia, the lush summer vegetation and the rich autumn colors, and the picturesque setting of many small southern towns. They wanted pictures of these scenes, and the artists seldom failed them. Leslie recognized the scenic value of war illustrations when he described war as a "fearful and wonderful teacher of topography." Forbes was enchanted with the magnificent scenery in Virginia; his Shenandoah sketches were some of the best landscape illustrations to come out of the war. Even Brady, Lovie, and Alf Waud, who ordinarily preferred the company and conversation of men, sometimes sought the pleasures of nature. Early in the Missouri war, Lovie climbed to the top of Pilot Knob, a local promontory, to enjoy the magnificent view of the surrounding country and of the army camped far below. Whatever their individual interests, the artists and photographers provided the readers of the illustrated weeklies with a grand tour of the southern Confederacy.[15]

But if the artists were also interested in feminine scenery, this was not apparent from their pictures. Women appeared only infrequently in the illustrations. After the surrender of Vicksburg, Fred Schell sent Leslie a sketch showing several young women at an army commissary asking for provisions. He reported that each family with a pretty daughter sent her to soften the hearts of the commissary officers. On the few occasions when artists mentioned personal encounters with women, they described them lightheartedly. When Davis visited the Cincinnati Sanitary Fair, he told Harper he felt like a swindler for paying only twenty-five cents for a plate of food and the privilege of looking at the "fairest of the daughters of Cincinnati." But he added: "I compromised with my conscience by giving only one look, and then addressing myself to my food. I would gladly have given twice as much for two looks without the food." Both Davis and Forbes sketched the studied haughtiness of southern girls, particularly the way they turned up their noses and pulled in their crinoline petticoats whenever they came near a Yankee. Forbes once greeted a young southern woman with "a sly wink," only to be coldly snubbed in return. Not at all taken aback, he reported to Leslie that it was a pity the "fair rebels" behaved this way, but he predicted that when the war was over a "little love-making will make it all straight again."[16]

No marching army was complete without its stragglers, men who for various reasons and excuses could not meet the pace. They slued off from the column and fell behind, or found a tree or rail fence for shelter and rested until they were able to march again. Some had no better excuse than that they wanted to heat a dipper of coffee, but the majority of stragglers were simply exhausted. Forbes remembered seeing men fall out of ranks "too foot-sore to proceed a single step further, and after receiving the captain's admonition to return to duty as soon as possible, [they] would retreat to the shelter of a fencecorner and fall into the sleep of sheer exhaustion, oblivious to the clatter and noise." Even though the sketch artists rode on horseback, they knew enough about marching to treat stragglers gently in their pictures. Occasionally they added a touch of humor; Alf Waud did one study of a ragged and disheartened straggler leaning against a crate with one hand inside his shirt— his sole problem of the moment to relieve himself of innumerable itches. On the other hand, some of their most pathetic portraits were of tired-eyed stragglers with slumped shoulders, bowed heads, and knees that were bent and probably shaking—fagged men who had been on their feet too long and were about to collapse.[17]

Another reason to leave the ranks was to forage. Because soldiers had to march with short rations, they saw no reason why they should not supplement their diets with whatever nature and nearby farms could provide. Henri Lovie saw a good deal of unofficial foraging in Missouri. One of his sketches showed a squad of soldiers ravaging a persimmon tree, a half-dozen grown boys clinging to the branches and fighting among themselves for the ripe fruit. Many a farmer stood by in helpless frustration, as Lovie showed in another sketch, while hungry soldiers stalked through his barnyard and chicken coop. At the end of a hard day of marching, an unguarded haystack was a temptation that tired men could not resist. In many ways the most valuable of all foragable items were fence rails; they were useful for reenforcing breastworks, made excellent temporary shelters, and provided convenient firewood. Forbes reported that the men became "animated" whenever they sighted a fence. Waud, Lovie, Forbes, and Frank Beard, who occasionally sent Leggett sketches, were delighted with the avidity of their assaults against the rails. "It is astonishing how rapidly the fences would disappear," one trooper recalled, "they seemed literally to be alive." In a few moments every man was back in ranks, his gun on one shoulder, a fence rail on the other.[18]

Where foraging stopped and looting began was a question that defied adequate answer. One of the main tenets of the editorial artists was that the enemy violated the sanctity of Federal dead, yet the Union army was full of "souvenir hunters" who boasted of the mementos they had taken from Confederate dead. The artists were not exceptions. In March of 1862, Alf Waud and several newspaper friends scavenged the abandoned Confederate fortifications at Manassas. The correspondent of the *New York Times* proudly reported to his editor: "It was a sight to see the independent journalists when they rode away from the deserted rebel camp. Many with muskets slung over their shoulders and knapsacks to their backs, all with pockets distended and sides laden with all manner of secession trophies. The artist of *Harper's* was enveloped in a red shirt and in his hand bore a lance of the rebel cavalry with the *guidon* attached." Six months later at Antietam, Waud was disgusted at seeing Maryland farmers doing the same thing.[19]

But when sketch artists submitted illustrations of Federal looting, their publishers refused to print them. In 1863 Lumley sent Leggett a sketch from Fredericksburg showing soldiers running rampant, breaking into houses, and throwing valuables through the windows to their comrades in the streets. Leggett did not print the picture. During Sherman's campaign in Georgia, Davis sketched a group of soldiers holding high carnival in the hotel at Big Shanty, tearing the feather beds to pieces, smashing the chinaware and furniture, and devouring all the food and liquor. A reporter for the *New York Tribune* told his readers to watch for Davis' "excellent sketch" of the scene in a coming edition of *Harper's Weekly*. It never appeared. All that readers of the *Weekly* saw of Sherman's army at Big Shanty was an innocuous picture of the railroad depot.[20]

It was easy enough to understand the hesitancy of the publishers. They were not anxious to portray their own soldiers doing things for which they condemned the enemy; there was always the possibility of censorship or suppression by the War Department; and they were also afraid that their readers would not make a clear distinction between vandalism and the army's program of planned destruction. But there was a more fundamental reason. Harper, Leslie, and Leggett still believed that warfare should be confined to military personnel. They thought that destruction of non-military property was needless and wanton, particularly if it meant hardship for women and children. They understood the need to maintain home front morale, but they shied away from proposals to undermine enemy morale. In this respect they were still thinking in terms of a crusade rather than of total war. Until late in 1864 they did not realize that the march was more than a means to other ends, but indeed that it was by itself an extremely effective way to wage war.

Consequently they ignored the new strategy of wholesale desolation as practiced by Sheridan in the Shenandoah and by Sherman in Georgia. Two veteran artists, Alf Waud and James E. Taylor, sketched Sheridan's whirl-wind campaign up the Shenandoah. Waud made only a few sketches; Taylor, who spent two years in the army as a private before joining *Leslie's*, a great many. But readers of *Harper's* and *Leslie's* saw very little evidence of Sheridan's devastation of the valley. Theo Davis was the only artist with Sherman's army on the march from Atlanta to Savannah, and he sketched the destruction left in the wake of the marching columns. But Harper published only a few of these sketches. One of these showed a squad of soldiers destroy-ing a section of railroad line, ripping up the track and burning the ties in huge bonfires, and several others showed the public buildings of Atlanta in flames when Sherman's army abandoned the city. Otherwise the published illustra-tions did not distinguish this campaign from many others that had preceded it. Harper and Leslie never published a single sketch of one of the most famous, and infamous, group of characters to emerge from the war—Sher-man's Bummers.[21]

The army was not so timid. The Quartermaster Corps and the Engineers employed cameramen to photograph all the construction and destruction done by both armies. Two of Brady's former operators, C. N. Barnard and J. F. Coonley, accompanied Sherman and photographed scenes that showed the war-making capacity of a marching army. Their pictures were filled with views of coiled rails and charred ties, punctured boilers from dismantled locomotives, grotesquely twisted girders in demolished depots, and fields of rubble that testified to the effectiveness of Sherman's artillery. Their photo-graphs were not published at the time and therefore did not contribute directly to the new marching images, but the fact that the army was making a pictorial record of the devastation influenced the publishers.[22]

Thus, early in 1865, when Sherman's army left Savannah to begin the march through the Carolinas, Harper and Leslie were less reluctant to advertise the work of destruction. Moreover, the army was in South Carolina, the seedbed of secession and war. Northerners were hungering for revenge. Everyone expected Sherman's tough westerners to exact retribution. The publishers made their preparations. Leslie dispatched Taylor to Savannah to join Sherman's army, and Harper detached William Waud from Petersburg to assist Davis.

Illustrations and photographs from the march through the Carolinas were a fitting culmination to four years of marching pictures. The swampy Carolina terrain, dissected by dozens of rivers and streams, was a marching man's nightmare. Waud sketched infantry and cavalry units wading shin-deep through flooded lowland forests. The enemy felled huge trees across the route of the advance, and Davis showed how Sherman's men cut them away so the train of the army could move through. Both artists praised the speed with which the Engineers bridged the major rivers and built corduroy roads across the swamps. Even the Confederates expressed their dismayed admiration. Towns and installations in the path of the army felt the flame of northern anger. McPhersonville was only the first of many towns in South Carolina to be burned. Taylor sketched many instances of demolition—a cotton press near Flat Rock, a railroad depot on the outskirts of Columbia, and a burning still at Bentonville in North Carolina, a sight sure to warm the heart of reform-minded readers. Yet he did not attribute all the conflagrations to Sherman's army. He wrote Leslie that the disastrous fire at Orangeburg was the work of the rebels, and for that reason he felt sorry for the inhabitants. "It was a painful sight," he reported, "to see women and children wandering houseless and penniless among the ruins of their once comfortable homes."[23]

There was little remorse, however, at the burning of the state capital at Columbia. Mystery surrounded the origin of the fire that destroyed a large section of the city, both armies claiming the other was responsible. Waud and Davis sketched the fire at its height. Waud showed the flames destroying a number of buildings and the refugees who huddled in small groups under the heavy pall of smoke. A number of Union soldiers watched the fire, and Waud added a bold touch of his own by sketching one of them servicing a bottle of whiskey. Davis' and Barnard's pictures after the fire showed scenes reminiscent of Roman ruins—rubble covering the ground in every direction, three or four columns stripped of their marble casings to expose the drab brick insides, and the hollow shells of gutted buildings. To many readers, the latter was symbolic of the shell of the now-dying Confederacy.[24]

Sherman's men created a legend even as they marched. After leaving Savannah, they cut through the swamp and forest land of South Carolina at a speed equal to that with which they had crossed the black-soil country of Georgia. Other men could fight as well, but none could march like these westerners. They seemed invincible. Wading through swamps, cutting away obstacles, corduroying roads, rebuilding bridges, and skirmishing and fighting with the Confederates never seriously slowed their advance. They were a hard breed of men, and they set themselves apart from the rest of the army by wearing soft black-felt hats as their special badge. If they were cocksure and arrogant as they pushed through North Carolina to join forces with Grant, no group of soldiers had better justification.

Their impact on the marching images, however, was not as great as it would have been if they had made the march earlier. The transfer of sketches from Sherman's army to New York took at least two weeks, and some of the sketches made at the beginning of the campaign were not published until two months later. Most of Taylor's illustrations did not appear in *Leslie's* until April 8, 1865, and then the war was nearly over. Unfortunately this was the only extensive series of marching illustrations since Fremont's Missouri fiasco. Moreover, marching pictures did not usually have the starkly dramatic impact of battle illustrations or the human interest appeal of camp scenes, and many casual readers probably gave them only a cursory examination. There was also a technical hazard. The field artists sometimes did not give the engravers sufficiently-detailed instructions, and consequently many of the published marching pictures contained stereotyped poses and appearances. For these reasons, the army on the march was the most unobtrusive of the New War images.

Illustrations and photographs of troops at ease, under fire, and on the march interpreted the war as the men in the front lines actually experienced it. But at the same time, editorial artists were again active on the home front. Throughout the summer and autumn of 1864, when Grant and Sherman were bringing the new strategy to full fruition, northerners were also engrossed with a bitterly-contested political campaign.

XIII

The Lincoln Image

The severe and relentless nature of the New War forced Fletcher Harper to make several important decisions. During the summer and autumn of 1864, as Grant moved from the repulse at Cold Harbor to the siege of Petersburg, and Sherman besieged Atlanta and then marched to the sea, Harper was worried about the election of 1864. He knew that discouragement with the military campaigns could have vast repercussions in the battle of the ballots. The cost of the war had reached frightening heights, and morale ebbed to new lows with each new list of casualties. Many northerners held the Lincoln administration responsible. There was also dissension within the Republican party. So in order not to embarrass Lincoln's campaign for a second term, Harper refused to publish sketches that reflected unfavorably on Union troops, and he also printed new atrocity illustrations.[1] Furthermore, he decided to refurbish the Lincoln image.

Prior to the war, Harper was a Democrat, but during the 1860 campaign he lost faith with the southern branch of the party. After hearing a southerner speak in New York, he confided to a friend: "I shall have hard work not to vote for Lincoln." However, he feared that a Republican victory would threaten his firm's extensive business interests in the South, and so he refused to throw the *Weekly* into the maelstrom of the campaign. Frank Leslie and T. B. Leggett also had many southern subscribers they did not want to lose. Like Harper, they would not support any of the candidates. They wrote guarded editorials about the issues, but kept their illustrations and cartoons basically neutral. Henry Louis Stephens drew a half-dozen Lincoln cartoons for *Vanity Fair,* but he did not show any particular favor or animosity. All agreed that nonpartisanship was the wisest policy.[2]

Consequently, photographers and cartoonists created the original Lincoln image. By 1860 Lincoln had been photographed more than thirty times, but only three of these portraits were generally available. In 1857 Alexander Hesler photographed Lincoln with his hair tousled, a portrait that cartoonists used three years later to caricature Lincoln as a frontier roughneck. In February of 1860 Mathew Brady made a full-length portrait showing a clean-shaven man who was self-assured despite his lack of good looks. Soon after Lincoln's nomination, Hesler produced a second portrait, this time of a thoughtful and serious man whose sharp hard features promised unusual strength. Republican campaign managers distributed more than a hundred thousand copies of the Brady and Hesler portraits. All three were primary references for the cartoonists.[3]

Currier and Ives had published cartoons in every campaign since 1848, and by 1860 most of the commercial publishers exploited this source of profit. These cartoons were mainly amused interpretations of the candidates and the issues, and because they cost only a few pennies, they were enormously popular. But the publishers also prepared special cartoons for distribution by the party managers, which were often brutal caricatures of the other candidates' personality and appearance.[4]

Anti-Lincoln cartoonists characterized Lincoln as an unprincipled opportunist.[5] They used the "Railsplitter" motif to show Lincoln straddling a rail representing the Republican platform. Louis Maurer, Currier and Ives' talented German-born cartoonist, pictured Lincoln at the head of a procession of free-lovers, Mormons, disgruntled spinsters, feminists, communists, Negroes, and other "lunatic" reformers. Several cartoonists condemned Lincoln as the tool of Horace Greeley; Maurer caricatured him as a monkey dancing to the tune of the *Tribune* organ grinder. They also portrayed him as an abolitionist. In "An Heir to the Throne," Maurer depicted Lincoln looking approvingly on a Negro: "How fortunate that this intellectual and noble creature should have been discovered just at this time to prove to the world the superiority of the Colored over the Anglo-Saxon race; he will be a worthy successor to carry out the policy I shall inaugurate." " 'The Nigger' in the Woodpile" exposed Lincoln trying to hide the slavery issue behind the "rails" of the Republican platform. Maurer also played upon the fear that southern extremists would use Lincoln's election as an excuse for secession. "Letting the Cat out of the Bag" showed Charles Sumner, one of the abolitionist senators, releasing a ferocious wildcat representing the "Spirit of Discord," while Greeley and Lincoln complained that it was not supposed to be turned loose until after the election.[6]

Friendly cartoonists characterized Lincoln as a common man uncommonly qualified to be president. "Honest Abe" promised a house cleaning. Maurer pictured Lincoln "wide awake" to Democratic plots to slip another of their candidates into the White House by a back window. A cartoonist for *The Railsplitter,* a campaign sheet published in Chicago by the Republican managers, showed Lincoln prying Buchanan from the presidency with a rail. They also used the "Railsplitter" motif to associate Lincoln with the workingmen, and taking the Brady and Hesler portraits as models, they divested Lincoln of his coat and necktie, and then showed him hard at work in dress shoes, dress trousers, and a spotless white dress shirt. In other cartoons they argued that only Lincoln could provide the nation with vigorous leadership: Lincoln firmly held the throttle of the Republican locomotive, but Douglas and Breckinridge, the two candidates of the divided Democratic party, tried to drive a wagon in opposite directions at the same time.[7]

Despite these efforts, friendly cartoonists succeeded only in creating a fundamentally bland personality for Lincoln. In "Uncle Sam Making New Arrangements," Maurer showed Lincoln thanking Uncle Sam for a four-year lease on the White House with the inspired words: "I will endeavor to do my best." The "Honest Abe" and "Railsplitter" devices were attempts to distract attention away from slavery and abolitionism. Only two cartoons from this campaign endowed Lincoln with a strong individuality. Frank Bellew did "A 'Rail' Old Western Gentleman" for a New York printer, a powerful scarecrow caricature of Lincoln's head on a body of rails. Maurer's "Honest Abe Taking Them on the Half Shell" showed a gleeful Lincoln about to devour Douglas and Breckinridge, each cowering on an oyster shell: "These fellows have been planted so long in Washington that they are as fat as Butter. I hardly know which to swallow first." But with these two exceptions, the initiative in creating the original Lincoln image lay with the opposition. Maurer was usually much more imaginative in his attacks on Lincoln than in his cartoons supporting him, simply because it was easier to burlesque Lincoln than to praise him. Even Harper published a cartoon showing Lincoln walking a tightrope with a Negro perched on his shoulders.[8]

Even the best of the sketch artists did not appreciably strengthen the Lincoln image. Henri Lovie sketched Lincoln in Springfield after the election, and in February 1861 he illustrated Lincoln's trip from Springfield to Washington. Harper sent Winslow Homer to the capital to get illustrations and photographs of the inauguration activities. Leggett assigned Thomas Nast to the Lincoln entourage. Nast was an enthusiastic admirer of the President-elect; in New York he pushed through a crowd to shake his hand. He also sympathized with the ordeal of Lincoln at numerous receptions, rallies, and flag-raisings along the route from New York to Washington, and he prepared a cartoon showing Lincoln with stretched arm and swollen hand after a day of "enthusiastic handshaking." But all of their sketches were of occasions where the public expected Lincoln to act with the studied formality of his high office. Many people testified to the mobility of his features and the animation of his gestures when speaking; George Templeton Strong saw him in New York and reported in his diary that the "great railsplitter's face was visible to me for an instant, and seemed a keen, clear, honest face, not so ugly as his portraits." But the illustrations in the weekly newspapers merely showed a tall, lean, expressionless man stiffened into a frozen rigidity.[9]

There was one set of vigorous pictures from the pre-inauguration period, but they dealt the Lincoln image a hard blow. Having reached Harrisburg in Pennsylvania, Lincoln mysteriously disappeared, and then suddenly reappeared again in Washington. According to the first reports, when Lincoln learned that southern sympathizers planned to assassinate him in Baltimore, he furtively disguised himself in a Scotch plaid cap and cape, slipped onto a special train in Harrisburg, and sneaked into Washington in the dead of night. Nast interviewed the stationmaster at Harrisburg and learned that the reports about the disguise were untrue. On the basis of this evidence, he sent Leggett a sketch showing Lincoln in a coat and hat walking calmly through Camden Station in Baltimore. But Leggett preferred the sensational rumors then current in New York, and he instructed his engravers to alter Nast's sketch to include the elaborate disguise. Cartoonists immediately exploited the incident. Henry Stephens did one cartoon for *Vanity Fair* showing Lincoln dancing a highland fling in the Harrisburg Station, and another showing him slinking through the depot in disguise. Harper published John McLenan's four-panel cartoon showing Lincoln thoroughly frightened as friends awakened him, then hurriedly dressing, rushing through the station in his cap and cape, and finally arriving at the White House with a bad case of the jitters.[10]

The bombardment of Fort Sumter shifted attention away from Lincoln. Sketch artists much preferred to make portraits of the generals; when Alf Waud arrived in Washington, the one man he most wanted to sketch at work was Winfield Scott. They did not seek out Lincoln in the White House, except for Francis B. Carpenter, who spent several months there preparing a painting of the president reading the emancipation proclamation. Occasionally they sketched one of his visits to the army, but then it was the sight of the army in review or the presence of the commanding general that attracted them. Brady photographed Lincoln's meeting with McClellan after Antietam, but the artists did not sketch it. Joseph Becker illustrated the dedication ceremonies at the Gettysburg cemetery, but he was so busy sketching the memorial arch, the battlefield, and the crowd, that he did not make a single sketch of Lincoln on the occasion later generations consider one of the most memorable of his life.[11]

Photographers were more attentive, but their pictures had a very limited circulation. Lincoln had seven sittings with Brady and three with Alexander Gardner, the last only four days before his assassination. Several lesser-known photographers also made portraits. But only one or two of these pictures ever captured Lincoln in a relaxed moment. Brady's portrait of the president wearing his spectacles and reading to his son Tad would have added immeasurably to a favorable image, but it was not widely distributed during the war years. Commercial publishers occasionally issued engraved copies of these portraits, but the quality of their reproduction was often quite poor. "The current portraits are all failures," Walt Whitman wrote, "most of them caricatures."[12]

Cartoonists continued to have the greatest impact on the image. During the Sumter crisis, they pictured Lincoln's dilemma. Leslie's cartoonists showed him caught on the points of a dozen bayonets—"A President-elect's Uncomfortable Seat." Stephens compared him to a circus acrobat trying to balance War and Peace. Harper was sometimes sympathetic with Lincoln's problems, sometimes critical of his vacillation. One of his cartoonists portrayed Lincoln trying to unravel a hopelessly-snarled ball of yarn representing the Union; but McLenan's "Presidential Merrymen" showed him joking with his cronies while a funeral procession for the Constitution passed by outside the window. Following the bombardment, Harper sprang to Lincoln's support. Several cartoons showed the president protecting national property from the thievery of Jefferson Davis. In July, Harper stated that he could not detect a single error of judgment in the record of the administration: "We submit that Mr. Lincoln is entitled to the candid support of every honest man in the country." Pictorial opinion in *Leslie's,* the *Illustrated News,* and *Vanity Fair* momentarily was just as favorable.[13]

But repeated failures by the armies brought disillusionment with the Lincoln leadership. Hostile cartoonists criticized members of the cabinet and then the president himself. In the summer of 1862, Lincoln incurred more disfavor with the preliminary proclamation of emancipation. His prestige dropped to an all-time low after the costly repulse at Fredericksburg. William Newman of *Leslie's* depicted Lincoln having a nightmare review of all the failures of the war. In one of *Harper's* cartoons, "Columbia" asked Lincoln about all her sons slain at Fredericksburg; Lincoln replied, "This reminds me of a little joke." Columbia angrily retorted, "Go tell your joke at Springfield." In another, Lincoln appeared as the manager of a theater sheepishly apologizing to his audience that the "Tragedy entitled The Army of the Potomac, has been withdrawn on account of Quarrels among the leading Performers. . . ."[14]

By 1863 master cartoonists like Frank Bellew, Henry Stephens, and Thomas Nast began to dominate the field. They relied less on situation comedy and more on caricature and personality stereotypes. Lincoln's face and figure were a cartoonist's delight; his critics might have described them as nature's own caricature. Skillful artists shaped his thin face, deep-set eyes, and heavy brows into expresssions of benign wisdom and kindness or they twisted the same features into the face of a sneering tyrant. In favorable cartoons, his height let him tower in superior majesty over smaller men, but in critical cartoons his huge hands and feet and long limbs were simply grotesque. Even friendly cartoonists usually caricatured him. Critics of *Vanity Fair* accused Stephens of disloyalty, but Stephens praised Lincoln more often than he condemned him. Many of Nast's early Lincoln cartoons were extremely crude portraits.[15]

Nevertheless, it was fortunate for Lincoln that the cartoons of his two severest critics were not widely distributed in the North. The first of these was John Tenniel, the stately and beloved English artist perhaps best remembered for his illustrations of Lewis Carroll's *Alice in Wonderland* and *Through the Looking-Glass.* Tenniel was the leading cartoonist for the *London Punch,* and his editorial illustrations were one reason *Punch* had a considerable influence in shaping British public opinion. He and other members of the *Punch* editorial board had always been aloofly suspicious of the United States, and during the war they favored the South. In 1861, the "Trent Affair," involving the seizure of two Confederate agents from a British man-of-war, seemed to prove Lincoln's perfidy.

Tenniel had developed a cartoon figure to represent Americans—a scrawny, bumptious fellow named "Brother Jonathan," who blustered, boasted, and bragged with monotonous regularity. In 1861 Tenniel noticed the physical resemblance between Brother Jonathan and Abraham Lincoln, and gradually he used the most objectionable of Jonathan's characteristics to create a grotesque caricature of the president. But whereas Jonathan had been an irritating but somehow likeable prankster, Tenniel characterized Lincoln as a diabolical villain. At times he only scorned him as an incompetent, but on other occasions he sat down at his drawing board with acid on his pen. He portrayed Lincoln subverting American civil rights by suppressing the press and suspending *habeas corpus*, a president who sent thousands of young men to be maimed and killed on the battlefield, and then told jokes when "Columbia" asked about her sons. He interpreted the emancipation proclamation as a gambler's black ace-in-the-hole. Shortly after the New York draft riots, Tenniel depicted Lincoln turning his back on Negroes being beaten and lynched in the streets. With each new cartoon, Lincoln's eyes took on a brighter glow, his hairline descended, and his posture became more stooped, until there was a definitely simian cast to his appearance.[16]

But even Tenniel's caricature was mild in comparsion to the work of a Baltimore dentist-artist named Adalbert Volck. In 1861 he issued a series of engravings so vicious that the Federal government ordered their suppression. Volck fled to Europe. He then tried to smuggle the plates for some new engravings back into the Confederacy on a blockade runner, but the ship was captured and the plates destroyed. Volck later published twenty-nine engravings entitled *Confederate War Etchings,* but these too aroused such a storm of indignation that he withdrew them from circulation. His engravings never had a wide distribution, but because the other anti-Lincoln cartoons issued by southern publishers were so dull and unimaginative by comparison, they enjoyed a great popularity among Confederates. His Lincoln cartoons were unusually brutal. "Under the Veil" portrayed Lincoln as a dancer who suddenly threw away his last veil to expose himself as a Negro. Another showed Lincoln's face twisted with hate as he wrote the emancipation proclamation under a picture showing the rapine and murder in Santo Domingo following emancipation there. Several others were no less savage.[17]

Lincoln desperately needed a cartoonist on his side with the talents of a Tenniel or a Volck. Such a man was Thomas Nast. But Nast worked for Harper, and until 1863 Harper publicly avoided aligning the *Weekly* with either political party. Inevitably, however, he became involved in many partisan controversies. None of these were more important in forcing him to play an open and aggressive role in domestic wartime politics than emancipation and the military utilization of Negroes.

Prior to the war, most of the publishers and artists looked upon the Negro as only the symbol of a national problem. George William Curtis lamented that anti-slavery sentiment in the North was motivated by abstract philanthropy, hatred of slave holders, and jealousy for white labor, and not by "consciousness of wrong done, and the wish to right it." Harper, Leslie, and Leggett would not discuss emancipation for fear it would stiffen the resistance of the South and prolong the war. Henry L. Stephens thought that "all the gammon preached about immediate emancipation is a dodge for bringing political capital to the miners of the black diamonds." A few publishers catered to northern anti-abolitionist sentiment; G. W. Cottrell published a cartoon showing Senator Sumner giving coins to a little Negro girl, while an empty-handed white girl pleaded, "I'm not to blame for being white, Sir!" Artists usually pictured Negroes either as buffoons or as "Uncle Toms." Nast and Bellew suggested that slaves would make good carriages for the artillery or excellent horses for the cavalry. William T. Crane of *Leslie's* and Theodore Davis were frankly disgusted when they saw Negroes looting the deserted homes of their masters. Nearly every artist sketched the "contraband" slaves who worked in the Union camps, but Leggett angrily published a picture showing a group of contrabands asleep under a shade tree while white soldiers dug entrenchments.[18]

But as the publishers' tolerance of southerners declined, their admiration for the Negroes increased. Sketch artists showed how slaves helped the army by bringing in information, by caring for exhausted and wounded soldiers, and by sheltering and feeding soldiers who had escaped from southern prisons—an Underground Railroad for white men. Crane illustrated the success of a Federally-sponsored experiment on the South Carolina Sea Islands, where Negroes were paid wages to raise cotton. Pictures of whipping posts, iron neckbands, and other instruments of personal torture, and illustrations showing how the enemy forced their slaves to load their artillery while exposed to the fire of Federal sharpshooters, and used the bodies of dead slaves as booby traps, made good atrocity pictures to elicit sympathy for the slaves.[19]

Harper did not originally favor wartime emancipation, but Confederate atrocities and the promise of a long and difficult war convinced him that emancipation was necessary. Characteristically, he justified his new position as a matter of principle, and he supported Lincoln's preliminary proclamation with enthusiasm. Leggett and Leslie were more restrained. A large illustration in the *Illustrated News* showed the emancipated Negroes of New York City strutting down Fifth Avenue and shouldering white couples into the gutter.[20]

Having committed himself, Harper then made the *Weekly* the foremost pictorial journal in the Negro crusade. He next considered using Negroes as combat troops. To counter the widespread resistance to this measure, he encouraged Nast to draw editorial illustrations supporting Curtis' contention that the Negro was an intelligent and responsible human being, "swayed by the same emotions, inspired by the same hopes, capable of the same human development, as those of us who belong to another race." Field artists sent in pictures showing that Negroes were already making many contributions to the war effort. Crane supplied Leslie with pictures of the martial qualities of Negro regiments in South Carolina. Theo Davis did a series of sketches from Vicksburg about Gordon, a former slave and scout for Grant's army who suffered mistreatment at the hands of southerners. Other sketch artists submitted still more evidence of Confederate atrocities against Negro troops. The climax came in the spring of 1864 with the Fort Pillow Massacre. Confederate soldiers in Tennessee were supposed to have indulged in an orgy of murder when they captured a fort defended by Negro troops. Illustrations in all the pictorials showed the fiendish glee with which they slaughtered the helpless Negro prisoners. The resultant outcry in the North again demonstrated how easily northerners believed the worst about the enemy.[21]

Leslie and Leggett supported the use of Negro combat troops as a matter of military expediency. But Harper argued that Negroes had a right to fight, and that eventually they should have other rights as well. This indicated that by 1864 he recognized the political and social implications of the war. Moreover, as the election of 1864 approached, he was anxious to work for Lincoln's re-election.[22]

Previously, Harper had pretended that the *Weekly* was nonpartisan: "These columns . . . are neither Democratic nor Republican; they are simply Union. *Harper's Weekly* has no politics." During the 1862 Congressional elections, he did not try to influence the voters. Even so, there was criticism of the *Weekly's* discussion of political questions. Henry E. Smith wrote Curtis that he could no longer tolerate having the *Weekly* in his home, because he believed it was not the purpose of an illustrated newspaper "to dabble in the dirty pool of partisan politics." He objected to the attempt of the *Weekly* to pose as politically neutral, and then under the guise of illustrations seek to impose views that were impalpable to many readers. Curtis denied Smith's accusations, stated that the *Weekly's* only loyalty was to the government, and then added: "You, Mr. Smith, ought to understand that you confer no favor upon anybody but yourself in buying the paper. . . ." Harper's espousal of controversial causes lost him some subscribers like Smith, but it also gained him many new ones. The historian-diplomat J. L. Motley wrote all the way from Vienna requesting a subscription.[23]

Harper's role in the campaign made it strikingly clear that he supported Lincoln and not any of the many other Republican factions. Dissident Republicans who opposed the president received short treatment. During the summer, he all but ignored the candidacy of John C. Fremont, and he argued that the "ill-tempered spirit" of the Wade-Davis manifesto denouncing a presidential veto "proves conclusively the unfitness of either of the gentlemen for grave counselors in a time of national peril."[24]

Harper was even more determined because the other two illustrated weeklies either slighted or opposed Lincoln's re-election. The tone of Leslie's editorials indicated that he preferred Lincoln, but he told his subscribers that his paper had never been "the organ of a party" and was interested only in the restoration of the Union. "This has been the sole aim and object of our editorials, carefully avoiding those sectional views and personal prejudices which are distasteful to all Americans." The careless reader of *Leslie's* might have spent the entire summer and autumn of 1864 unaware of the election.[25]

Early in 1864, W. Jennings Demorest bought the *New York Illustrated News* and threw its support behind the most extreme faction of the Republican Party. Several indignant editorials criticized Lincoln's arbitrary arrests and seizures of property, and suggested that as long as he had sworn to defend the constitution, he might begin to do so. On June 18 Demorest announced his support of Fremont. A month later he claimed that the government had refused the use of the mails to the *News,* solely because of "the feelings of hostility which we have never disguised towards Mr. Lincoln's imbecile administration." He added: "We look upon him as a weak yet obstinate man, incompetent for his high office, temporizing with traitors in arms, despotic towards patriots who honestly differ with him in opinion, and dishonestly engaged in using the means for his own re-election which ought to be employed in putting down the rebellion. All these things we have not hesitated to say, and for these things we are promised, not to be brought to justice, but to be shut up in Fort Lafayette."[26]

The commerical publishers sold pictures to both parties. Printmakers and envelope manufacturers issued vehement anti-Lincoln cartoons one week and pro-Lincoln cartoons the next. When the Democrats nominated General McClellan at the Chicago convention, the publishers accorded him the same treatment. Portrait publishers and manufacturers of campaign badges supplied both parties, and oftentimes included portraits of Lincoln and McClellan on the same sheet or badge. A few of the Lincoln portraits, particularly those copied from recent Brady or Gardner photographs, were excellent likenesses, but most of them were extremely crude.[27]

Meanwhile, Harper worked for Lincoln by stressing one basic idea—loyalty. The election turned upon a single issue, he stated, and that was "whether the national government has the right to defend its existence by force against foreign enemies and domestic enemies, or whether it is a mere partnership with the states in which the prosperity of the whole is at the whim of the smallest part." Accordingly, the voter faced a simple decision: "Whoever believes that the Union and Government shall be unconditionally maintained will vote for Lincoln and Johnson, all others will vote for McClellan and Pendleton." The implication was that a vote for McClellan and the Democrats was a disloyal vote.[28]

At Chicago the Democrats adopted a platform that in effect called for an armistice to end the war and reunite the nation. Republicans believed that the Chicago platform meant abandoning most of the objectives for which northerners were fighting the war. To make matters worse for his party,

McClellan refused to subscribe to all the planks of the Chicago platform. Harper was not alone in exploiting these circumstances. Frank Bellew did cartoons for both *Harper's* and *Leslie's* depicting McClellan as an acrobat trying to balance precariously between war and peace. Prang of Boston and Currier and Ives published prints arguing that McClellan was perfectly willing to sacrifice millions of Negroes and thousands of Federal martyrs merely to achieve the presidency. While McClellan humbled himself before Jefferson Davis, Lincoln stood firm in his determination to continue the war.[29]

Nast made a ferocious cartoon attack on the Chicago platform. In one large multi-panel illustration, he answered the accusations of the platform with counter-accusations of his own. Where the Democrats claimed Lincoln had violated civil rights, Nast retorted with the emancipation proclamation, and when the platform claimed that only the Democratic party could reunite the nation, Nast answered with a pictorial review of Confederate atrocities. Harper was delighted with Nast's "Chicago Platform," and he offered to let Union clubs and committees use the electrotype plates to print and distribute their own copies throughout the country.[30]

Nast's attack on McClellan infuriated the opposition. Two Ohioans wrote Harper: "You will much oblige [us] . . . if you will keep your dam Blagard Sheet at home, or send it to them that can Stumic it. We can no longer gow it any longer." Opposition cartoonists attacked Lincoln's violations of the constitution. They argued that his reputation as a jokester demonstrated his lack of sober responsibility. They also prophesied that his abolitionist policies threatened the country with miscegenation. Bromley's of New York issued a cartoon showing Lincoln promenading in the park with a Negro woman. Auguste Laugel, a Frenchman traveling through the North during the campaign, noticed the large lamp-lit transparencies in a Democratic parade in Philadelphia that showed the long thin silhouette of the president with a plump Negro woman on each arm. Toward the end of the campaign, one cartoonist showed a drunken Negro soldier preventing a crippled army veteran from casting his ballot for McClellan; the veteran could only lament, "I am an American citizen and did not think I had fought and bled for this. Alas my country."[31]

Nevertheless, Nast had seized the initiative in the cartoon campaign and he never relinquished it. From September to November he lashed out with a series of cartoons that combined savage criticism with a superb sentimental

176

appeal. He skillfully used such allegorical figures as "Columbia," "Peace," and "Victory," and then raised Lincoln to this pantheon of near-gods by showing the president freeing the slaves, mourning with the nation over its dead, and in a Christmas scene magnanimously welcoming the ragged Confederate orphans back into the family. He illustrated the devastation that war had brought to the South, and he pictured northern traitors collecting Democratic votes by taking names from the graves of Federal soldiers. His "Blessings of Victory" portrayed "Peace" and "Victory" holding the sword and palm leaf over scenes of prisons, freed slaves, and the returning veterans. "Blessings of Victory" inspired one old soldier of the Army of the Shenandoah to write Harper: "All honor to the elegant sheet. . . . Nothing could better represent the feelings of the soldiers—a glorious victory, and an honorable peace will soon follow."[32]

The one picture with the greatest impact on the campaign was Nast's "Compromise with the South." It showed Jefferson Davis with one foot on the grave of "Heroes Who Fell in a Useless War," shaking the hand of a crippled Union veteran. "Columbia" was weeping by the grave. In his original sketch, Nast surrounded this scene with a number of smaller pictures, but Harper eliminated them and enlarged the central sketch to full-page size. Both the regular and extra editions of the *Weekly* containing this picture were immediately sold out, and Harper then released the plates so other publishers might circulate a million additional reprints.[33]

Letters praising "Compromise with the South" poured into Harper's office. *"God bless you for the high and noble patriotism of your sheet!"* wrote one cavalryman from West Virginia. "Oh, that these cowards at the North who desire 'peace at any price' could be fired with one spark of the high and self-sacrificing spirit that animates the army! We who risk most and suffer most by the war desire *no peace until every black and crime-stained traitor heart is crushed in the dust, and every seed of future treason and rebellion annihilated."* A Michigan soldier recovering from a wound received before Atlanta, wrote Harper that he was taking copies of "Compromise with the South" and "Blessings of Victory" back to the front so he could show them to the other men in his regiment. Numerous letterwriters suggested that Harper reprint the picture on durable paper so they could hang it in every "hotel, railroad depot, and other places of general resort throughout the North as being the most truthful and powerful explanation of the issues to be settled by our armies and by the November election."[34]

Harper printed many of these testimonials from the army to create the impression that the men in the service were voting as a unit for Lincoln. A private with the army near Petersburg thanked Harper for "the manly, patriotic tone" of the *Weekly,* and then reported that he was going to vote for Lincoln, and he thought all good soldiers and citizens should do likewise. Nast used this idea in several editorial illustrations. "Rally Round the Flag" said in effect "Rally around Lincoln, boys!" His last cartoon of the campaign, "Election Day," showed "Columbia" proudly casting a ballot for Lincoln, while marginal sketches under the caption "No Compromise" portrayed soldiers and civilians voting for Lincoln.[35]

When Lincoln won a second term, the men at the *Weekly* were jubilant. Curtis told his readers that the election proved the northern people were determined to fight on to victory. Frank Bellew helped them celebrate with one of the best cartoons of the war, "Long Abraham Lincoln a Little Longer," showing an extremely elongated Lincoln holding a newspaper announcing his re-election. Though he portrayed the president as careworn and tired, Bellew's happy good humor permeated the cartoon, and it expressed perfectly the general feeling of relief and satisfaction.[36]

The Lincoln image was the product of the frenzied excitement of wartime politics. Lincoln was obliged to make decisions that led people either to hate or to idolize him. Consequently, they believed that he was either an ugly uncouth tyrant who abused his extraordinary war powers for personal and political advantage, or that he was a humble but resolute statesman who inspired and led the nation through its most serious crisis. After the election of 1864, everyone turned his attention back to the war, and in the warm flush of approaching victory, the publishers issued new illustrations of enemy atrocities and by implication promised a day of judgment and retribution. In this mood there occurred the tragic event of April 14, 1865 at Ford's Theater. The impact of the assassination was so great that Democrats joined with various varieties of Republicans to honor the man so many of them had earlier damned. The post-war image of Lincoln as the martyred self-sacrificing president came quite easily, despite the fact that it bore little resemblance to the image of the war years.

XIV

Roundup

The hate and suspicion fostered by Nast and other editorial artists during the campaign did not subside with Lincoln's re-election. Republican leaders appreciated the value of propaganda too much to confine its use to political campaigns. As the war moved into the final months, the radical faction of the Republican party kept northern tempers at a high pitch. The Committee on the Conduct of the War issued new reports on enemy atrocities to prepare public opinion for a harsh settlement with the South. Harper and Leslie published pictures that supported the allegations of the Committee. Northerners were aroused when the war came to an end, and the assassination of Lincoln seemed to be the final and most monstrous crime of all. The joy and thanksgiving engendered by the victory were submerged by a desire for vengeance that boded ill for the South in the years of Reconstruction.

Harper and Leslie were unintentional allies of the Committee even though neither considered himself a Radical. Demorest had joined the Radicals when he endorsed Fremont for the presidency, but his influence stopped when he ceased publication of the *Illustrated News* at the end of the campaign. Leslie's reluctance to take a partisan position was primarily responsible for the decline in the circulation of his newspaper to less than a hundred thousand copies a week. Even so, *Leslie's* still reached a considerable audience. Harper, on the other hand, supported Lincoln's program of moderation and opposed Radical attempts to sabotage the president. The *Weekly's* circulation of a hundred and twenty thousand copies a week was at an all-time high. But like Lincoln, both Harper and Leslie accepted many of the specific proposals if not the vindictive spirit of the Radicals. Every picture supporting the Negro crusade, demanding the unqualified surrender of the South or illustrating Confederate atrocities strengthened the Radicals.

The revival of the atrocity campaign began in May of 1864 when the

Committee on the Conduct of the War issued a report on the condition of the men recently released from the Richmond prisons. The report included eight frightening photographs of living cadavers that had once been Federal soldiers. Both Harper and Leslie republished the photographs and quoted extensively from the report. Harper was unusually angry. These atrocities were the work, he wrote, "of desperate and infuriated men whose human instincts have become imbruted by the constant habit of outraging humanity." Yet he would not support a Committe recommendation that the Federal government retaliate by starving Confederate prisoners. The idea might be correct in the abstract, he argued, but he did not think it was wise under the circumstances.[1]

The release of more prisoners allowed the sketch artists to present their own evidence. Their illustrations were not as sensational as those in the Committee's report, but for that very reason they were more convincing to many northerners who were suspicious of any evidence from the partisan Committee. In November, William Waud sent Harper two sketches of some recently-released prisoners. They lay helplessly in their rags on the decks of the exchange ships, sick in body and crippled of limb. Yet their spirits were strong; several pulled themselves up on one elbow and cheered the flag. Waud's original sketches were objective and matter-of-fact, but Harper's engravers embellished the appearance of the prisoners with the limp postures, sad faces, and upward-turned eyes of Christian martyrs. The following month Waud sketched another group of ragged and barefoot prisoners in Charleston. But some of these men were strong enough to play fiddles and dance jigs of joy, and others were quite spry as they accepted new clothes, tobacco, and other gifts distributed by the Sanitary Commission.[2]

Illustrations and photographs from Federal armies in the South told an even more frightening tale of horror. Sherman's army captured the abandoned prison pen at Millen, Georgia, and Theo Davis and Lieutenant T. A. Prime sent Harper and Leslie several sketches of the filthy hovels and pits in the crowded compounds where the prisoners had lived. J. E. Taylor sketched similar scenes in the prison pen at Columbia, South Carolina. Joseph Becker was in North Carolina when the Federal army found some prisoners who had formerly been at Millen, but had been moved from pen to pen along with the retreating Confederates. His sketch showed a dozen emaciated men on the brink of death, three of whom had already become idiots from "sheer horror and destitution." He was further shocked to discover that one of the prisoners was a former schoolmate, but so changed after only three years that Becker had failed to recognize him.[3]

These pictures, together with a new Committee report on atrocities, altered the original attitudes of the publishers. By April of 1865, Harper and Leslie were writing editorials that spoke more of revenge than of reconciliation. Leslie angrily denounced the "savage barbarity" of an enemy whose crimes included "wanton, needless murder . . . robbery, imprisonment and starvation. . . ." Harper threatened retaliation by publishing three associated sketches showing a group of Confederate prisoners and views of the Federal prison at Elmira and a cell in Fort Lafayette. Both men agreed that soon there would be a final reckoning.[4]

Then in the second week of April, the war came to an unexpectedly-sudden end. Throughout the winter of 1864–65, Gardner, Brady, and the other cameramen with the Army of the Potomac had been photographing the consequences of Grant's war of attrition. The depots at City Point burst with supplies for Grant's troops, but Lee's veterans suffered severe privation in the Petersburg trenches. For many months they had not had enough food to eat nor warm clothes to cover their bodies. Young boys fourteen and fifteen years old and middle-aged men in their fifties filled the thin ranks of the army. Fort Malone—known to its inhabitants as "Fort Damnation"—was perhaps the worst place in the Confederate lines. Brady later photographed the pools of stagnant leaden water lapping against the slimy muddied banks of the entrenchments from which twisted tree roots hung like skeletal fingers. From out of these pits late in March, Lee made his last assault, and was repulsed. On April first, Sheridan's cavalry shattered Pickett's troopers at Five Forks, and the following morning the Ninth Corps cracked the Confederate defenses at Fort Malone. It was then that Brady photographed young barefoot boys in their early teens lying face down in the mud where they had been killed.[5]

The next day Union armies occupied Petersburg and Richmond. John R. Hamilton and A. W. Warren sketched the triumphant entry of the troops and the crowds of Negroes that lined the roadsides to greet them. Then they rushed off to rejoin the armies still pursuing Lee. Joseph Becker illustrated Lincoln's tour of Richmond, showing him acknowledging the cheers of the Negroes from an open carriage, and then visiting the home that Jefferson

Davis had occupied throughout the war. Becker and Brady examined the ruins of Richmond; "most melancholy," Becker thought, when he saw that most of the city had been burned. He sent Leslie sketches showing former home owners looking among the rubble for valuables they had left behind when the fire got out of control. Brady's photographs depicted a desolation more complete than that in Columbia after Sherman's occupation. In some places, the camera eye could not find a single habitable building. The notorious prisons of the capital were also shocking. In the last week of the war, Becker and Warren added to the mounting northern anger with detailed illustrations of Libby, Belle Isle, and Castle Thunder.[6]

Lee's surrender at Appomattox[7] inspired the picturemen to moments of retrospection. Harper told Curtis he was glad the North had lost the first battle of Bull Run because otherwise slavery would not have been destroyed and the war would have been for nought. Nast drew a double-panel cartoon showing Fort Sumter in 1861 threatened by lightning bolts of war, and the same scene in 1865 with the female figure of "Peace" hovering over the battered fort. Another *Harper's* artist drew the last of the Lincoln cartoons when he showed the bespectacled president seated on a camp chair at City Point writing a dispatch on a drum-head: "All seems well with us."[8]

The events of April 14 and 15 abruptly shattered their celebration. Lincoln returned to Washington, and on the evening of the 14th he attended Ford's Theater. John Wilkes Booth, a disgruntled actor, shot him while he watched the play. He died the following day. Harper's and Leslie's inclination to be lenient with southerners immediately evaporated. "The commencement, the progress, and the close of rebellion—treason, wanton barbarity, assassination!" Leslie raged. "Unrelieved by a single trait, lightened up by no single act of generosity, it stands in history one black, hideous blotch on civilization and mankind."[9]

Artists and photographers recorded every significant event in the weeks after the assassination. Harper and Leslie recalled artists from the armies to assist their staff artists. They re-created the assassination scene in Ford's Theater, and showed the small room across the street where the president died. F. C. H. Bonwill sketched the funeral in Washington for Leslie, and William Waud followed the cortege across the country to the final internment in Springfield. Other artists remained in the capital to show the "conspirators" in their cells and to illustrate their trial. Of necessity, they sketched many incidents they did not witness personally; a picture in *Leslie's* showing two army officers sinking Booth's body in the Potomac illustrated an event that never even occurred. The culmination of their work came on July 7 when they depicted in graphic detail the hanging of four of the convicted conspirators.[10]

Still the public was not satisfied. They agreed with Leslie that the assassination was a reminder for northerners not to be sympathetic with treason. Artists still in Richmond sent in more sketches of the prisons, and pictured the stubborn defiance of southern women who snubbed Federal officers and soldiers. The cartoonists concentrated on Jefferson Davis. One Cincinnati lithographer portrayed the Devil, Benedict Arnold, and Jefferson Davis gathered around the "treason toddy bowl." Cartoons showing how Davis would be hanged were especially popular. In May, the artists were delighted to hear that Davis had been captured disguised as an old woman. More than a dozen publishers from St. Louis to Boston issued cartoons showing the once-distinguished president of the Confederacy dressed in a faded sunbonnet and dress and wearing a pair of men's boots beneath his petticoats. But after Davis' capture, many people were angry that the government imprisoned rather than executed him. Nast compared the horrors of Andersonville prison with the rumored comforts that Davis enjoyed in Fortress Monroe. He showed veterans looking on in disgust, and in angry captions, he shouted: "Shall the rebel leaders be restored to power?" and "Soldiers! Have you fought in vain?"[11]

Such was the spirit of the Bloody Shirt.

* * *

The cooperation of the sketch artists and the editorial artists at the end of the war was unique. Heretofore they had followed parallel but separate paths, each creating their own images. Generally they agreed on long-range objectives, but differed on the nature of war and its impact on the troops. Consequently, there emerged not one but two new images from the Civil War.

Nast, Bellew, Stephens, McLenan, Tenniel, Volck, and the dozens of unidentified cartoonists who worked for the commercial publishers created images that garnered support for the war. The Civil War cast American society into the worst confusion since the Revolution, but editorial artists interpreted the issues with a simple clarity that was extremely satisfying to people seeking easy solutions. The enemy represented evil. He subverted the Union to preserve an unholy institution, hurled the nation into the maelstrom of war, and then fought with ferocious barbarity. Southern sympathizers and laggards on the home front shared the guilt of treason. But northerners fought heroically in a great moral crusade, and inevitably they triumphed. The enemy was crushed and the states were reunited once again. In brief, these were the images of the editorial artists. They were strong and intoxicating.

The field sketchers' artistic concept of warfare was vastly more complex. Images of heroism underwent a thorough transformation. Sketch artists no longer portrayed spectacular acts of individual bravery. Soldiers who defiantly exposed themselves to the bullets of the enemy were merely foolhardy. Death was seldom heroic, and there was nothing inspirational in the pictures of the slaughtered men at Gettysburg and Cold Harbor. The new images emphasized patient and self-reliant performance of duty. The true heroes were men who endured the fatigue, the waiting, and the uncertainty of the war of attrition.

Artists also revised their thinking about the structure of the army. The battle of Bull Run proved that civilians did not become soldiers merely by putting on a uniform, and that combat was only one facet of army life. By the summer of 1862 the artists recognized the importance of training and discipline, and consequently they had a much greater respect for professional officers. They learned that combat regiments depended upon a large number of auxiliary services—clerks and couriers to implement the system of command, adjutant-generals and inspector-generals, quartermasters and teamsters, medical officers and signal corpsmen, engineers, and even provost marshals. Moreover, they realized that the majority of each soldier's life was spent in camp, on patrol and along the picket line, marching from one campaign to another, and in the cold isolation of winter quarters.

The images of leadership also changed. The fascination of artists with the activities of the generals declined even before McClellan left the army. Gone were the field portraits in full-dress uniforms and the gallant equestrian poses.[12] Pope, Burnside, Halleck, Hooker, and Meade arrived and departed too quickly to leave lasting impressions. When Grant and Sherman and their lieutenants assumed command, the artists and photographers were more discriminating. Nevertheless, they were impressed by the quiet competence of these new leaders, as they showed in occasional portraits depicting the field generals attending unostentatiously to the details and responsibilities of command. The new images demanded performance rather than showmanship.

The greatest change was in the image of the common soldier. After 1863 he monopolized the attention of the field artists. In 1861 he was a crusader engaged in a holy cause; by 1863 he looked upon his personal role in the war as an obligation to complete, but he did not particularly like the army, and he did not intend to stay in it any longer than necessary. The new images portrayed him as a disciplined and thoroughly competent man who nevertheless retained his civilian independence of mind. He waited patiently through the tension of sieges and the inactivity of winter, marched efficiently, and fought with superb skill and courage. The paraphernalia and ceremonialism of The Heroic War irritated him, and after Lee's surrender the once-eager young men who marched down Broadway four years earlier were anxious to get home. But in the moment of victory, the old traditions had a resurgence, and tired veterans had to parade down Pennsylvania Avenue in Washington "to satisfy the curiosity of civilians. . . ."[13]

The post-war survival of these new images suffered because many of the artists were not available to perpetuate them. Henri Lovie and William Crane died soon after Appomattox. Winslow Homer did a number of war paintings, but his primary interest was in landscapes and marine subjects. Alex Simplot gave up sketching and went into business in Dubuque. Arthur Lumley, William Waud, and Joseph Becker continued to work as illustrators, but the Civil War was not a subject that any longer concerned them.[14]

Other picturemen, however, consolidated the work of the war years. Many of the photographs made by Brady and the other cameramen were eventually published and finally given a mass distribution. In 1876 and 1891, Edwin Forbes used only the new images when he published two sets of engravings based on his field sketches. He ignored battlefield heroics, and instead depicted the routine of army life, the weary exhaustion of the march, the quiet solitude of the picket line, and the functional performance of veteran troops under fire. When the publishers of the Century Company wanted a complete set of Civil War illustrations, they employed Alf Waud, Theodore Davis, and Frank Schell, and for pictures of the Confederate army, Allen Redwood, an outstanding artist who had fought for the South. All four subscribed unreservedly to the new images. The Century illustrations were especially significant because other publishers reprinted them extensively throughout the late nineteenth and early twentieth centuries.[15]

The new field images were never completely triumphant. The traditional images of the editorial artists were too strongly entrenched. Thirty years after Appomattox, Theodore Roosevelt spoke the language of the heroes when he referred to the Spanish-American War as "a splendid little war," and volunteer soldiers embarked for Cuba with a fanfare that recalled the frenzied excitement in April of 1861. But a new corps of sketch artists and photographers recorded their struggle.[16] The jungles and malaria of Cuba undermined the heroics of San Juan Hill just as the mud of Virginia enveloped the illusions fostered by Colonel Elmer Ellsworth and the gallant charge of Company B at Fairfax Court House. History was not repeating itself; human nature merely remained unchanged. In every war since 1865, more realistic images eventually prevailed because War itself proved to be the artists' best ally.

Notes

CHAPTER I: THE IMAGE MAKERS

[1] James A. Connolly, *Three Years in the Army of the Cumberland,* edited by Paul M. Angle (Bloomington, Indiana, 1959), 120–121, 253.

[2] John D. Billings, *Hardtack and Coffee.* . . . (Boston, 1888), 25.

[3] "Art in America," in *Godey's Lady's Book and Magazine,* 62:269–270 (March, 1861); Virgil Barker, *American Painting, History and Interpretation* (New York, 1950), 392, 460–461; "How to Make a Picture," in the *American Review,* 15:400–410 *passim* (May, 1852); *Harper's Weekly,* Feb. 9, 1861, 83; *New York Illustrated News,* Sept. 29, 1860, 322, hereinafter cited as *NYIN;* Suzanne LaFollette, *Art in America* (New York, 1929), 119–120, 126–128, 142, 153; Edgar W. Martin, *The Standard of Living in 1860* (University of Chicago, 1942), 358–359; Anthony Trollope, *North America,* edited by Donald Smalley and Bradford Allen Booth (New York, 1951), 203; Edward Douglas Branch, *The Sentimental Years, 1836–1860* (New York, 1934), 161–162; James Flexner, *A Short History of America Painting* (Boston, 1950), 49, 53–54; and for a discussion of the same taste in literature, see Paul Fatout, "Yarning in the Eighteen Fifties," in the *American Scholar,* 3:281–284 (Summer, 1934).

[4] See the chapters on the Revolution, War of 1812, and the Mexican War in Roy Meredith, *The American Wars, A Pictorial History from Quebec to Korea, 1755–1953* (Cleveland and New York, 1954), *passim.*

[5] Harry T. Peters, *Currier and Ives, Printmakers to the American People* (New York, 1942), 2–3, 10–12, 16, 18, 29, 32, 36; Samuel Simkin, ed., *A Currier & Ives Treasury* (New York, 1955), iii–v, opposite plate 13; Russel Crouse, *Mr. Currier and Mr. Ives, A Note on Their Lives and Times* (New York, 1930), 6–7; Barker, *American Painting,* 512–514; LaFollette, *Art in America,* 93–94; *The Diary of George Templeton Strong,* edited by Allan Nevins and Milton Halsey Thomas (4 vols., New York, 1952), 3:36; *NYIN,* Oct. 18, 1862, 370.

[6] The most complete collection of paintings and prints from the Revolution is in *The American Heritage Book of the Revolution,* by the editors of *American Heritage Magazine* (New York, 1958), *passim.* Also see Meredith, *American Wars, passim;* "Battle Art of Currier and Ives," in *The Old Print Shop Portfolio,* 7:194–216 (May, 1948); Mark Twain, *The Adventures of Huckleberry Finn* (Harper & Brothers edition, New York, 1912), 140.

[7] Meredith, *American Wars, passim;* "Battle Art of Currier & Ives," *op. cit.,* 194–216.

[8] Strong, *Diary,* 1:157, 162, 195–196; Robert Taft, *Photography and the American Scene, A Social History, 1839–1889* (New York, 1942), 125–126, 148–150, 158–159, 478 footnote 186; James D. Horan, *Mathew Brady, Historian with a Camera* (New York, 1955), 21–22, 46; Barker, *American Painting,* 391; *Harper's Weekly,* Feb. 16, 1861, 99, July 9, 1864, 442; *Frank Leslie's Illustrated Newspaper,* Jan. 2, 1864, 225, hereinafter cited as *Leslie's.* "Whatever may be said in praise of Daguerreotyping, we must all pronounce it a foe-to-graphic art." *Vanity Fair,* March 29, 1862, 158.

[9] Taft, *Photography,* 223–224, 233–234.

[10] For the development of illustrated journalism in Europe and the United States, see Clement K. Shorter, "Illustrated Journalism: Its Past and its Future," in *The Contemporary Review,* 75:482–486 (April, 1899); Frank Luther Mott, *A History of American Magazines, 1850–1865* (Cambridge, Massachusetts, 1938), 43–45; Taft, *Photography,* 419–420. For a general discussion of the factors encouraging illustrated journalism, see Shorter, *op. cit.,* 482, and Will Jenkins, "Illustration of the Daily Press in America," in *International Studio,* 16:254 (June, 1902). Critics did not fail to challenge the work of the illustrated newspapers. Shorter, *op. cit.,* 494, quotes a poem by William Wordsworth entitled "Illustrated Journalism":

> Discourse was deemed Man's noblest attribute,
> And written words the glory of his hand;
> Then followed printing with enlarged command
> For thought—dominion vast and absolute
> For spreading truth, and making love expand.
> Now prose and verse, sunk into disrepute,
> Must lacquey a dumb Art that best can suit
> The taste of this once-intellectual land.
> A backward movement surely have we here,
> From manhood,—back to childhood; for the age—
> Back towards caverned life's first rude career.
> Avaunt this vile abuse of pictorial page!
> Must eyes be all-in-all, the tongue and ear
> Nothing? Heaven keep us from a lower stage!

[11] *Leslie's,* Dec. 15, 1855, 6; Mott, *American Magazines,* 192–193; Frank Luther Mott, *American Journalism, A History of Newspapers in the United States through 260 years, 1690 to 1950* (New York, 1950), 319, 332, 379.

[12] Phineas Taylor Barnum, *Struggles and Triumphs; or Forty Years' Recollections of P. T. Barnum* (Buffalo, New York, 1874), 268, 380–381; William C. Edgar, "An Old Timer and other Journalistic Memories," in the *Bellman,* 26:714–719 (June 28, 1919).

[13] "Frank Leslie," in the *Dictionary of American Biography,* edited by Allen Johnson and Dumas Malone (22 vols., New York, 1928–1944), 11:186–187, hereinafter cited as *DAB; National Cyclopedia of American Biography* (19 vols., New York, 1898–1922), 3:370; Mott, *American Magazines,* 452–453; Madeleine Bettina Stern, *Purple Passage, The Life of Mrs. Frank Leslie* (Norman, Oklahoma, 1953), 34; Edgar, *op. cit.,* 714, 718.

[14] Stern, *Purple Passage,* 33–35, 47–48, 63–64; *NYIN,* Sept. 29, 1860, 323; J. C. Derby, *Fifty Years Among Authors, Books and Publishers* (New York, 1884), 692.

[15] *Leslie's,* Nov. 24, 1860, 2, Dec. 15, 1860, 53.

[16] *Ibid.,* Aug. 2, 1856, 124–125, Dec. 15, 1860, 53, Dec. 14, 1905, 566, 568; Mott, *American Magazines,* 458–459, Trollope, *North America,* 273–274, and Edward Dicey, *Six Months in the Federal States* (2 vols., London, 1863), 1:57–58, reflect the reaction of foreign visitors to the way vendors hawked illustrated newspapers through railroad cars.

[17] Mott, *American Magazines,* 469–473; "Fletcher Harper," in the *DAB,* 8:281; Horan, *Brady,* 49 and plate #241; Joseph Henry Harper, *The House of Harper, A Century of Publishing in Franklin Square* (New York, 1912), 223–224; Joseph Henry Harper, *I Remember* (New York, 1934), 7–9.

[18] Harper, *House of Harper,* 91: Harper, *I Remember,* 18–19, 27, 37; Mott, *American Magazines,* 475–476.

[19] Mott, *American Magazines,* 45.

[20] Frederic Hudson, *Journalism in the United States, from 1690 to 1872* (New York, 1873), 705; Louis M. Starr, *Bohemian Brigade: Civil War Newsmen in Action* (New York, 1954), 242: Clement Eaton, *A History of the Southern Confederacy* (New York, 1954), 221, 223, 225–227, 231; Mary Elizabeth Massey, *Ersatz in the Confederacy* (Columbia, South Carolina, 1952), 142–143; Lamont Buchanan, *A Pictorial History of the Confederacy* (New York, 1951), 215; *Leslie's,* Sept. 27, 1862, 3, Jan. 31, 1863, 299; *NYIN,* Dec. 20, 1862, 98–99. The Confederacy had artists and several of them sketched the war, but more for their personal satisfaction than for publication, and their sketches had little or no influence on the contemporary war images. Frank Vizetelly, a sketch artist for the *Illustrated London News,* spent some time in 1862 and 1863 in the Confederacy. Most of his illustrations appeared in the *News,* but a few fell into the hands of the Federal Navy when Vizetelly tried to pass them through the blockade, and eventually they saw publication in *Harper's Weekly.* See W. Stanley Hoole, *Vizetelly Covers the Confederacy* (Tuscaloosa, 1957).

[21] For Nast's illustrations, see the *Illustrated London News* and the *New York Illustrated News* for July–December, 1860, particularly *NYIN,* Nov. 3, 1860, 405, for a self-portrait of Nast in the Italian army. Also see George M. Trevelyan, "The War Journal of 'Garibaldi's Englishman,'" in *Cornhill Magazine,* 97:824,

848 (June, 1908); Evelyn Ashley, "A Garibaldian Reminiscence," in *The National Review*, 33:492–500 (May, 1899); Albert Bigelow Paine, *Th. Nast, His Period and His Pictures* (New York, 1904), 49–50, 67.

CHAPTER II: THE CRUSADE

[1] John Q. Anderson, ed., *Brokenburn, The Journal of Kate Stone, 1861–1868* (Baton Rouge, 1955), 14, 24; *NYIN*, Jan. 19, 1861, 141, Jan. 26, 1861, 178, Feb. 9, 1861, 211; *Harper's Weekly*, Feb. 9, 1861, 83, Feb. 16, 1861, 98, May 25, 1861, 322, June 8, 1861, 354; W. A. Swanburg, *First Blood, The Story of Fort Sumter* (New York, 1957), 179. Sketches from Harper's officer-artists at Sumter prior to the bombardment appeared in the *Weekly* between January 12, 1861 and April 27, 1861. Their original sketches were better than one would suspect, because all West Point graduates had training in sketching and drawing, as explained in Meredith, *American Wars*, 98–100. For Harper's trip to the South, see Harper, *House of Harper*, 132–133.

[2] *Leslie's*, Jan. 26, 1861, 145, Feb. 23, 1861, 209. A brief biography of Waud appeared in *Harper's Weekly*, Nov. 30, 1878, 947.

[3] Waud's pre-bombardment sketches from the South, over thirty-five in number, appeared in *Leslie's* between November 24, 1860 and April 20, 1861. See particularly *Leslie's*, Feb. 23, 1861, 216–217, March 2, 1861, 237.

[4] *Ibid.*, Jan. 19, 1861, 129, 136–137, Jan. 26, 1861, 145, Feb. 2, 1861, 161, 168, Feb. 23, 1861, 212, March 16, 1861, 257, March 23, 1861, 280–281, March 30, 1861, 292–293, 296, April 27, 1861, 353.

[5] *Ibid.*, April 27, 1861, 353, 356–357, 360, May 4, 1861, 388–397.

[6] *Harper's Weekly*, April 27, 1861, 260, 264–265, May 4, 1861, 273.

[7] *NYIN*, April 27, 1861, *passim*, May 4, 1861, 405, 412. For Osbon's career, see *Albert Bigelow Paine, A Sailor of Fortune. Personal Memoirs of Captain B. S. Osbon* (New York, 1906).

[8] *Leslie's*, May 4, 1861, 388, 392–393, 397.

[9] *Ibid.*, May 4, 1861, 387; *Harper's Weekly*, May 4, 1861, 277; Strong, *Diary*, 3:124, 127, 128.

[10] "Off for the War" and "The Brave at Home" in Folder #4420 in the Library of Congress Print Collection; *Leslie's*, April 20, 1861, 352, May 4, 1861, 287; Georgeanna Woolsey Bacon and Eliza Woolsey Howland, eds., *Letters of a Family During the War for the Union, 1861–1865* (2 vols., privately printed, 1899), 1:55–56. For a southern reaction to the beginning of the war, see Susan Leigh Blackford, comp., *Letters From Lee's Army, or Memoirs of Life in and Out of The*

Army in Virginia During the War Between the States (New York and London, 1947), 3–4.

[11] *Leslie's,* May 4, 1861, 396; *Harper's Weekly,* June 22, 1861, 388; *NYIN,* May 11, 1861, 1, June 1, 1861, 49.

[12] *Leslie's,* April 20, 1861, 344, 345, April 30, 1861, 381, May 4, 1861, 389; *Harper's Weekly,* May 4, 1861, 281, 282, May 11, 1861, 298, May 25, 1861, 329; *NYIN,* May 4, 1861, 413; Strong, *Diary,* 3:124, 126.

[13] *Harper's Weekly,* March 16, 1861, 162, April 20, 1861, 242, May 4, 1861, 274, May 18, 1861, 306, June 22, 1861, 386, July 13, 1861, 447; *NYIN,* Aug. 26, 1861, 258, May 10, 1862, 11; *Leslie's,* April 27, 1861, 353, May 4, 1861, 385, 389, June 1, 1861, 33, July 6, 1861, 113, Nov. 16, 1861, 403.

[14] W. A. Cooper, "Mr. Henry Mosler," in *Godey's Lady's Book and Magazine,* 130:563–570 (June, 1895); Manuscript Memoirs in the Alexander Simplot Papers, 1; *Leslie's,* April 30, 1861, 371; Robert Taft, *Artists and Illustrators of the Old West* (New York, 1953), 294 footnote 9; Yda Addis Storke, *A Memorial and Biographical History of the counties of Santa Barbara, San Luis Obispo and Ventura, California* (Chicago, 1891), 485–486.

[15] *Leslie's,* May 11, 1861, 403, Nov. 9, 1861, 391, July 11, 1863, 243; Meredith, *American Wars,* 342–344; John H. Brinton, *Personal Memoirs of John H. Brinton* (New York, 1914), 231, 285–287; *Harper's Weekly,* Oct. 26, 1861, 675, Feb. 21, 1863, 125–126; *NYIN,* Nov. 4, 1861, 11, Sept. 5, 1863, 290; *National Cyclopedia of American Biography,* 9:365; *The New York Times,* March 9, 1888, 5.

[16] Roy Meredith, *Mr. Lincoln's Camera Man; Mathew B. Brady* (New York, 1946), 77; Horan, *Brady,* 37 and plates #224–231 for examples of soldiers' portraits.

[17] Meredith, *Brady,* 88–89; Horan, *Brady,* 35.

[18] *Harper's Weekly,* May 4, 1861, 280, May 11, 1861, 304, May 18, 1861, 305.

[19] *Ibid.,* May 4, 1861, 283; *NYIN,* May 4, 1861, 408–409

[20] *Leslie's,* April 30, 1861, 376–377, July 13, 1861, 137, 144.

[21] *NYIN,* May 4, 1861, 402, May 18, 1861, 26. There are brief biographies of Alf Waud in *American Artists and their Work* (2 vols., Boston, 1889), 2:401–409; *Appleton's Annual Cyclopedia and Register of Important Events of the Year 1891* (New York, 1892), new series, 16:661. See also the obituaries in *Harper's Weekly,* April 18, 1891, 279; *The New York Times,* April 10, 1891, 5; the *Atlanta Constitution,* April 8, 1891, 7.

[22] *NYIN,* May 18, 1861, 26, July 6, 1861, 138, July 22, 1861, 180, 183. For examples of Scott in the prints, see Frank Weitenkampf, "Political Caricature in the United States in Separately Published Cartoons, an Annotated List," in the

Bulletin of the New York Public Library, 56:515–528, 557–574 (October and November, 1952), hereinafter cited as Weitenkampf, *NYPLB,* the Scott cartoons being listed on page 526; several envelopes in the Durkee Collection; and *Harper's Weekly,* June 8, 1861, 355. William Howard Russell, correspondent for the London *Times,* noticed the portraits of Scott in the New York shop windows: "Innumerable 'General Scotts' glower at you from every turn, making the General look wiser than he or any man ever was," quoted in Bayrd Still, *Mirror for Gotham, New York as seen by Contemporaries from Dutch Days to the Present* (New York, 1956), 179.

[23] *Harper's Weekly,* June 8, 1861, 356, June 15, 1861, 376, June 22, 1861, 392–394, July 6, 1861, 422, July 20, 1861, 453, July 27, 1861, 474, *Leslie's,* June 15, 1861, 76–77, July 6, 1861, 124–125; *NYIN,* June 1, 1861, 61. For lithographed prints, see Folder #4452 in the Library of Congress Print Collection. Also see Fred A. Shannon, "The Life of the Common Soldier in the Union Army, 1861–1865," in *The Mississippi Valley Historical Review,* 13:477–478 (March, 1927).

[24] *Leslie's,* June 29, 1861, 102; *Harper's Weekly,* June 8, 1861, 358, July 20, 1861, 452.

[25] The artists were followed by curiosity seekers who stripped the staircase and building for souvenirs. Allen Kingsbury, who was later killed at Yorktown in 1862, sent his family a piece of the stair on which Ellsworth had been shot: "Be careful of it, show it to the people as a trophy of *war.* I worked hard to get it," Allen Alonzo Kingsbury, *The Hero of Mefield; containing the journals and letters of Allen Alonzo Kingsbury.* . . . (Boston, 1862), 34.

[26] *Harper's Weekly,* May 25, 1861, 321, June 8, 1861, 357, May 11, 1861, 289, May 18, 1861, 308, June 15, 1861, 369; *NYIN,* June 8, 1861, 65; *Leslie's,* June 1, 1861, 33, 40–41, 48; and three envelopes in the Durkee Collection.

[27] Strong, *Diary,* 3:146.

CHAPTER III: THE PICNIC WAR

[1] Mott, *American Magazines,* 452, 460; *Leslie's,* May 19, 1860, 383, July 6, 1861, 113; *Harper's Weekly,* June 15, 1861, 369; *Vanity Fair,* Feb. 18, 1860, 127.

[2] The "flying gallop" was a pictorial representation dating back to ancient times of a running horse with the two fore legs stretched out in front, the two hind legs to the rear, and none of the hooves touching the ground. The impression was one of great flying speed. Not until after the Civil War did photographers prove that a running horse never took such a position; rather, at all times one or more legs are curved under or are on the way foward. See A. L. Kroeber, *Anthropology, Race, Language, Culture, Psychology, Prehistory* (New York, 1948), 497–503.

3 *NYIN,* July 22, 1861, 187, July 15, 1861, 168–169; *Harper's Weekly,* June 15, 1861, 377, July 20, 1861, 454; *Leslie's,* May 25, 1861, 17, June 8, 1861, 53, Aug. 3, 1861, 183; Strong, *Diary,* 3:154.

4 *Leslie's,* June 8, 1861, 56–57. For self-portraits of Schell, see *ibid.,* June 28, 1862, 205, Feb. 11, 1865, 324.

5 *Ibid.,* June 22, 1861, 88–89; *Harper's Weekly,* June 29, 1861, 408, 413.

6 *Leslie's,* June 22, 1861, 82; *NYIN,* July 6, 1861, 144. The printmakers also issued cartoons criticizing "militia generals"; see "Militia General in Action" in Weitenkampf, *NYPLB,* 525.

7 *Leslie's,* Nov. 24, 1860, 4, Dec. 22, 1860, 73–76, March 9, 1861, 245, March 2, 1861, 232–233, 236, March 16, 1861, 268, March 23, 1861, 276–277, Feb. 14, 1863, 322, 334.

8 *Ibid.,* June 22, 1861, 85, June 29, 1861, 106.

9 *Cincinnati Daily Gazette,* June 29, 1861, 1.

10 *Leslie's,* June 29, 1861, 101, 104–105, July 20, 1861, 149, 152–153, July 27, 1861, 161, 168–169, Aug. 3, 1861, 181, Aug. 10, 1861, 193; *Harper's Weekly,* July 27, 1861, 468; *Cincinnati Daily Gazette,* July 22, 1861, 2.

11 Note the reaction, for instance, of George Templeton Strong, *Diary,* 3:167; *Leslie's,* Jan. 4, 1862, 112; *NYIN,* Nov. 18, 1861, 36–37, Nov. 25, 1861, 50, Dec. 2, 1861, 80, March 15, 1862, 302, April 5, 1862, 350; *Harper's Weekly,* Sept. 21, 1861, 600–601, Jan. 25, 1862, 49, June 7, 1862, 367; five envelopes in the Durkee Collection; two prints in Folder #4420 in the Library of Congress Print Collection.

12 Meredith, *Brady,* 2–3; Horan, *Brady,* 38.

13 Meredith, *Brady,* 3–6; for a self-portrait of Waud at Bull Run, see *NYIN,* July 29, 1861, 196.

14 *American Art Annual,* 10:78 (1903); Begrüdet von Ulrich Thieme and Felix Becker, *Allgemeines Lexikon der Bildenden Künstler von der Antike bis zur Gegenwart* (37 vols., Leipzig, 1907–1950), 23:463; *The New York Times,* Oct. 21, 1890, 1, Sept. 28, 1912, 13; *Leslie's,* May 4, 1861, 389. For a self-portrait of Lumley at Bull Run, see *ibid.,* Aug. 3, 1861, 180.

15 Meredith, *Brady,* 6–7.

16 Lumley's Bull Run illustrations appeared in the August 3, 1861 issue of *Leslie's.*

17 Waud's Bull Run illustrations appeared in the July 29, August 5, and August 12, 1861 issues of *NYIN;* one of his original wash drawings from Bull Run is in the Waud Collection in the Library of Congress. Bull Run illustrations in *Harper's Weekly* appeared in the issues of August 3 and 10, 1861.

[18] Meredith, *Brady*, 8–12 and plates #127, 128. His photographs of the retreat have since disappeared.

[19] *NYIN*, Sept. 23, 1861, 330, Aug. 12, 1861, 232–233; *Leslie's*, July 27, 1861, 164–165; *Harper's Weekly*, Aug. 10, 1861, 500.

[20] J. Cutler Andrews, *The North Reports the Civil War* (Pittsburg, 1955), 91; Meredith, *Brady*, 10–14.

[21] Strong, *Diary*, 3:169; *Harper's Weekly*, Aug. 10, 1861, 499, Aug. 17, 1861, 514, Sept. 7, 1861, 562–563; *Leslie's*, Aug. 3, 1861, 178–179, Aug. 10, 1861, 194.

[22] Strong, *Diary*, 3:170; *Harper's Weekly*, Aug. 17, 1861, 522, 525, 528; *NYIN*, Aug. 5, 1861, 213, Aug. 12, 1861, 234.

[23] *Leslie's*, Aug. 3, 1861, 178, 189, Nov. 2, 1861, 381, 382; *NYIN*, Oct. 21, 1861, 385.

[24] Strong, *Diary*, 3:169.

[25] Shelby Foote, *The Civil War. A Narrative. Fort Sumter to Perryville* (New York, 1958), 70.

CHAPTER IV: McCLELLAN IN COMMAND

[1] George B. McClellan, *McClellan's Own Story* . . . (New York, 1887), 68; Foote, *Civil War*, 99–101, 109–110; Warren W. Hassler, Jr., *General George B. McClellan, Shield of the Union* (Baton Rouge, 1957), 23–30; Kenneth P. Williams, *Lincoln Finds A General* (4 vols., New York, 1949–1956), 1:113, 127, 131–132; Camille Ferri Pisani, "A French Visit to Civil War America," in *American Heritage*, 8:72 (August 1957).

[2] Williams, *Lincoln Finds A General*, 1:104; Foote, *Civil War*, 69, 100.

[3] For Brady's portraits of McClellan, see Meredith, *Brady*, Lecture Book Plate #119; David Donald, Hirst D. Milhollen, Milton Kaplan, and Hulen Stuart, *Divided We Fought, A Pictorial History of the War, 1861–1865* (New York, 1952), 26. Also see the portraits and the advertisements of the lithographers in *Leslie's*, Nov. 9, 1861, 399, Jan. 18, 1862, 131; *NYIN*, Nov. 18, 1861, 36–37, Nov. 25, 1861, 50, Dec. 2, 1861, 80, June 7, 1862, 80; *Harper's Weekly*, Sept. 21, 1861, 600–601, Jan. 25, 1862, 49. The Durkee Collection contains at least five envelopes with McClellan portraits. For prints with children playing at being McClellan, see "The Brave at Home" and "The Brave Wife" in Folder #4420 in the Library of Congress Print Collection. McClellan also became a favorite character in the cartoons, as in *Harper's Weekly*, Sept. 21, 1861, 608, Feb. 8, 1862, 96; *NYIN*, Oct. 21, 1861, 400.

[4] *NYIN*, Oct. 21, 1861, 387.

NOTES

⁵ *Leslie's,* Jan. 11, 1862, 117; *NYIN,* Sept. 23, 1861, 330, 332–333, Oct. 21, 1861, 389, Dec. 16, 1861, 100, Dec. 28, 1861, 113, Jan. 4, 1862, 128, April 5, 1862, 340, 349.

⁶ *Leslie's,* Dec. 28, 1861, 81, 82.

⁷ *NYIN,* Jan. 4, 1862, 138. Most of Waud's field sketches were prepared for the engravers by Thomas Nast, who did not hesitate to add his own ideas and to impose his own strong style upon Waud's sketches. On a few occasions, Nast even added his own signature to a sketch that was actually Waud's. Moreover, soon after Nast followed Waud to *Harper's Weekly,* one of the first illustrations he did for Harper, "The Rebel Army Crossing the Potomac," was almost an exact copy of a sketch Waud had submitted to the *News* several months earlier. The original Waud sketch is in the Alfred R. Waud Collection in the Library of Congress, and the Nast illustration in *Harper's Weekly,* Sept. 27, 1862, 613. For these reasons, Waud had an intense dislike of Nast; on one occasion he wrote a friend that he "detested" Nast; see letter from Waud to Paul D. (?), July 5, 1862, also in the Waud Collection. In Nast's defense, it should be stated that as an editorial artist he was virtually dependent upon the field sketches for most of his knowledge and information about the war.

⁸ *Harper's Weekly,* March 15, 1862, 162. After Waud joined the *Weekly,* most of his field sketches were prepared for the engravers by Henry L. Stephens, who was better known at the time as the cartoonist for *Vanity Fair.* Unlike Nast, Stephens redrew Waud's sketches without altering the details or the style. See a letter from Frank Weitenkampf to Charles K. Bolton, Dec. 13, 1940, in the Alfred R. Waud Folder, Art Room, New York Public Library.

⁹ Notices of Lumley's association with the *Illustrated News* appeared in the issues of March 8, 1862, 274, and March 15, 1862, 290. *Leslie's,* May 3, 1862, 1, July 26, 1862, 273.

¹⁰ Meredith, *Brady,* 90–93; Horan, *Brady,* 40.

¹¹ *Leslie's,* May 3, 1862, 4.

¹² Meredith, *Brady,* 98–99 and plates #59, 60, 62; Donald, *Divided We Fought,* 42, 43, 44, 49.

¹³ *NYIN,* May 3, 1862, 410–411, May 17, 1862, 17, 21, May 24, 1862, 43. For a self-portrait of Lumley on the Peninsula, see the issue of June 14, 1862, 89.

¹⁴ *Ibid.,* May 17, 1862, 24–25, 26, June 7, 1862, 78, June 21, 1862, 100–101, 107.

¹⁵ *Ibid.,* May 31, 1862, 52, 57, 61; *Harper's Weekly,* June 7, 1862, 364. Lumley's sketches of Fair Oaks appeared in the *NYIN* for June 21 and 28 and July 5, 1862, *passim.* Waud wrote Harper, "I was flat on my back" at the time of the battle. His sketch of a bayonet charge at Fair Oaks appeared in *Harper's Weekly,* Aug. 16, 1862, 523.

[16] Photographs by Brady's assistants in Donald, *Divided We Fought*, 56, 57, and also see page 61 for Waud's original sketch of the burial parties at work. Lumley's sketch in the *NYIN*, July 5, 1862, 129.

[17] *Leslie's*, July 26, 1862, 276–285; Meredith, *Brady*, plates #64–67; Donald, *Divided We Fought*, 73.

[18] Donald, *Divided We Fought*, 71; Waud's sketches of the Seven Days appeared in the July 26, August 2 and 9, 1862 issues of *Harper's Weekly, passim*. His brother William made most of *Leslie's* sketches of the same actions, *Leslie's*, July 26, 1862, 273, 280, 281, and all the illustrations in the August 2, 1862 issue. For Lumley's sketches, see *NYIN*, July 19, 1862, 168–169, Aug. 2, 1862, 195.

[19] *An Album of American Battle Art* (Washington, 1947), 166–167; *NYIN*, July 19, 1862, 171; Alfred R. Waud to Paul D. (?), July 5, 1862, in the Waud Collection.

[20] *Leslie's*, Sept. 20, 1862, 402. On May 3, Leslie published a cartoon showing McClellan and several other Union generals holding pieces of the Confederate alligator which they have dissected. From one reader, Leslie got the following letter: "Permit me, in the name of myself and a party of friends, to ask you a few questions, which, of course, you need not answer. By what right did you, or your artist, give the biggest slice of the alligator to McClellan? By what right or logic can McClellan or his friends claim for him the head of the reptile; does it belong to him? If so, how? Has he ever hurt the rebels anywhere since he took the command? Where and when did he do anything of vital importance beside stopping others from pushing vigorously ahead? Is not your drawing a misrepresentation, not worthy of a respectable newspaper? Are you, too, capable of toadyism?" *Leslie's*, May 3, 1862, 16, May 17, 1862, 59; *NYIN*, Aug. 2, 1862, 492.

[21] *Leslie's*, Oct. 4, 1862, 25; Otto Eisenschiml and Ralph Newman, *The Civil War, The American Iliad as Told by Those Who Lived It* (New York, 1957), 261.

[22] Meredith, *Brady*, 124; *Leslie's*, Oct. 4, 1862, 17, 24; *Harper's Weekly*, Sept. 27, 1862, 613, 621, Oct. 4, 1862, 631.

[23] Edwin Forbes, *Thirty Years After, An Artist's Story of the Great War* (2 vols., New York, 1890), 2:257.

[24] *Ibid.*, 1:73 and 2:257–258; *Leslie's*, Oct. 11, 1862, 33, 40–41; Waud's and Davis' sketches appeared in *Harper's Weekly*, Oct. 11, 1862, 641, 644–645, 648–649; Eisenschiml and Newman, *Civil War*, 266; Meredith, *Brady*, 126–127, 129, plate #71 and Lecture Book plates #6 and 84.

[25] Meredith, *Brady*, 129 and Lecture Book plate #96. *Harper's Weekly*, Oct. 18, 1862, 664–665, published eight of Brady's Antietam photographs; *Leslie's*, Oct. 18, 1862, 49, 52, 62, Oct. 25, 1862, 70; Josiah Marshall Favill, *The Diary of a Young Officer, serving with the armies of the United States during the war of the rebellion* (Chicago, 1909), 190. By way of contrast, Waud sent Harper a sketch

of some civilians helping to care for the wounded after the battle; see the original Waud sketch in Donald, *Divided We Fought*, 133, and *Harper's Weekly*, Oct. 11, 1862, 645, 649.

CHAPTER V: THE WESTERN WAR

[1] Flexner, *American Painting*, 53–54; for panoramas and reactions to them, see Richardson Wright, *Hawkers & Walkers in Early America* (Philadelphia, 1927), 135, 180, 183–184; Barker, *American Painting*, 447–450; Branch, *Sentimental Years*, 161; Martin, *Standard of Living*, 361; Taft, *Photography and the American Scene*, 3–4; Dicey, *Six Months*, 2:41; *NYIN*, May 10, 1862, 4, Feb. 8, 1863, 215; Still, *Mirror for Gotham*, 102. For the printmakers, see Peters, *Currier and Ives*, plates #29, 34, 40, 56, 87, 112, 119, 139, 189; Crouse, *Currier and Ives*, plate opposite p. 4. Also see Meredith, *American Wars*, 84–97, and the paintings and drawings in the serialized article, "How the West Was Won," beginning in the April 6, 1959 issue of *Life*.

[2] Foote, *Civil War*, 91–92; *Harper's Weekly*, June 1, 1861, 349; *Leslie's*, June 29, 1861, 97; Weitenkampf, *NYPLB*, 525.

[3] Lovie's sketches from Cairo appeared in *Leslie's* from the late summer of 1861 until the later spring of 1862; also see *ibid.*, Aug. 24, 1861, 232–233, Aug. 31, 1861, 248–249; *Harper's Weekly*, Aug. 31, 1861, 545; *NYIN*, Aug. 26, 1861, 264–265.

[4] *Leslie's*, Aug. 24, 1861, 225; *NYIN*, Aug. 26, 1861, 260, May 10, 1862, 14; also see the Currier and Ives lithographed print of Lyon's death in the Print Collection of the Library of Congress. The image of the Heroic Death was one of the first romantic images to disappear. Franc Wilkie recalled: "I saw many men die during the war, and in no case was there anything distressing in the occurrence. When a man was hit, and believed the wound to be a deadly one, he never grew excited or frantic over his condition. The conviction seemed to quiet him, to stun him a little, to be something of the nature of an opiate. I do not believe there was a single instance in the entire war in which a soldier, knowing that he was about to die, arranged any of the beautiful sentiments so frequently published in some of the newspapers and in a certain class of books. 'Tell them that I have cheerfully given my life for my flag and my country,' is an absurd invention. No dying man ever said it, and no dying man ever thought it." Franc B. Wilkie, *Pen and Powder* (Boston, 1888), 248–249.

[5] *Leslie's*, Sept. 7, 1861, 260, 266, 268, 269, Sept. 28, 1861, 309, 317, Oct. 12, 1861, 344–345, Nov. 16, 1861, 403, Jan. 11, 1862, 113. Lovie's concern at missing Lexington was heightened when he learned that Harper had a part-time artist there named Orlando Richardson, *Harper's Weekly*, July 6, 1861, 431, Oct. 12, 1861, 645, 646, 653, Oct. 19, 1861, 657.

[6] For biographical material on Simplot, see *The History of Dubuque County, Iowa* . . . (Chicago, 1880), 881–882; Weston Arthur Goodspeed and Kenneth

Cornell Goodspeed, *History of Dubuque County, Iowa.* . . . (Chicago, 1911), 690–691; *The Iowa Journal of History and Politics,* 13:145 (1915); an unidentified newspaper obituary (perhaps the *Dubuque Telegraph*), undated, in the Simplot Collection; John Hunter, "Alexander Simplot, Forgotten Bohemian," in the *Wisconsin Magazine of History,* 41:256–261 (Sumner, 1958). The Simplot Collection also contains a tintype of Simplot taken at the time of his wedding in 1866. His early sketching at Cairo and St. Louis is described in the Simplot Manuscript Memoirs, 1, 3–6, 8; his sketches published in *Harper's Weekly,* May 25, 1861, 327, 331, Oct. 12, 1861, 642, Oct. 19, 1861, 667. Simplot's doodles are informative: to one undistinguished sketch, he added his own comment: "Fine (in my estimation)," and on the inside cover of one of his sketch books, he lettered elaborately, "Drawn from Nature by Alex Simplot, Our Special Artist upon the spot." A list of the sketches he sent Harper and the prices he asked and received for them appear in his Sketch Book I. For evidence that A. S. Leclerc was in reality Alexander Simplot, compare the original sketches entitled "Confluence of the Ohio & Miss. Rivers" and "Camp Houghton" in the Large Sketch Book with the illustrations credited to Leclerc in the *NYIN,* Aug. 5, 1861, 221, and Sept. 9, 1861, 293. See also the sketch of Birds' Point, Missouri, in the Large Sketch Book, to which he added the following note, "Sent twice. Price to Harper's Weekly, 8 dollars. Price to NY Illustrated News, 2," and the list on page 1 of Sketch Book I of the four sketches he sent to the *Illustrated News* and the prices he asked for them. The pseudonym, A. S. Leclerc, was based upon his own initials and the French form of his mother's maiden name, LeClair. Simplot stopped sending sketches to the *Illustrated News* after he joined the Fremont expedition in September, 1861, and the last of the sketches submitted to the *News* was credited to his true identity; see *NYIN,* Oct. 28, 1861, 405.

[7] Foote, *Civil War,* 89–90, 95–97.

[8] Simplot Clipping Book, 6; *Harper's Weekly,* Oct. 19, 1861, 664, Oct. 26, 1861, 679; *Leslie's,* Oct. 26, 1861, 363.

[9] Simplot Manuscript Memoirs, 8–10; Simplot Clipping Book, 5, 10–11; Albert D. Richardson, *The Secret Service, the Field, the Dungeon, and the Escape* (Hartford, Connecticut, 1865), 189–192; Wilkie, *Pen and Powder,* 9–10, 16–17, 23–24, 39–40, 52, 71–72, 132–134; Thomas W. Knox, *Camp-Fire and Cotton-Field: Southern Adventure in Time of War. Life with the Union Armies, and Residence on a Louisiana Plantation* (Philadelphia, 1865), 95–97; Junius Henri Browne, *Four Years in Secessia: Adventures within and beyond the Union Lines: embracing a great variety of facts, incidents, and romance of the war.* . . . (Hartford, Connecticut, 1865), 28; Emmet Crozier, *Yankee Reporters, 1861–65* (New York, 1956), 68–69; Sylvanus Cadwallader, *Three Years with Grant, As Recalled by War Correspondent Sylvanus Cadwallader,* edited by Benjamin P. Thomas (New York, 1955), 99.

[10] Simplot Clipping Book, 6–7; Richardson, *Secret Service*, 304; Crozier, *Yankee Reporters*, 169; Wilkie, *Pen and Powder*, 56–57; *Leslie's*, Nov. 2, 1861, 369, Nov. 16, 1861, 405; *Harper's Weekly*, Nov. 2, 1861, 698, Nov. 16, 1861, 727, 728.

[11] Simplot Clipping Book, 7–13; Wilkie, *Pen and Powder*, 61–63; *Harper's Weekly*, Nov. 16, 1861, 722, Nov. 23, 1861, 737, 738, Dec. 7, 1861, 775; *Leslie's*, Nov. 9, 1861, 396, Feb. 22, 1862, 212.

[12] Crozier, *Yankee Reporters*, 170; Wilkie, *Pen and Powder*, 49, 64, 75–77.

[13] Foote, *Civil War*, 98–99.

[14] Simplot Clipping Book, 13–14; *Harper's Weekly*, Nov. 16, 1861, 728, Nov. 23, 1861, 738; *Leslie's*, Oct. 26, 1861, 368, Nov. 23, 1861, 13; *NYIN*, Nov. 11, 1861, 24–25.

[15] Simplot Clipping Book, 15–16; Wilkie, *Pen and Powder*, 70–71; *Leslie's*, Dec. 7, 1861, 35. Lovie had had enough of Missouri: "I hope to change my field of action shortly, and to get out of this state of misery and scrub oaks." *Leslie's*, Dec. 28, 1861, 86.

[16] Simplot Manuscript Memoirs, 7; *Harper's Weekly*, Oct. 5, 1861, 630, Oct. 12, 1861, 646, Dec. 28, 1861, 821; *Leslie's*, Dec. 21, 1861, 68–77. Until 1863–64, the western photographers did not show the imagination and enterprise of their eastern counterparts. With few exceptions, their pictures were of ships of the western river flotillas, gun emplacements, and group photographs. For the Western River War in the photographs, see Francis Trevelyan Miller, ed., *The Photographic History of the Civil War* (10 vols., New York, 1957), 1:171–249, 2:179–226, 6:205–234.

[17] Simplot Clipping Book. 16–19; *Leslie's*, Feb. 22, 1862, 209, March 15, 1862, 268, March 1, 1862, 229.

[18] *Leslie's*, March 1, 1862, 232–233. Two more examples appeared soon after, *ibid.*, April 19, 1862, 384. The first example in the *NYIN* did not appear until Jan. 24, 1863, 177. Fletcher Harper later justified horror pictures as portraying the brutal character of the enemy; *Harper's Weekly*, May 21, 1864, 322.

[19] Foote, *Civil War*, 195–215.

[20] Simplot Clipping Book, 19–20; his Small Sketch Book contains three of his sketches made late on the afternoon of the 15th.

[21] *Leslie's*, March 15, 1862, 257, 270; Simplot Clipping Book, 19–20.

[22] *Harper's Weekly*, March 1, 1862, 129, March 8, 1862, 148, March 15, 1862, 161, 164; *Leslie's*, March 8, 1862, 244–253, March 15, 1862, 257, 277, 287–288; *NYIN*, March 8, 1862, 277–278; Wilkie, *Pen and Powder*, 117–118.

[23] Simplot Clipping Book, 23–26; Wilkie, *Pen and Powder*, 150–151; *Harper's Weekly*, April 5, 1862, 212, May 3, 1862, 285; *Leslie's*, April 5, 1862, 328–329,

April 19, 1862, 377. J. M. McLaughlin replaced Lovie as *Leslie's* artist at Island No. 10 after Lovie left to rejoin Grant, *ibid.*, April 26, 1862, 401, May 31, 1862, 144.

[24] Late in the war, Leslie claimed that William Waud had been impressed into the "rebel" service by Beauregard during the time of the firing on Sumter; *Leslie's*, March 25, 1865, 7. For his sketches from Florida, see *ibid.*, April 19, 1862, 372–381, 382, and for his New Orleans sketches, *ibid.*, May 17, 1862, 59, May 24, 1862, 88–89, 97, 98, 100, 101, 108–109, May 31, 1862, 113, 120, 121, 129, 132, 133, 134, 141. B. S. Osbon reported the action for Fletcher Harper; see F. Lauriston Bullard, *Famous War Correspondents* (Boston, 1914), 402–406; Andrews, *North Reports the Civil War*, 241; *Harper's Weekly*, May 24, 1862, 327.

[25] Bruce Catton in his *Grant Moves South* (Boston, 1960), 216–264 *passim*, discusses the question of surprise at Shiloh. Catton is not nearly as critical of Sherman and Grant as were the newspaper reporters on the scene. At the time, however, Lovie accepted the contention that the Federal army had been surprised on the morning of the 6th.

George W. Cable actually wrote that New Orleans "had never been really glad again after the awful day of Shiloh." George W. Cable, "New Orleans Before the Capture," in *Battles and Leaders*, 2:18.

[26] *Leslie's*, May 3, 1862, 18, 20–29, May 17, 1862, 56–57, 64, 68, 69, 72–73, 76.

[27] *Ibid.*, May 17, 1862, 66, 77.

[28] *Ibid.*, May 17, 1862, 65–66.

[29] Simplot Clipping Book, 26–28; *Leslie's*, May 17, 1862, 60; *Harper's Weekly*, April 26, 1862, 265–266, May 3, 1862, 286; *NYIN*, April 26, 1862, 389.

[30] *Leslie's*, May 3, 1862, 18, 20–29, May 17, 1862, 66, 72–73, 77; William Bircher, *A Drummer-Boy's Diary: comprising Four Years of Service with the Second Regiment Minnesota Veteran Volunteers, 1861 to 1865* (St. Paul, 1899), 32–36. For public reaction to Lovie's Shiloh sketches, see *Leslie's*, June 28, 1862, 195, 198; Eisenschiml and Newman, *Civil War*, 188.

[31] But until the very end of the war, Walt Whitman noticed distinct qualities in the western troops; see Walt Whitman, *The Wound Dresser. Letters written to his mother from the hospitals in Washington during the Civil War*, edited by Richard M. Buche (New York, 1949), 144; Walt Whitman, *The Complete Poetry and Prose of Walt Whitman as prepared by him for the Deathbed Edition* (2 vols., New York, 1948), 2:69–70.

CHAPTER VI: ARTISTS AT WORK

[1] Most of the biographical information upon which this and the following paragraphs are based is cited elsewhere in the text and the footnotes. For com-

parison with the regular newspaper correspondents, see Bullard, *War Correspondents*, 378–379, and for a treatment of the special problems of sketch artists, see Harry V. Barnett, "The Special Artist," in (Cassell's) *The Magazine of Art*, 6:163–170 (1883).

[2] For biographical information on Eugene Benson, see Mantle Fielding, *Dictionary of American Painters, Sculptors and Engravers* (Philadelphia, 1926), 26; H. W. French, *Art and Artists in Connecticut* (Boston, 1879), 149–150; Clara Erskine Clement and Laurence Hutton, *Artists of the Nineteenth Century and their Works* (2 vols., Boston, 1879), 1:55–56; "Eugene Benson" in the *DAB*, 2:204–205; *The New York Times*, March 1, 1908, 9.

[3] *Harper's Weekly*, May 18, 1861, 310–311, June 1, 1861, 338, 341, 343, June 22, 1861, 394, 397, July 13, 1861, 447, July 20, 1861, 450; William Howard Russell, *My Diary North and South* (Boston, 1863), 46, 62, 78, 94, 155, 198–199, 232, 235; *New York Tribune*, July 21, 1861, 4.

[4] James G. Randall, "The Newspaper Problem in its Bearing upon Military Secrecy during the Civil War," in *The American Historical Review*, 23:317–318 (1917–1918); Cadwallader, *Three Years with Grant*, 11–12; Wilkie, *Pen and Powder*, 11–12.

[5] *Leslie's*, Oct. 12, 1861, 343, Dec. 7, 1861, 35, April 12, 1861, 365; Forbes, *Artist's Story*, 1:98; Meredith, *Brady*, 90; George Augustus Sala, *My Diary in America in the midst of war* (2 vols., London, 1865), 1:303.

[6] Taft, *Photography and the American Scene*, 231–232; Horan, *Brady*, 56; Meredith, *Brady*, 144–145; *Official Records of the War of the Rebellion*, Series I, Vol. 28, Part 1, pp. 597, 601, 603; *Leslie's*, Sept. 12, 1863, 389; Theodore R. Davis, "Grant Under Fire," in *The Cosmopolitan*, 14:339 (January, 1893).

[7] *Harper's Weekly*, April 12, 1862, 237; *Leslie's*, April 5, 1862, 323, Nov. 21, 1863, 129, Feb. 13, 1864, 327.

[8] For an example of Davis "boosting" an officer, see *Harper's Weekly*, Aug. 1, 1863, 487. Josiah Favill, *Diary*, 127–128, records the reaction of a subordinate officer to "boosting." Alf Waud was perhaps the artist most respected by high officers in the army as testified by letters to him from G. K. Warren, June 29 and 30, 1880, and from O. O. Howard, undated, in the Waud Collection.

[9] George Alfred Townsend, *Rustics in Rebellion, A Yankee Reporter on the Road to Richmond, 1861–1865* (Chapel Hill, North Carolina, 1950), 219, 240–241; Wilkie, *Pen and Powder*, 272–274; Connolly, *Three Years*, 99.

[10] Townsend, *Rustics in Rebellion*, 177; Starr, *Bohemian Brigade*, 253.

[11] Wilkie, *Pen and Powder*, 178–180, 275; Simplot Clipping Book, 27; *Leslie's*, Sept. 20, 1862, 416, Aug. 6, 1864, 307.

[12] Rachel Sherman Thorndike, ed., *The Sherman Letters. Correspondence between General and Senator Sherman from 1837 to 1891* (New York, 1894), 81,

187–194 *passim,* 197, 220; Mark A. DeWolfe Howe, ed., *Home Letters of General Sherman* (New York, 1909), 241; William Tecumseh Sherman, *Memoirs of General W. T. Sherman . . .* (2 vols., New York, 1891), 2:408–409; *Leslie's,* Dec. 7, 1861, 34–35.

[13] Meredith, *American Wars,* 11; Howe, *Home Letters,* 24; Mark A. DeWolfe Howe, ed., *Marching with Sherman, Passages from the Letters and Campaign Diaries of Henry Hitchcock, major and assistant adjutant general of Volunteers, November 1864—May 1865* (New Haven, Connecticut, 1927), 217–218, 230, 250–251.

[14] *Harper's Weekly,* April 26, 1862, 260–261.

[15] *Official Records of the War of the Rebellion,* Series II, Vol. II, p. 286; *Harper's Weekly,* May 3, 1862, 274, May 17, 1862, 306, June 7, 1862, 354; Andrews, *North Reports the Civil War,* 198, 686 footnote 27; Harper, *House of Harper,* 181–182.

[16] *NYIN,* May 3, 1862, 410, May 17, 1862, 26, May 31, 1862, 58, June 21, 1862, 114.

[17] Starr, *Bohemian Brigade,* 253.

[18] There are only a few photographs of the war artists. A full-length portrait of Theo Davis appeared in Robert Taft, "The Pictorial Record of the Old West, IX. Alfred R. Waud and Theodore R. Davis," in *The Kansas Historical Quarterly,* 17: 358–359 (November, 1949). Brady photographed Alf Waud at Gettysburg, and the portrait has been reprinted in Meredith, *Brady,* plate #3. There are also two wartime portraits of Alf Waud in the Waud Collection. Nearly everyone of the artists sometime during the war included a self-portrait in his sketches. Henri Lovie usually traveled with the minimum baggage, but once he mentioned taking a Negro servant named John with him to carry three heavy suitcases and trunks; *Leslie's,* Feb. 14, 1863, 334. The information about drawing materials is based upon the original sketches, largely those of Forbes, the Wauds, and Simplot.

[19] This is also based upon the original sketches. For published copies of some of the original sketches, consult Donald, *Divided We Fought, passim,* and several examples in James G. Randall, *The Civil War and Reconstruction* (Boston, 1937), *passim.*

[20] Forbes, *Artist's Story,* 1:81; Forbes wrote: "I fully expected when I started for the front, to accompany the troops into the battle and seat myself complacently on a convenient hillside and sketch exciting incidents at my leisure; but how greatly reality differed from imagination. . . ." *ibid.,* 2:257–258, 309–310; *Harper's Weekly,* Aug. 9, 1862, 503, Oct. 10, 1863, 646; Charles A. Page, *Letters of a War Correspondent* (Boston, 1899), 20, 237; *Leslie's,* Aug. 30, 1862, 358.

[21] *Leslie's,* Oct. 12, 1861, 344–345, Nov. 16, 1861, 403, March 8, 1862, 244–253; Wilkie, *Pen and Powder,* 117–118. Until the summer of 1863, the engravings in

the *New York Illustrated News* rivaled those in *Leslie's,* but thereafter they deteriorated badly.

²² *Harper's Weekly,* Aug. 16, 1862, 523–524.

²³ *Leslie's,* Feb. 14, 1863, 334, July 11, 1863, 251, Oct. 31, 1863, 83, May 21, 1864, 130, Aug. 13, 1864, 331; *Harper's Weekly,* Sept. 27, 1862, 612, Oct. 3, 1863, 635; *NYIN,* June 7, 1862, 78; Starr, *Bohemian Brigade,* 193.

²⁴ *Leslie's,* May 17, 1862, 66, Aug. 30, 1862, 358; Forbes, *Artist's Story,* 1:138; *Harper's Weekly,* Sept. 26, 1863, 621, Simplot Manuscript Memoirs.

²⁵ Bernard A. Weisberger, *Reporters for the Union* (Boston, 1953), 128; *New York Herald,* April 24, 1864, 1; *Leslie's,* May 21, 1864, 130, June 4, 1864, 167.

CHAPTER VII: THE ENEMY

¹ Peters, *Currier and Ives,* 39 and plates #81 and 123; *Leslie's,* Feb. 2, 1861, 162, 176, Feb. 23, 1861, 209, March 2, 1861, 240; Wilkie, *Pen and Powder,* 15; Harper, *House of Harper,* 173, 177–178; *Harper's Weekly,* Feb. 9, 1861, 96, March 9, 1861, 146, April 27, 1861, 272; *NYIN,* Jan. 12, 1861, 146.

² *Harper's Weekly,* June 13, 1863, 371; *Vanity Fair,* June 8, 1861, 266. Among other names, southerners cursed the editor of the *Illustrated News* as a "lying, infamous scoundrel," a "thief," and a "black republican son of a bitch . . ." *ibid.,* Jan. 26, 1861, 178, Feb. 9, 1861, 211, Jan. 19, 1861, 161.

³ For the general themes of northern propaganda, see William B. Hesseltine, "The Propaganda Literature of Confederate Prisons," in *The Journal of Southern History,* 1:56–57 (February, 1935); George Winston Smith, "Union Propaganda in the American Civil War," in *The Social Studies,* 35:26–32 (January, 1944); T. Harry Williams, "Benjamin F. Wade and the Atrocity Propaganda of the Civil War," in *The Ohio State Archaeological and Historical Quarterly,* 48:34–38 (1939); also see Alonzo H. Quint, *The Potomac and the Rapidan. Army notes from the failure at Winchester to the reenforcement of Rosecrans, 1861–3* (Boston, 1864), 161.

⁴ *Harper's Weekly,* June 13, 1863, 371.

⁵ *Leslie's,* Jan. 4, 1862, 110, April 19, 1862, 371; Harper, *House of Harper,* 132–133.

⁶ *Harper's Weekly,* Sept. 21, 1861, 595, Oct. 26, 1861, 688; *NYIN,* Nov. 11, 1861, 32, Nov. 25, 1861, 64; *Leslie's,* Dec. 21, 1862, 80.

⁷ *Leslie's,* Aug. 2, 1862, 289, Aug. 16, 1862, 333, Aug. 30, 1862, 353; *NYIN,* Jan. 10, 1863, 156; *Harper's Weekly,* June 15, 1861, 380, Aug. 23, 1862, 541. "Of course it is impossible for photography to lie. . . ." *ibid.,* July 9, 1864, 442. How-

ever, amateur artists who submitted sketches to the weeklies often did not hesitate to exaggerate. See the original sketch by C. K. Iwansky in the Waud Collection of a drunken Confederate bivouac in Texas, and the published illustration in *ibid.*, June 15, 1861, 375.

[8] For material on cartooning, see Peters, *Currier and Ives,* 23; "Cartoons of the Presidents," in the *DAR Magazine,* 67:547–552 (1933); "National Humor," in the *American Whig Review,* 16:311 (October, 1852); "Vanity Fair," in *Atlantic Monthly,* 10:252–254 (August, 1862); "The Comic Paper in America," in the *Critic,* 39:229–230 (September, 1901); Florence Seville Berryman, "Cartoons that have made or marred careers," in the *DAR Magazine,* 61:821–822 (1927); James Parton, "Caricature in the United States," in *Harper's New Monthly Magazine,* 52:39, 42 (December, 1875); E. L. Godkin, "The 'Comic Paper' Question," in *The Nation,* 11:434–436 (December 29, 1870); George Haven Putnam, *Some Memories of the Civil War, together with an appreciation of the career and character of Major General Israel Putnam, leader in the colonial wars and in the American Revolution* (New York and London, 1924), 124, 157–158, 164–166; and a brief article on the state of American comic art during the war in the *New York Tribune,* July 21, 1861, 2.

For information on patriotic stationery, consult A. Jay Hertz, "Campaign Covers of the Nineteenth Century," in *The American Philatelist,* 61:948–953 (September, 1948); Raymond Marsh, "Some Early Patriotics," in *The American Philatelist,* 64:95–100 (November, 1950); George N. Malpass, "Publishers and Vendors of Civil War Patriotic Envelopes," in *The American Philatelist,* 65:282–293 (January, 1952); Catherine S. Overson, "Civil War Envelopes," in *The Magazine Antiques,* 13:490–492 (June, 1928); and "Pictorial Envelopes of the Civil War," in the *Bulletin of the Missouri Historical Society,* 5:306–310 (July, 1949).

[9] Paine, *Nast,* 1–82 *passim;* Albert Bigelow Paine, "Harper's Weekly and Thomas Nast," in *Harper's Weekly,* Jan. 5, 1907, 14–16.

[10] Paine, *Nast,* 82, 120; Edward Cary, *George William Curtis* (Boston, 1894), 190–191; William Murrell, "Nast, Gladiator of the Political Pencil," in *American Scholar,* 5:472–473 (Autumn, 1936). Publishers of the illustrated weeklies estimated that ten people usually saw each copy of an illustrated weekly; the figure "half a million" is then a conservative estimate for weekly circulation of 100,000.

[11] Paine, *Nast,* 89–90, 94; Murrell, "Nast," 472; James Parton, "Caricature in the United States," in *Harper's New Monthly Magazine,* 52:40 (December, 1875).

[12] *Harper's Weekly,* Jan. 3, 1863, 8–9, Jan. 5, 1907, 16; Paine, *Nast,* 84–85; John Beatty, *Memoirs of a Volunteer* (New York, 1946), 161.

[13] Quint, *Potomac and Rapidan,* 166. On several occasions, artists made composite illustrations summarizing all the types of enemy atrocities; consult *Harper's*

Weekly, Feb. 7, 1863, 88–89, May 21, 1864, 328–329; *Leslie's,* April 4, 1863, 24–25, Feb. 20, 1864, 344–345.

[14] *Harper's Weekly,* Feb. 22, 1862, 117, 119, Jan. 18, 1862, 45. Compare these with the matter-of-fact sketch by Alf Waud showing a group of released prisoners returning to their regimental camp, in *ibid.,* Feb. 1, 1862, 387. *Leslie's,* Jan. 11, 1862, 113, Oct. 26, 1861, 363. The *Illustrated News* criticized the government's failure to arrange for an exchange of prisoners as "a barbarity," *NYIN,* Oct. 21, 1861, 387.

[15] *Harper's Weekly,* June 13, 1863, 373, Dec. 5, 1863, 781.

[16] *NYIN,* Nov. 14, 1863, 41, Nov. 28, 1863, 65, 72, 80; *Leslie's,* Nov. 22, 1862, 136–137, June 18, 1864, 193; *Harper's Weekly,* March 5, 1864, 145, June 18, 1864, 385, 387, Dec. 10, 1864, 788–789, Jan. 14, 1865, 28–29; and two original sketches by William Waud in the Waud Collection.

[17] For the photographic record of southern and northern prisons, see Miller, *Photographic History,* 7:19–186 *passim. Harper's Weekly,* April 15, 1865, 236, included a picture of Elmira prison, but it was carefully prepared to show the prison at its best. Sketch artists with Sherman's army in Georgia also submitted sketches of prisons there; see *Harper's Weekly,* Jan. 7, 1865, 9, Jan. 14, 1865, 28–29, Feb. 18, 1865, 109; *Leslie's,* Jan. 14, 1865, 256, Jan. 28, 1865, 296–297, April 8, 1865, 37. Also consult *Harper's Weekly,* April 5, 1862, 215, April 25, 1863, 261, Aug. 29, 1863, 549; Buchanan, *Pictorial History of the Confederacy,* 217.

[18] Williams, "Wade and Atrocity Propaganda," 38; Sala, *Diary,* 2:319–322; *Harper's Weekly,* May 17, 1862, 306, May 21, 1864, 322.

[19] *Leslie's,* May 11, 1861, 414, 416, June 15, 1861, 71, Sept. 28, 1861, 305, 318, Nov. 23, 1861, 5, July 30, 1864, 296–297.

[20] For an example, see *ibid.,* August 6, 1864, 305.

[21] *NYIN,* Feb. 8, 1862, 220, April 19, 1862, 376–377; *Leslie's,* Feb. 13, 1864, 321, March 19, 1864, 416; *Harper's Weekly,* Oct. 25, 1862, 680–681. For a contrary viewpoint on stripping dead soldiers, see Sala, *Diary,* 1:296–297.

[22] Buchanan, *Pictorial History of the Confederacy,* 123, 220, 248. For a cartoonist's portrayal of a Confederate picket, see *Leslie's,* March 5, 1864, 384.

[23] Buchanan, *Pictorial History of the Confederacy,* 130–132, 206; Simplot Clipping Book, 21–23; Bruce Catton, "A Southern Artist on the Civil War," in *American Heritage,* 9:117–120 (October, 1958); *Leslie's,* July 27, 1861, 176; Weitenkampf, *NYPLB,* 528. John McLenan, *Harper's* cartoonist, argued that Butler's proclamation brought a distinct improvement in the manners of the women of New Orleans; *Harper's Weekly,* July 12, 1862, 448.

[24] *Harper's Weekly,* Sept. 14, 1861, 582–583, Dec. 28, 1861, 817, March 1, 1862, 140, March 29, 1862, 193, Nov. 21, 1863, 749, May 14, 1864, 310, 313.

[25] *NYIN,* April 12, 1862, 360–361; *Harper's Weekly,* Sept. 13, 1862, 592; *Leslie's,* Oct. 12, 1861, 338, Sept. 14, 1861, 274.

[26] *Harper's Weekly,* Aug. 30, 1862, 548, 555. Henri Lovie was home in Cincinnati at the time of Morgan's raid against northern Kentucky, and he crossed the river to sketch the action for *Leslie's.* His pictures showed the raiders shooting their pistols as they rode through the town, but that was the extent of the "atrocities"; *Leslie's,* Aug. 9, 1862, 305, 310, Aug. 16, 1862, 321, 325, 329; *NYIN,* Aug. 16, 1862, 225.

[27] *Harper's Weekly,* Sept. 27, 1862, 616–617; see also another Nast fantasia entitled "War on the Border" in *ibid.,* Jan. 17, 1863, 40–41.

[28] *Leslie's,* Sept. 21, 1861, 292, March 29, 1862, 309–316, 311, Sept. 12, 1863, 389, Feb. 6, 1864, 311, 317; *Harper's Weekly,* Sept. 5, 1863, 561, 564, Sept. 19, 1863, 594, 604, Oct. 29, 1864, 690, 701. For two examples of Nast's caricature at its best, see his "Baltimore Gorilla" and "First Family Virginian," in *NYIN,* May 18, 1861, 32, June 15, 1861, 96, and also Nov. 24, 1862, 44; Sala, *Diary,* 2:351. For complaints against Alf Waud's portraits of southern women during his postwar southern tour, see *Harper's Weekly,* July 14, 1866, 422.

[29] Forbes, *Artist's Story,* 2:173; George R. Agassiz, ed., *Meade's Headquarters, 1864–1865, Letters of Colonel Theodore Lyman from the Wilderness to Appomattox* (Boston, 1922), 100, 152, 186–187; Camille Ferri Pisani, "A French Visit to Civil War America," in *American Heritage,* 8:76 (August, 1957).

[30] *Leslie's,* May 17, 1862, 64; *Harper's Weekly,* June 7, 1862, 368; Quint, *Potomac and Rapidan,* 111; Page, *Letters,* 10; Charles W. Wills, *Army Life of an Illinois Soldier. Including a day by day record of Sherman's march to the sea; letters and diary of the late Charles W. Wills* (Washington, 1906), 60–61; Nathaniel Hawthorne, "A Peaceable Man," in *The Atlantic Monthly,* 10:51 (July, 1862); Sala, *Diary,* 1:323–324; Dicey, *Six Months,* 2:240–242; Lester Frank Ward, *Young Ward's Diary. A human and eager record of the years between 1860 and 1870 as they were lived in the vicinity of the little town of Towanda, Pennsylvania; in the field as a rank and file soldier in the Union army; and later in the nation's capital, by Lester Ward who became the first great sociologist this country produced,* edited by Bernhard J. Stern (New York, 1935), 103–105.

CHAPTER VIII: THE HOME FRONT

[1] Roy Franklin Nichols, *The Disruption of American Democracy* (New York, 1948), 23: Sala, *Diary,* 1:365–366. For scattered examples of patriotism in a pictorial context, see Catherine S. Overson, "Civil War Envelopes," in *The Magazine Antiques,* 13:492 (June, 1928); Edwin F. Palmer, *The Second Brigade; or, Camp Life* (Montpelier, Vermont, 1864), 124. Or, as Leslie ex-

pressed it, "a deed of patriotic valor . . . is a joy for ever." *Leslie's*, Nov. 8, 1862, 109.

[2] Sala, *Diary*, 2:329; Strong, *Diary*, 3:135; *NYIN*, Feb. 23, 1861, 241; *Leslie's*, May 4, 1861, 385; Ward, *Young Ward's Diary*, 103–105; Woolsey, *Family Letters*, 1:66–67. Three-year-old Theodore Roosevelt was particularly proud of the Zouave uniform his grandmother made for him; see Carleton Putnam, *Theodore Roosevelt; The Formative Years*, 1858–1886 (New York, 1959), 23–24, 48 footnote #50.

[3] Ward, *Young Ward's Diary*, 122; *NYIN*, July 13, 1861, 146, 152–153, Oct. 21, 1861, 386; *Harper's Weekly*, March 23, 1861, 188, May 18, 1861, 315, June 8, 1861, 368; *Vanity Fair*, April 27, 1861, 199; Currier and Ives print in Folder #4420 in the Library of Congress Print Collection.

[4] Trollope, *North America*, 162–163.

[5] Mott, *American Magazines*, 523; *Vanity Fair*, Dec. 31, 1859, 1.

[6] Overson, *op. cit.*, 491; George N. Malpass, "Publishers and Vendors of Civil War Patriotic Envelopes," in *The American Philatelist*, 65:288 (January, 1952); *Atlantic Monthly*, 10:254 (August, 1862).

[7] Curtis was a popular writer, lecturer, and journalist, and an espouser of causes from Transcendentalism to anti-slavery. At the same time, he was also active in the Republican party, serving as a county chairman throughout the war. As a publicist, he smoothly blended realism with idealism. For material on Curtis in relation to Fletcher Harper, the *Weekly*, abolitionism, and Lincoln, see Charles Eliot Norton, *Letters of Charles Eliot Norton*, edited by Sara Norton and Mark A. DeWolfe Howe (2 vols., Boston, 1913), 1:203; Cary, *Curtis*, 77–78, 120, 147, 153, 155–156, 158ff, 166–169, 177–179, 183–185, 203; Curtis to Salmon P. Chase, Feb. 24, 1862, Salmon P. Chase Papers in the Library of Congress. Curtis wrote a column for the *Weekly*, "The Lounger," which generally expressed opinions on controversial issues somewhat in advance of those in the regular editorial columns. In 1863, Harper appointed Curtis political editor of the *Weekly;* Harper, *I Remember*, 50.

[8] *Harper's Weekly*, Aug. 3, 1861, 496, Aug. 10, 1861, 512, Jan. 25, 1862, 64, March 29, 1862, 208, April 5, 1862, 224, June 14, 1862, 384, *NYIN*, March 22, 1862, 320; one envelope in the Durkee Collection.

[9] The *Illustrated News* suspected that the War Department refused permission to circulate the *News* within the army. This claim came into the open during the 1864 campaign in which the *News* opposed the re-election of Lincoln; *NYIN*, July 16, 1864, 604.

[10] *Harper's Weekly*, June 15, 1861, 384, Aug. 17, 1861, 528, Aug. 24, 1861, 531, 544, Feb. 1, 1862, 80, Jan. 3, 1863, 16, Jan. 10, 1863, 32; *NYIN*, Aug. 9, 1862, 224, Sept. 27, 1862, 336, Jan. 10, 1863, 160, Feb. 7, 1863, 224.

[11] *Harper's Weekly,* Aug. 31, 1861, 560, Jan. 11, 1862, 32, Jan. 18, 1862, 48, Feb. 1, 1862, 80, Feb. 22, 1862, 128, March 22, 1862, 192, April 12, 1862, 240; *Leslie's,* May 3, 1862, 32, Nov. 29, 1862, 160, July 18, 1863, 272; *Vanity Fair,* Aug. 30, 1862, 97, Dec. 27, 1862, 306; Weitenkampf, *NYPLB,* 557; Currier and Ives print in the Library of Congress Print Collection. George Alfred Townsend of the *New York Herald* thought that the lithographs of Welles reminded him of the biblical Abraham; Townsend, *Rustics in Rebellion,* 190.

[12] For a cross section of Lincoln cartoons, see Rufus Rockwell Wilson, *Lincoln in Caricature* (New York, 1953), *passim.* For examples of anti-British and anti-French cartoons, see *Leslie's,* Oct. 5, 1861, 336, Nov. 23, 1861, 16, Dec. 7, 1861, 48; *Harper's Weekly,* Aug. 3, 1861, 496, Aug. 10, 1861, 512, Aug. 24, 1861, 544, Sept. 28, 1861, 624; *NYIN,* Aug. 26, 1861, 256.

[13] *NYIN,* Dec. 2, 1861, 74, 76; *Harper's Weekly,* Sept. 6, 1862, 568–569. Artists also suggested the proper feminine reception for the returning hero; *NYIN,* Feb. 14, 1863, 232; *Harper's Weekly,* June 13, 1863, 381, Jan. 23, 1864, 56–57, Feb. 25, 1865, 120–121; Currier and Ives print on the same subject in Folder #4420 in the Library of Congress Print Collection.

[14] *Harper's Weekly,* Sept. 6, 1862, 568–569, April 9, 1864, 229.

[15] *Ibid.,* June 29, 1861, 401; *Leslie's,* April 23, 1864, 65–66. Frank Bellew did a cartoon for Leslie's showing two gentlemen and a young lady in a parlor. The lovely young thing, showing the "profound interest and deep sympathy of our wives and daughters for everything which concerns the honor and glory of the republic," listens intently as one of the gentlemen remarks: "We haven't heard anything lately of Stewart's raids and charges," and then brightly interrupts with, "Oh dear no. Stewart's rates and charges are very moderate now, you can get real beautiful foulard silks there for two dollars"; *Leslie's,* June 6, 1863, 176.

One possible reason that there are not many of the original field sketches of the *Leslie's* artists still available is that Leslie donated many of them to the New York Sanitary Commission Fair in the spring of 1864 for auction; *Leslie's,* April 16, 1864, 56–57, 60–61, April 23, 1864, 65, 68, 69, 72–73, 76–77, April 30, 1864, 81, 84.

[16] *Ibid.,* Sept. 6, 1862, 369; *NYIN,* Oct. 21 1861, 392–393; Still, *Mirror for Gotham,* 182; Francis Colburn Adams, *The Story of a Trooper, with much of interest concerning the campaign on the peninsula, not before written* (New York, 1865), 50–51.

[17] *Harper's Weekly,* Aug. 10, 1861, 510, Sept. 7, 1861, 576, Aug. 2, 1862, 496, Sept. 20, 1862, 608; Billings, *Hardtack and Coffee,* 25–26.

[18] *Harper's Weekly,* Sept. 14, 1861, 592, Aug. 31, 1861, 560, Aug. 16, 1862, 528, Aug. 23, 1862, 544; *Vanity Fair,* Aug. 2, 1862, 54, May 4, 1861, 207, May 11, 1861, 216, May 18, 1861, 234, June 15, 1861, 280, June 29, 1861, 293, Oct. 5, 1861, 160. The envelope described is in the Durkee Collection. Northern cartoonists,

particularly those employed by the commercial printers, argued that in contrast to the volunteer system in the North, the Confederates were forced to drive recruits into the southern army at bayonet point; see Weitenkampf, *NYPLB*, 526, 558–559.

[19] Dicey, *Six Months*, 2:23, 79; *Leslie's*, Aug. 2, 1862, 291, Nov. 15, 1862, 124, Sept. 19, 1863, 420; *Harper's Weekly*, Aug. 30, 1862, 560, Oct. 11, 1862, 656; *Vanity Fair*, July 26, 1862, 39, Aug. 9, 1862, 70, Aug. 30, 1862, 108, June 6, 1863, 98.

[20] Randall, *Civil War and Reconstruction*, 410–416.

[21] *Leslie's*, July 25, 1863, 282–283, Aug. 1, 1863, 293, 300–301, 305, Aug. 29, 1863, 372; *NYIN*, July 25, 1863, 200, 201, Aug. 1, 1863, 208, 216, 217, Aug. 8, 1863, 232–233, 236, Aug. 15, 1863, 244, Aug. 29, 1863, 295.

[22] Harper, *House of Harper*, 188–189; Cary, *Curtis*, 165.

[23] *Harper's Weekly*, Aug. 1, 1863, 484–485, 493–494, 496; Paine, *Nast*, 92–93.

[24] Weitenkampf, *NYPLB*, 51.

[25] *Leslie's*, May 23, 1863, 144, June 20, 1863, 208; *Harper's Weekly*, Feb. 28, 1863, 144, Oct. 22, 1864, 688; *Vanity Fair*, Nov. 8, 1862, 217, May 30, 1863, 87; and an envelope in the Durkee Collection.

[26] *Leslie's*, July 25, 1863, 292; *NYIN*, July 18, 1863, 178, 181; *Harper's Weekly*, July 11, 1863, 448; C. T. Congdon, "The Limits of Caricature," in *The Nation*, 3:55 (July 19, 1866).

"But it has been fortunate for us that we have had McClellan, and Seymour, and Banks and all the rest of the incapables, and that by their management the war has been prolonged. We needed a severe moral training. Had the rebellion been put down easily we would have had slavery fastened upon us for a new term of years, and honest men would have had new reason for patriotic shame and regret. The delays, the disasters, the misconduct, the vacillations, the meanness which have hindered our success, have made success certain. Vallandigham, Fernando Wood, William B. Reed have helped our cause more than they could have done had they been patriots. The New York Riots were almost as great a help to us as a victory, and now we are approaching the end," Charles Eliot Norton to Squire, July 20, 1864, in the Ephraim George Squire Papers in the Library of Congress. Norton was a protegy of George William Curtis; Squire was, for a time, editor of *Frank Leslie's Illustrated Newspaper*.

CHAPTER IX: VICKSBURG AND GETTYSBURG

[1] Simplot Clipping Book, 28–34, and Manuscript Memoirs: *Harper's Weekly*, May 10, 1862, 300, June 28, 1862, 408–409, July 5, 1862, 418, Oct. 11, 1862, 647, Nov. 1, 1862, 692–701.

[2] "It was his especial delight in the innumerable skirmishes and battles which attended the movement [to the south and rear of Vicksburg], to select a portion of the skirmish line which was most conspicuous, and to place himself well in the front with the most advanced of the sharpshooters. In case the enemy's line was driven back,—as it always was in this series of operations,—and there were any dead Confederates left on the ground, it was one of Davis' queer fancies to exchange clothes with a dead man. This he would do in full view of the combatants, and not infrequently when under sharp fire. It did not seem to be his desire to exchange for the purpose of getting a better suit, for he frequently lost in quality by the transaction, but simply for the novelty of the change." Wilkie, *Pen and Powder*, 318–319. Davis' own letters to Harper testify that he was careful to protect himself whenever under fire; *Harper's Weekly*, June 27, 1863, 405, Sept. 19, 1863, 603.

[3] There are brief biographies of Davis in Theodore R. Davis, "Grant Under Fire," in *The Cosmopolitan*, 14:333 (January, 1893); *Harper's Weekly*, Sept. 7, 1867, 564, Nov. 24, 1894, 1114; *New York Tribune*, Nov. 11, 1894, 7. A description of Davis appeared in Russell, *Diary North and South*, 46; a photographic portrait probably taken about 1863 in Robert Taft, "The Pictorial Record of the Old West, IX. Alfred R. Waud and Theodore R. Davis," in *The Kansas Historical Quarterly*, 17:358–359 (November, 1949); a self-portrait in *Harper's Weekly*, Sept. 7, 1867, 564. His coverage of the tour of the Prince of Wales is summarized in *NYIN*, Oct. 13, 1860, 354. For details and illustrations of his tour through the Confederacy with Russell, see Russell, *Diary, passim, Harper's Weekly* from May 8, 1861 to August 3, 1861, and the *New York Tribune*, July 21, 1861, 4.

[4] *Leslie's*, May 17, 1862, 66, Aug. 9, 1862, 305, Aug. 16, 1862, 321, 325, 329, Sept. 27, 1862, 8–9, 13, Oct. 4, 1862, 20–21, Oct. 18, 1862, 56–57, 60, Oct. 25, 1862, 76, Dec. 27, 1862, 216–217, 220, Jan. 3, 1863, 225, 228, 232–233, Jan. 10, 1863, 244–245, 248, Jan. 17, 1863, 268, Feb. 28, 1863, 356, 360–361.

[5] *Ibid.*, March 28, 1863, 14.

[6] *Ibid.*, April 19, 1862, 377; *Harper's Weekly*, April 11, 1863, 225; *NYIN*, May 2, 1863, 1.

[7] *Leslie's*, March 28, 1863, 8–9, 14, April 4, 1863, 28, 29.

[8] *Ibid.*, March 28, 1863, 14, April 11, 1863, 34, 45.

[9] Wilkie, *Pen and Powder*, 227–228, 360.

[10] There is a short biography of Fred B. Schell in *American Art and American Art Collections* (2 vols., Boston, n.d.), 2:924–928.

[11] *Leslie's*, May 16, 1863, 120–121.

[12] Cadwallader, *Three Years with Grant*, 64; *Harper's Weekly*, May 30, 1863, 341, June 13, 1863, 369, 372, June 20, 1863, 392–393, 395, 396, June 27, 1863, 404–405; *Leslie's*, July 13, 1863, 184–185; *NYIN*, June 20, 1863, 120–121.

[13] *Leslie's*, June 20, 1863, 200–201; *NYIN*, June 27, 1863, 136–137; *Harper's Weekly*, July 4, 1863, 420–421.

[14] *Harper's Weekly*, July 11, 1863, 446, Aug. 1, 1863, 487.

[15] *Ibid.*, Aug. 8, 1863, 501; *Leslie's*, July 4, 1863, 232–233, July 25, 1863, 280, Aug. 8, 1863, 312.

[16] These were the subjects that Brady did so well, yet until late in 1863, the western war photographers took pictures only of ships, fortifications, gun emplacements, and soldier groups; Miller, *Photographic History*, 2:179–226.

[17] *Harper's Weekly*, June 20, 1863, 113, June 27, 1863, 405, July 4, 1863, 427, July 11, 1863, 437; *Leslie's*, July 13, 1863, 241, July 25, 1863, 277, 288.

[18] *Harper's Weekly*, July 25, 1863, 468–469, Aug. 8, 1863, 501; *Leslie's*, July 25, 1863, 273, 285, 288, Aug. 1, 1863, 296.

[19] Eisenschiml and Newman, *Civil War*, 449; Davis, "Grant Under Fire," 339; *Harper's Weekly*, Aug. 1, 1863, 481, 487.

[20] Henry Steele Commager, *The Blue and the Gray* (New York, 1950), 673; *Leslie's*, Aug. 8, 1863, 309, Aug. 15, 1863, 332–333; *Harper's Weekly*, Aug. 1, 1863, 488–489.

[21] In January of 1862, W. R. McComas, Leslie's artist in Kentucky, portrayed Grant on horseback in a feint against Columbus, Kentucky. But as portraiture, this single sketch added nothing to northerners' knowledge of Grant's appearance; *Leslie's*, Feb. 15, 1862, 196, 206.

[22] *Leslie's*, March 28, 1863, 14; Simplot Clipping Book, 17; Davis, "Grant Under Fire," 334–336, 338.

[23] *Battles and Leaders of the Civil War* (4 vols., New York, 1887), 1:352; Davis, "Grant Under Fire," 334; *NYIN*, March 22, 1862, 316, June 7, 1863, 81, Dec. 19, 1863, 120–121; *Leslie's*, March 15, 1862, 261, June 13, 1863, 177; *Harper's Weekly*, March 8, 1862, 145, June 6, 1863, 365, June 13, 1863, 376–377. Examples of the error in the prints can be found in the Print Collection in the Library of Congress, and in "Battle Art of Currier & Ives," in *The Old Print Shop Portfolio*, 7:196, 208 (May, 1948); Cadwallader, *Three Years with Grant*, 138–139.

[24] Cadwallader, *Three Years with Grant*, 350–352; *Harper's Weekly*, July 25, 1863, 465, 478, Feb. 6, 1864, 81, May 28, 1864, 340, June 25, 1864, 415, July 16, 1864, 449; Horan, *Brady*, 55–56; *Leslie's*, March 19, 1864, 408–409. Grant was still so little known by 1863 that Leslie included the following in a description: "He has a good form, very square shoulders, and generally stands squarely on his feet, never resting on one leg or lounging against a support. He never uses profane or extravagant language. He is almost a model of temperance, seldom drinking at all. . . ." *ibid.*, July 4, 1863, 227. Compare this with a description

left by a staff officer who saw Grant on frequent occasions: "Grant is a man of a good deal of rough dignity; rather taciturn; quick and decided in speech. He habitually wears an expression as if he had determined to drive his head through a brick wall, and was about to do it"; Lyman, *Meade's Headquarters*, 81.

The problem of acquiring recent portraits was even more acute in the case of Confederate generals. Until 1863, the northern illustrated weeklies used a portrait of Robert E. Lee made while he was a professor at West Point and showing him with dark hair and mustache and with no signs of age on his face; *Leslie's*, Oct. 4, 1862, 29; *Harper's Weekly*, Aug. 24, 1861, 541. However, early in 1863 Harper published portraits of Lee and Thomas Jackson by Frank Vizetelly, artist for the *Illustrated London News; Harper's Weekly*, Feb. 14, 1863, 103, 109, March 14, 1863, 173–174; Meredith, *Brady*, 196.

25 *New York Herald*, June 24, 1863, 4, June 25, 1863, 1; Forbes, *Artist's Story*, 1:77–78.

26 Brief biographies of Forbes appear in Clement and Hutton, *Artists of the Nineteenth Century*, 1:261–262; Michigan State Library, *Biographical Sketches of American Artists* (5th ed., Lansing, Michigan, 1924), 117; "Edwin Forbes," in *DAB*, 6:504; *The New York Times*, March 7, 1895, 3; *New York Herald*, March 7, 1895, 12.

27 Forbes, *Artist's Story*, 1:1–2, 2:257–258; *Leslie's*, July 5, 1862, 226, 228–229. Forbes' field sketches, as is apparent from the original sketches in the Forbes Collection, were usually made from a great distance whenever battle conditions existed.

28 Forbes, *Artist's Story*, 1:29–30, 138, 2:257.

29 *Leslie's*, July 11, 1863, 253; *New York Herald*, June 24, 1863, 1; *Leslie's*, Sept. 22, 1860, 273, July 18, 1863, 260; Paine, *Nast*, 90–91; *Harper's Weekly*, July 18, 1863, 460, July 25, 1863, 477.

30 There are brief biographies of Bellew in "Caricature in America," in *All the Year Round*, 41:300–301 (September 28, 1878); "Frank Bellew," in *DAB*, 2:165–166; Wilson, *Lincoln in Caricature*, xi; *The New York Times*, June 30, 1888, 5. For his sketches of the Gettysburg campaign, *NYIN*, July 4, 1863, 145, July 18, 1863, 181, 185, July 25, 1863, 193, 196–205, Aug. 8, 1863, 237; Starr, *Bohemian Brigade*, 204.

31 Meredith, *Brady*, 151–154; Horan, *Brady*, 53–54.

32 Meredith, *Brady*. plate #3; *Harper's Weekly*, July 25, 1863, 472–473.

33 *Harper's Weekly*, July 25, 1863, 472–473, Aug. 8, 1863, 504–505, 508; several of the originals are in the Waud Collection. Frank A. Haskell, a staff officer at Gettysburg, recognized the difficulty of describing the battle there: "A full account of the *battle as it was* will never, can never be made. Who could sketch the changes, the constant shifting of the bloody panorama: It is not possible."

Frank A. Haskell, *The Battle of Gettysburg,* edited by Bruce Catton (Boston, 1958), 156.

[34] *Leslie's,* July 18, 1863, 261; the note to Leslie is on the original sketch in the Forbes Collection.

[35] Forbes, *Artist's Story,* 2:177–178, 274; *Leslie's,* July 18, 1863, 268–269, July 25, 1863, 281, 284; and the original sketches in the Forbes Collection.

[36] Forbes, *Artist's Story,* 2:178; *Harper's Weekly,* Aug. 22, 1863, 532–534; the note to Leslie in the Forbes Collection.

CHAPTER X: AT EASE

[1] *Leslie's,* Sept. 26, 1863, 2, Jan. 9, 1864, 249. On the other hand, Leslie introduced an illustration of a foraging party as "those commoner scenes of war that may be termed its prose, the poetry being the stern and breathless clash of battle"; *ibid.,* March 14, 1863, 385.

[2] Connolly, *Three Years,* 136.

[3] Frank Weitenkampf, "Winslow Homer and the Wood Block," in the *Bulletin of the New York Public Library,* 36:731–736. (November, 1932); William Howe Downes, *The Life and Works of Winslow Homer* (Boston, 1911), 8–9, 34–35; Flexner, *American Painting,* 61–64.

[4] Downes, *Homer,* 42–43; Starr, *Bohemian Brigade,* 111; *Harper's Weekly,* June 14, 1862, 376; Meredith, *American Wars,* 131–132.

[5] Downes, *Homer,* 41–42; *Harper's Weekly,* May 2, 1863, 274, May 17, 1862, 305, 308, 309, June 14, 1862, 378, July 5, 1862, 424–425, July 12, 1862, 436, 440–441, Nov. 15, 1862, 724; *NYIN,* May 16, 1863, 34. The best collection of Homer's field sketches is in the Print Division of the Cooper Union Institute in New York City. Meredith, *American Wars,* 145–147, has copies of several of the Homer originals. Homer's preference for teen-age subjects is supported by the fact that he did many of these in greater detail than his other work and also because he worked many of them into water colors.

[6] For examples, see Donald, *Divided We Fought,* 242, 322, 343; Meredith, *Brady,* Lecture Book plate #36. Western artists contributed very little to the images of the army at ease. Western armies did not spend as much time in winter quarters, and even when one of the western armies was stalemated, artists like Henri Lovie and Alex Simplot or Theodore Davis either went home on furlough or transferred to another army that was active in the field. This was perhaps unfortunate because according to the letters and diaries, the westerners were a more relaxed and less disciplined group of soldiers than their comrades on the eastern front. For a reporter's description of the western army and

a western artist (Theo Davis) at ease, see W. F. G. Shanks, "Chattanooga and How we held it," in *Harper's New Monthly Magazine*, 36:146–147 (January, 1868).

[7] *Harper's Weekly*, Dec. 7, 1861, 776–777; *Leslie's*, Dec. 14, 1861, 52–53; *NYIN*, Dec. 9, 1861, 88–89, 90. The editor of the *Dayton* [Ohio] *Daily* thought that Waud's "miserable" sketch of the review was the work of an amateur, and that the editors of the *News* "ought to be ashamed of it"; *NYIN*, Dec. 28, 1861, 115. For sketches of other reviews, see *Harper's Weekly*, July 6, 1861, 424–425, May 2, 1863, 280–281, Oct. 10, 1863, 648–649; *NYIN*, Oct. 25, 1862, 397.

[8] Charles Sterling Underhill, comp., *Your Soldier Boy Samuel* (privately printed, 1929), 101, 131.

[9] Forbes, *Artist's Story*, 2:213–214, 225; *Leslie's*, Oct. 12, 1861, 343; *NYIN*, July 12, 1862, 145, Oct. 21, 1861, 396, May 9, 1863, 298; *Harper's Weekly*, Sept. 23, 1861, 330.

[10] *NYIN*, Jan. 4, 1862, 129, March 22, 1862, 305; *Harper's Weekly*, Jan. 30, 1864, 68.

[11] *NYIN*, July 12, 1862, 145; *Leslie's*, July 2, 1864, 225; *Harper's Weekly*, Oct. 8, 1864, 643. The Waud description is on the back of one of his sketches in the Waud Collection.

[12] Forbes, *Artist's Story*, 2:301; *Leslie's*, June 29, 1861, 112, 114, June 12, 1862, 181; *Harper's Weekly*, June 1, 1861, 348, June 28, 1862, 411, 412; *NYIN*, March 7, 1863, 273.

[13] Favill, *Diary*, 253; Forbes, *Artist's Story*, 1:153–154; *Harper's Weekly*, Dec. 28, 1861, 828, Jan. 25, 1862, 60, Sept. 26, 1863, 616–617; *Leslie's*, Jan. 4, 1862, 104–105; *NYIN*, Dec. 28, 1861, 117–124.

[14] Abner R. Small, *The Road to Richmond*, edited by Harold Adams Small (Berkeley, California, 1939), 198; *Harper's Weekly*, July 15, 1865, 445; *Leslie's*, Sept. 20, 1862, 401, 407; Wilkie, *Pen and Powder*, 229–230.

[15] Whitman, *The Wound Dresser*, 163; "In camp, on the march, nay, even in the solemn hour of battle, there was ever and anon a laugh passing down the line, or some sport going on inside the tents. Seldom was there wanting someone, noted for his powers of storytelling, to beguile the weary hours about the camp-fire in front of our shelters, or out among the pines on picket. Few companies could be found without some native-born wag or wit, whose comical songs or quaint remarks kept the boys in good humor, while at the same time each and all, according to the measure of their several capacities, were given to playing practical jokes of one kind or other for the general enlivenment of the camp"; Bircher, *Diary*, 183–184.

[16] *NYIN*, July 5, 1862, 137, Aug. 9, 1862, 212, Jan. 17, 1863, 172; *Harper's Weekly*, Nov. 9, 1861, 716, Jan. 17, 1863, 33; *Leslie's*, March 18, 1865, 412–413,

March 14, 1863, 397, May 7, 1864, 100, Dec. 10, 1864, 180; Forbes, *Artist's Story*, 2:182, 198, 261.

[17] Forbes, *Artist's Story*, 1:25; *Harper's Weekly*, Jan. 24, 1863, 52, Sept. 21, 1861, 599; *Leslie's*, July 19, 1862, 260, March 18, 1865, 413.

[18] Forbes, *Artist's Story*, 1:2, 5; *Leslie's*, Oct. 31, 1863, 81, 88–89, Jan. 9, 1864, 249, March 19, 1864, 412, April 9, 1864, 40, May 7, 1864, 100; and the originals in the Forbes Collection.

[19] *Harper's Weekly*, Aug. 22, 1863, 540, Feb. 1, 1862, 69; *Leslie's*, Nov. 29, 1862, 156; *NYIN*, Sept. 30, 1861, 348. But for sketches of muddy camps, see *NYIN*, Oct. 28, 1861, 412; *Harper's Weekly*, Jan. 18, 1862, 38.

[20] For a general treatment of this subject, see Bell Irvin Wiley, *The Life of Billy Yank, The Common Soldier of the Union* (Indianapolis and New York, 1952), 152–153; Fred A. Shannon, "The Life of the Common Soldier in the Union Army, 1861–1865," in *The Mississippi Valley Historical Review*, 13:480–481 (March, 1927); *Harper's Weekly*, June 22, 1861, 394, Nov. 2, 1861, 694, Feb. 6, 1864, 93, July 15, 1865, 444; *Leslie's*, Jan. 11, 1862, 120–121.

[21] *Leslie's*, Dec. 3, 1864, 169, Dec. 19, 1863, 193–194; *Harper's Weekly*, Nov. 29, 1862, 764, Dec. 3, 1864, 780.

[22] Jenkin Lloyd Jones, *An Artilleryman's Diary* (Wisconsin History Commission: Original Papers, No. 8, February, 1914), 291. For Grant and his staff in the same mood, see Cadwallader, *Three Years with Grant*, 279–280; *NYIN*, Jan. 4, 1862, 136–137, 138; *Harper's Weekly*, Jan. 1863, 1.

[23] *NYIN*, Jan. 10, 1863, 152–153; *Harper's Weekly*, Jan. 4, 1862; *Leslie's*, Jan. 18, 1862, 134, 136–137; Forbes, *Artist's Story*, 1:37–38.

[24] Wiley, *Billy Yank*, 153–154; Quint, *Potomac and Rapidan*, 95, 244–245, 247–8, 268, 311; Charles Benerlyn Johnson, *Muskets and Medicine, or Army Life in the Sixties* (Philadelphia, 1917), 188–189; Theodore Frelinghuysen Upson, *With Sherman to the sea; the Civil War letters, diaries, & reminiscences of Theodore F. Upson,* edited by Oscar Osburn Winther (Baton Rouge, 1943), 45; Charles H. Lynch, *The Civil War Diary, 1862–1865 of Charles H. Lynch, 18th Conn. Vol's.* (Hartford, Connecticut, 1915), 36, 137, 140, 148; M. Hamlin Cannon, "The United States Christian Commission" in *The Mississippi Valley Historical Review*, 38:71–72, 78 (June, 1951); Fred Emory Haynes, "Social Work at Camp Dodge," in *The Iowa Journal of History and Politics*, 16:482 (1918); Jones, *Artilleryman's Diary*, 97, 235, 305–306; Forbes, *Artist's Story*, 1:133; Robert Ferguson, *America during and after the war* (London, 1866), 226–227; Page, *Letters*, 244; B. F. Stevenson, *Letters from the Army* (Cincinnati, 1884), 291; Isaac Lyman Taylor, "Campaigning with the First Minnesota, A Civil War Diary," edited by Hazel C. Wolf, in *Minnesota History*, 25:248 (September, 1944).

[25] Cadwallader, *Three Years with Grant*, 290–291, 294; Oliver Willcox Norton, *Army Letters, 1861–1865* (Chicago, 1903), 51; *NYIN*, Jan. 4, 1862, 141, June 20, 1863, 114; *Leslie's*, March 29, 1862, 310, Oct. 31, 1863, 88–89; *Harper's Weekly*, June 14, 1862, 376–377; Ferguson, *America and the war*, 73–74.

[26] Wiley, *Billy Yank*, 154; Beatty, *Memoirs*, 161; Wills, *Army Life*, 164–165; *Harper's Weekly*, July 5, 1862, 423, Nov. 21, 1863, 750; the Waud original sketch and his warning to the engravers is in the Waud Collection; Quint, *Potomac and Rapidan*, 50–51; Stanton P. Allen, *Down in Dixie, Life in a Cavalry Regiment in the War Days, from the Wilderness to Appomattox* (Boston, 1893), 90–92; Henry N. Blake, *Three Years in the Army of the Potomac* (Boston, 1865), 104–105; *Vanity Fair*, Sept. 14, 1861, 130.

[27] Adams, *Story of a Trooper*, 31–32; *Harper's Weekly*, Nov. 15, 1862, 728–729, Nov. 29, 1862, 765, May 30, 1863, 344–345.

[28] Andrews, *North Reports the Civil War*, 643; Starr, *Bohemian Brigade*, 252–253; *Leslie's*, Nov. 21, 1863, 129, May 21, 1864, 130; *Harper's Weekly*, Nov. 21, 1863, 741; *NYIN*, Nov. 25, 1861, 61; *Vanity Fair*, May 24, 1862, 250, May 2, 1863, 42–43.

[29] *Leslie's*, Feb. 15, 1862, 194, April 9, 1864, 44; John Chipman Gray and John Codman Ropes, *War Letters, 1862–1865* (Boston, 1927), 185; O. W. Norton, *Letters*, 137–138; *Harper's Weekly*, Dec. 27, 1862, 819, March 21, 1863, 278, Feb. 18, 1865, 99, March 25, 1865, 179; Woolsey, *Letters of a Family*, 1:175, 2:364, 402–403.

[30] Compare Jones, *Artilleryman's Diary*, 279–280, with plate #11 in William Forrest Dawson, *A Civil War Artist at the Front. Edwin Forbes' Life Studies of the Great Army* (New York, 1957). Also see Underhill, *Soldier Boy Samuel*, 28, and Favill, *Diary*, 224–226.

CHAPTER XI: UNDER FIRE

[1] Frank Wilkeson, *Recollections of a Private Soldier in the Army of the Potomac* (New York, 1887), 37; Wirt Armistead Cate, ed., *Two Soldiers, The Campaign Diaries of Thomas J. Key, C.S.A. December 7, 1863–May 17, 1865, and Robert J. Campbell, U.S.A. January 1, 1864–July 21, 1864* (Chapel Hill, North Carolina, 1938), 246; *Leslie's*, May 28, 1864, 145; Meredith, *Brady*, 161–162; Horan, *Brady*, 55.

[2] *Harper's Weekly*, March 26, 1864, 197; Meredith, *Brady*, 162; Horan, *Brady*, 55–56.

[3] Horan, *Brady*, plate #260; Meredith, *Brady*, 163 and plate #90.

[4] The two Waud portraits are in the Print and Photograph Division of the Library of Congress, Photos of Officers, Lot #4187; Sala, *Diary*, 1:302–303, 314.

[5] *Leslie's Weekly*, Dec. 14, 1905, 570; *New York Tribune*, Jan. 29, 1910, 7; for a self-portrait of Becker in the field, see *Leslie's*, March 4, 1865, 372. Becker had previously sketched the dedication ceremonies at the Gettysburg cemetery, *ibid.*, Dec. 5, 1863, 168–169, and the coal mines at Hecksherville, Pa., *ibid.*, Dec. 26, 1863, 220.

[6] *Leslie's*, May 28, 1864, 148; some of Brady's photographs have been reproduced in Meredith, *Brady*, plates #100 above and 101 above, and in Donald, *Divided We Fought*, 298. For a selection of photographs from the Wilderness to Cold Harbor, see Miller, *Photographic History*, 3:28–92.

[7] Eisenschiml and Newman, *Civil War*, 561.

[8] *Leslie's*, May 28, 1864, 152–153, 157, June 4, 1864, 161, 168–169; *Harper's Weekly*, June 4, 1864, 356, 357, 360–361; Meredith, *Brady*, plate #100 below. Reproductions of two of Waud's original sketches from the Wilderness are in Donald, *Divided We Fought*, 300, 302.

[9] Reproduction of the original sketch in Donald, *Divided We Fought*, 304.

[10] *Leslie's*, May 28, 1864, 152–153, June 4, 1864, 164, June 11, 1864, 180, 189. Frank Bellew was at Spottsylvania for the *New York Illustrated News* to make the only on-the-spot sketches of this campaign for Leggett, *NYIN*, June 4, 1864, 505–506. *Harper's Weekly*, June 11, 1864, 376–377, 380; and the original in Donald, *Divided We Fought*, 308.

[11] *Leslie's*, June 25, 1864, 221. Robert Tilney, *My Life in the Army. Three Years and a Half with the Fifth Army Corps, Army of the Potomac, 1862–1865* (Philadelphia, 1912), 85–86, describes a scene at Cold Harbor very similar to Forbes' sketch; *Harper's Weekly*, June 25, 1864, 404; and originals in Donald, *Divided We Fought*, 316–317; Eisenschiml and Newman, *Civil War*, 579.

[12] *Harper's Weekly*, June 25, 1864, 404, 408–409, 412, and the originals in Donald, *Divided We Fought*, 319; *Leslie's*, June 25, 1864, 216–217.

[13] *Harper's Weekly*, May 28, 1864, 338.

[14] For examples, see *ibid.*, June 11, 1864, 372, Aug. 6, 1864, 508, Oct. 22, 1864, 681.

[15] *Leslie's*, June 4, 1864, 165, 172; *Harper's Weekly*, May 28, 1864, 344–345, June 4, 1864, 357. Meredith, *American Wars*, 179, reproduces a Homer painting of the Wilderness. There is some doubt that Homer actually went to Virginia during this campaign, despite the repeated assertions in most of the secondary sources that he was there.

[16] *Leslie's*, June 4, 1864, 165, June 11, 1864, 177, 180, 189; *Harper's Weekly*, June 4, 1864, 257, June 25, 1864, 408–409. The photographs have been reproduced in Donald, *Divided We Fought*, 312 and 313, and in Miller, *Photographic History*, 3:47, 49.

[17] Meredith, *Brady,* 166 and plate #85; Horan, *Brady,* plate #278; Miller, *Photographic History,* 3:61, 63, 65. The original of the Forbes' sketch is in the Forbes Collection (#237, Box 12). During the Peninsula campaign, Arthur Lumley made several detailed sketches of doctors amputating a soldier's leg in a field hospital–actually a barn–while waiting soldiers lay on the ground outside; *NYIN,* May 31, 1862, 57, 61. It is interesting to speculate why in the several following issues, Leggett then featured neat stone and brick government hospitals, all in strong contrast to what Lumley had portrayed; *NYIN,* Jan. 10, 1863, 145, Jan. 17, 1863, 161, June 14, 1863, 108. Also see *Leslie's,* Nov. 7, 1863, 109, and for a sketch by Andrew McCullum of "a typical field hospital" of the Ninth Corps, emphasizing cleanliness, fine diet, and other superb care, *Harper's Weekly,* March 11, 1865, 149–150.

[18] Original sketch in the Waud Collection; *Harper's Weekly,* June 11, 1864, 372.

[19] William Tecumseh Sherman, *Memoirs,* 2:394, commented on how seldom armies fought in neat formations and also described the true character of hand-to-hand fighting; *Harper's Weekly,* June 11, 1864, 276–277, June 25, 1864, 408–409.

[20] *Harper's Weekly,* Nov. 15, 1862, 725; Meredith, *Brady,* plate #105; Oliver Wendell Holmes, Jr., *Touched with Fire: Civil War Letters and diary of Oliver Wendell Holmes, Jr., 1861–1864* (Cambridge, Massachusetts, 1946), 149.

[21] *Leslie's,* July 23, 1864, 280–281; *Harper's Weekly,* July 23, 1864, 472–473, Aug. 13, 1864, 516, 520–521. William Waud first joined the Army of the James before moving up to Petersburg, and is mentioned in Page, *Letters,* 168–169.

[22] *Harper's Weekly,* Aug. 6, 1864, 504–505, Sept. 24, 1864, 612, Oct. 8, 1864, 648–649, Nov. 5, 1864, 717; Horan, *Brady,* plates #274, 275, 277; Meredith, *Brady,* plates #51, 52, 54, 99, 103 below.

[23] *Harper's Weekly,* Aug. 20, 1864, 529, 536–537, 542, Aug. 27, 1864, 548; *Leslie's,* Aug. 20, 1864, 337, 344–345, Aug. 27, 1864, 352, 356, 360–361.

[24] *Leslie's,* Aug. 27, 1864, 360–361, Sept. 3, 1864, 376; Lyman, *Meade's Headquarters,* 203.

[25] *Harper's Weekly,* Oct. 29, 1864, 696; Forbes, *Artist's Story,* 2:201; Meredith, *Brady,* plates #64, 86, 87.

[26] *Harper's Weekly,* Nov. 5, 1864, 712–713, Jan. 21, 1865, 33; *Leslie's,* Nov. 19, 1864, 136–137, Nov. 26, 1864, 145, Jan. 28, 1865, 292–293; William Waud to Alfred R. Waud, October 3, 1864, in the Waud Collection.

CHAPTER XII: ON THE MARCH

[1] As an example, see *Harper's Weekly,* July 30, 1864, 488–489.

[2] With the expanded scope of the war, the publishers also had to decide whether

to maintain an artist with each of the major armies or to concentrate their forces. Good artists were limited in number, and the costs of maintaining them in the field were constantly rising. Leslie continued to assign artists to all the major armies, and in the summer of 1864 he had ten full-time sketchers in the field, six with the eastern armies. But only two or three of these were veteran field sketchers. Harper, on the other hand, concentrated his artists. In 1864 he had only five men in the field, three with the Army of the Potomac, one with Sherman, and the fifth with Sheridan. For the other war theaters he relied upon sketches submitted by occasional contributors. But the important factor was that of the four artists who started the war in 1861, three of them—Davis and the two Wauds—were with the *Weekly*.

[3] For examples of the early marching images, see *Leslie's,* Nov. 16, 1861, 405; *Harper's Weekly,* Nov. 16, 1861, 727; Simplot Clipping Book, 13.

[4] *Leslie's,* Sept. 14, 1861, 273; *Harper's Weekly,* June 7, 1862, 364, Nov. 22, 1862, 744–745, Jan. 16, 1864, 33; *NYIN,* March 15, 1862, 292–301, May 31, 1862, 52, Nov. 29, 1862, 57; Bircher, *Diary,* 54.

[5] Quint, *Potomac and Rapidan,* 89; *Harper's Weekly,* Feb. 22, 1862, 121.

[6] *Leslie's,* June 14, 1862, 168–169, 171.

[7] *Harper's Weekly,* Feb. 14, 1863, 104–105; *NYIN,* Dec. 27, 1862, 124; *Leslie's,* Jan. 3, 1863, 228, Feb. 14, 1863, 328–329.

[8] *Leslie's,* Feb. 21, 1863, 352; *Harper's Weekly,* March 21, 1863, 192; Quint, *Potomac and Rapidan,* 89.

[9] Forbes, *Artist's Story,* 2:169; *Harper's Weekly,* Oct. 1, 1864, 628.

[10] Forbes, *Artist's Story,* 2:185–186; Fred A. Shannon, "The Life of the Common Soldier in the Union Army, 1861–1865," in *The Mississippi Valley Historical Review,* 13:471–473 (March, 1927); *Leslie's,* July 5, 1862, 229; Lyman, *Meade's Headquarters,* 8.

[11] Shannon, "Common Soldier," 474; Forbes, *Artist's Story,* 1:45–46; Lynch, *Diary,* 104, 105, 107–108.

[12] Connolly, *Three Years,* 121.

[13] *Harper's Weekly,* Aug. 6, 1864, 502, 508, Dec. 10, 1864, 792–793; *Leslie's,* March 26, 1864, 8–9. Also see Henry O. Dwight, "How We Fight at Atlanta," in *Harper's New Monthly Magazine,* 29:663–666 (1864); Bircher, *Diary,* 167–168.

[14] Henry Hitchcock's letters and diaries contain numerous references to Davis; Hitchcock, *Marching with Sherman,* 39, 54, 130, 153, 186–187, 188–189, 199, 256, 268. For another testimonial of Davis' work during this campaign, see the *New York Evening Post,* Dec. 22, 1864, 2; Andrews, *North Reports the Civil War,* 578.

[15] For evidence of the interest of soldiers and artists in scenery, see Stevenson, *Letters*, 118, 134; Lynch, *Diary*, 71; Bircher, *Diary*, 89; *Harper's Weekly*, Nov. 8, 1862, 718, Nov. 7, 1863, 711; Forbes, *Artist's Story*, 2:277; *Leslie's*, Sept. 7, 1861, 260, 269, Nov. 9, 1861, 389–390.

[16] *Harper's Weekly*, Jan. 9, 1864, 29, March 19, 1864, 187; *Leslie's*, Nov. 15, 1862, 117, Oct. 10, 1863, 33.

[17] Forbes, *Artist's Story*, 1:46; *Harper's Weekly*, March 28, 1863, 196, Aug. 6, 1864, 508, Oct. 22, 1864, 681.

[18] *Leslie's*, Sept. 28, 1861, 305, Oct. 12, 1861, 337, Dec. 13, 1862, 184–185; *NYIN*, Dec. 2, 1861, 72–73, Aug. 29, 1863, 284; a sketch in the Waud Collection never published; Forbes, *Artist's Story*, 1:97; Small, *Road to Richmond*, 200; Tilney, *Life in Army*, 52.

[19] *The New York Times*, March 14, 1862, 1, March 15, 1862, 3.

[20] The Lumley original is in the Waud Collection; Andrews, *North Reports the Civil War*, 560; *Harper's Weekly*, July 9, 1864, 444.

[21] *Harper's Weekly*, Oct. 1, 1864, 636, Oct. 15, 1864, 660, Jan. 7, 1865, 1.

[22] For the photographs, see Miller, *Photographic History*, 3:209–248; Horan, *Brady*, 56–57.

[23] *Leslie's*, April 8, 1865, 33–45; *Harper's Weekly*, March 4, 1865, 129, April 15, 1865, 225–229. Sketches from the Carolina phase of Sherman's campaign were disappointing only in the continued neglect of the "Bummers" and because the appearance of the uniforms of the marching men was too fine. This latter was undoubtedly due to hasty work by both the sketch artists and the engravers in New York.

[24] *Harper's Weekly*, April 8, 1865, 217; Donald, *Divided We Fought*, 419.

CHAPTER XIII: THE LINCOLN IMAGE

[1] For Harper's suppression of sketches, see Chapter 12, "On the March," pp. 161–162 and for Harper's revival of the atrocity illustrations, see the following chapter, "Roundup," pp. 179–181.

[2] Cary, *Curtis*, 137–138; *Leslie's*, Nov. 24, 1860, 1; the *Vanity Fair* cartoons are republished in Wilson, *Lincoln in Caricature*, 5, 13, 57, 61, 71, 73.

[3] Stefan Lorant, *Lincoln, A Picture Story of His Life* (New York, 1957), 282, 284–285; Frederick Hill Meserve and Carl Sandburg, *The Photographs of Abraham Lincoln* (New York, 1944), plates #6, 101, 20, 25, 26; Joseph B. Bishop, "Early Political Caricature in America," in *The Century Magazine*, 44:226 (June, 1892). For a critical analysis of the origin of the "tousle-head"

portraits, see Jay Monaghan, "A Critical Examination of Three Lincoln Photographs," in the *Journal of the Illinois State Historical Society,* 52:91–105 (Spring, 1959). Compare the 1857 Hesler portrait with the Currier and Ives cartoons, "An Heir to the Throne," and " 'The Nigger' in the Woodpile," both republished in Wilson, *Lincoln in Caricature,* 33, 65. Horan, *Brady,* 31–32; Meredith, *Brady,* 59; Taft, *Photography,* 194–195; Peters, *Currier and Ives,* 34. Ordinarily, photographers like Brady, Hesler, and Gardner made four exposures at a sitting.

[4] For the history of American political cartooning prior to 1860, see William Murrell, *A History of American Graphic Humor* (2 vols., New York, 1933); Allan Nevins and Frank Weitenkampf, *A Century of Political Cartoons, Caricature in the United States from 1800 to 1900* (New York, 1944); Bishop, "Political Caricature," *op. cit.,* 219–231; Frank Weitenkampf, *American Graphic Art* (New York, 1924). Also see *Caricatures pertaining to the Civil War. . . .* (New York, 1892); A. Jay Hertz, "Campaign Covers of the Nineteenth Century," in *The American Philatelist,* 61:948–953 (September, 1948); Raymond Marsh, "Lincoln Patriotics," in the *Lincoln Herald,* 52:48–53 (December, 1950); R. Gerald McMurty, "Lincoln Patriotics," in the *Journal of the Illinois State Historical Society,* 52:123–129 (Spring, 1959).

[5] Contemporary criticism of Lincoln is broadly covered in James G. Randall, "The Unpopular Mr. Lincoln," originally published in the *Abraham Lincoln Quarterly,* 2:255–280 (1943) and revised and republished in Randall's *Lincoln The Liberal Statesman* (New York, 1947), 65–87.

[6] Most of the Lincoln cartoons from the 1860 campaign are reproduced in Wilson, *Lincoln in Caricature, passim;* the specific cartoons here referred to are on pages 33, 65, 67.

[7] *Ibid.,* 5–73, *passim.* There were two publications named *The Railsplitter* published by the party managers during the campaign. The second was published in Cincinnati, thirteen issues appearing in August, September, and October of 1860.

[8] Wilson, *Lincoln in Caricature,* 9, 15, 55; *Harper's Weekly,* Aug. 25, 1860, 544. Also see *Vanity Fair,* March 23, 1861, 139.

[9] *Leslie's,* Nov. 24, 1860, 4, Dec. 22, 1860, 73, 76, March 2, 1861, 225, 232, 236, March 9, 1861, 244, 245, March 16, 1861, 261, 264–265, 269, March 23, 1861, 276–277, 281; Lovie's inauguration sketches appeared in the issues of March 16, 1861, 268, March 23, 1861, 276–277, April 6, 1861, 309; *Harper's Weekly,* March 2, 1861, 129, March 16, 1861, 161, 165, 168–169; *NYIN,* March 2, 1861, 264–265, March 9, 1861, 309, March 16, 1861, 300–301, 289, 297, March 23, 1861, 312–313, 317, 320, March 30, 1861, 327, 330, 325; Strong, *Diary,* 3:101.

[10] *NYIN,* March 9, 1861, 280–281; *Vanity Fair,* March 9, 1861, 113–114; *Harper's Weekly,* March 9, 1861, 160. Nast's sketch corrected one error but created another; Lincoln did not leave his railroad car as it passed through Baltimore, and con-

sequently the entire scene in Nast's illustration never occurred. See a copy of Nast's original sketch in Philip Van Doren Stern, *They Were There* (New York, 1959), 30.

[11] *NYIN*, July 22, 1861, 180; Meredith, *Brady*, plates #73, 74; *Leslie's*, Dec. 5, 1863, 168–169, March 26, 1864, 3; Robert Taft, "Joseph Becker's Sketch of the Gettysburg Ceremony, November 19, 1863," in *The Kansas Historical Quarterly*, 21:257–263 (Winter, 1954).

[12] Horan, *Brady*, plates #143, 146, 148, 149, 150–154, and page 55. *Harper's Weekly* engraved the Lincoln and Tad photograph in the May 6, 1865 issue, p. 273. Whitman, *Complete Poetry and Prose*, 2:66; Lorant, *Lincoln*, 289–299; *Harper's Weekly*, April 27, 1861, 268.

[13] *Leslie's*, March 2, 1861, 240; *Vanity Fair*, March 23, 1861, 139; *Harper's Weekly*, March 2, 1861, 144, March 30, 1861, 208, April 13, 1861, 240, May 18, 1861, 307, June 1, 1861, 352, June 22, 1861, 400, July 13, 1861, 434, 448.

[14] *Leslie's*, Feb. 14, 1863, 336; *Harper's Weekly*, Jan. 3, 1863, 16, Jan. 10, 1863, 32, Jan. 17, 1863, 48, Jan. 31, 1863, 80.

[15] For early Nast cartoons of Lincoln, see *NYIN*, March 23, 1861, 320, March 30, 1861, 330. For the attitude of Henry Louis Stephens, see Wilson, *Lincoln in Caricature*, xiii, xiv, and *Vanity Fair*, June 9, 1860–July 4, 1863, *passim*.

[16] The original cartoons can be found in the *London Punch*, vols. 39–48 (July 1860–June 1865). The full set was reproduced in William Shepard Walsh, ed., *Abraham Lincoln and the London Punch: Cartoons, Comments, and Poems, Published in the London Charivari, During the American Civil War (1861–1865)* (New York, 1909); and the Lincoln cartoons from *Punch* are reproduced in Wilson, *Lincoln in Caricature*. For the cartoons referred to here, see *Punch*, Oct. 18, 1862, 161, Aug. 8, 1863, 57, Sept. 24, 1864, 127, Dec. 3, 1864, 229. Tenniel eventually realized he had gone too far in his caricature of Lincoln, and immediately after Lincoln's assassination, he drew "Britannia Sympathizes with Columbia," *Punch*, May 6, 1865, 183, which attempted to redress his earlier cartoons. Nevertheless, Tenniel's cartoons were extremely popular in Britain among people who did not favor the North. George Augustus Sala wrote: "The general cast of Mr. Lincoln's features must be familiar to most English people through the photographic portraits in the London shop windows. His actual appearance is even nearer approached by the admirable cartoon sketches of Mr. John Tenniel in *Punch*. With a curiously intuitive fidelity of appreciation, Mr. Tenniel has seized upon that lengthy face, those bushy locks, that shovel beard, that ungainly form, those long, muscular, attenuated limbs, those bony and widespread extremities"; Sala, *Diary*, 2:147. British cartoon interpretation of Lincoln would also include the work of Matt Morgan in the *London Fun*, most of whose cartoons here been reproduced in Wilson, *Lincoln in Caricature*, *passim*.

NOTES

17 Wilson, *Lincoln in Caricature*, 109, 141, 181, 193; Bruce Catton, "A Southern Artist on the Civil War," in *American Heritage*, 9:117–120 (October, 1958); *DAB*, 19:288; Meredith, *American Battle Art*, 185,

18 Cary, *Curtis*, 150; *Vanity Fair*, July 5, 1862, 3, July 26, 1862, 43, Oct. 4, 1862, 162, Dec. 6, 1862, 271; *Harper's Weekly*, Jan. 26, 1861, 64, Feb. 2, 1861, 80, April 9, 1864, 237, May 7, 1864, 292; *Leslie's*, Oct. 26, 1861, 368, Dec. 7, 1861, 29, 44, Dec. 21, 1861, 65, 72–73; *NYIN*, April 13, 1861, 268, Nov. 18, 1861, 48, Aug. 2, 1862, 205, Aug. 23, 1862, 252–253. Also see a grotesque doodle of a Negro soldier in an Alf Waud sketch in the Waud Collection; "The Innocent Cause of the War" in the Durkee Collection; Forbes, *Artist's Story*, 1:158; Weitenkampf, *NYPLB*, 527–528.

19 *Leslie's*, Jan. 18, 1862, 144, Feb. 13, 1862, 206; *Harper's Weekly*, June 29, 1861, 406, Feb. 15, 1862, 108, May 10, 1862, 289, 299, June 14, 1862, 373, Aug. 16, 1862, 520–521, Nov. 8, 1862, 712–713, Sept. 19, 1863, 597, March 12, 1864, 164, April 2, 1864, 212; William Waud to Alfred R. Waud, October 3, 1864, in the Waud Collection.

20 *Harper's Weekly*, Aug. 24, 1861, 530, Sept. 14, 1861, 578, Oct. 19, 1861, 659, Aug. 16, 1862, 528, Jan. 17, 1863, 48; *Leslie's*, Aug. 24, 1861, 226, Oct. 12, 1861, 352, April 5, 1862, 336, June 7, 1862, 146; *NYIN*, Feb. 9, 1861, 210, Oct. 14, 1861, 370, Dec. 2, 1861, 80, April 12, 1862, 368, Jan. 31, 1863, 186; George William Curtis to W. Dean Colman, September 23, 1862, Curtis Folder in Miscellaneous Manuscripts in the New York Public Library.

21 *Harper's Weekly*, Jan. 24, 1863, 50, 56–57, March 14, 1863, 168–169, May 16, 1863, 307, May 30, 1863, 338, June 20, 1863, 386, July 4, 1863, 429, Aug. 15, 1863, 514–515, 528, Jan. 23, 1864, 52, Jan. 30, 1864, 71, May 14, 1864, 306; Cary, *Curtis*, 161; *Leslie's*, June 7, 1862, 145, Aug. 30, 1862, 360, Jan. 24, 1863, 276, Dec. 19, 1863, 193, Jan. 16, 1864, 264–265, March 5, 1864, 369, Aug. 20, 1864, 349; *NYIN*, Feb. 7, 1863, 217, March 19, 1864, 321; the Currier and Ives print, another by the Chicago printers, Kurz and Allison, and a Frank Bellew print are in the Library of Congress Print Collection.

The Fort Pillow illustrations are in *NYIN*, April 30, 1864, 424; *Leslie's*, May 7, 1864, 97, July 16, 1864, 259; *Harper's Weekly*, April 30, 1864, 283. Public interest in the Fort Pillow Massacre was high because of a report by the Committee on the Conduct of the War about the massacre and the abusive treatment of prisoners in Confederate camps; see William E. Doster, *Lincoln and Episodes of the Civil War* (New York, 1915), 243.

22 *Harper's Weekly*, May 20, 1865, 306, Aug. 5, 1865, 488–489.

23 *Ibid.*, Oct. 11, 1862, 643, Jan. 10, 1863, 18, Oct. 17, 1863, 658; Harper, *House of Harper*, 147; for a general summary of the *Weekly's* editorial history, see *ibid.*, Jan. 7, 1865, 2, and a brief article in the "Critical Notices" section of the *North American Review*, 100:623–625 (April, 1865). For cartoons that did

appear during the 1862 campaign, see *Vanity Fair,* Nov. 22, 1862, 247; Folder #4421 in the Library of Congress Print Collection; Weitenkampf, *NYPLB,* 557.

[24] *Harper's Weekly,* Aug. 20, 1864, 530. For Curtis' position in respect to the Radical faction of the Republican Party, see Cary, *Curtis,* 177–179.

[25] *Leslie's,* June 25, 1864, 224, July 2, 1864, 240, Dec. 10, 1864, 178.

[26] *NYIN,* June 11, 1864, 514, July 16, 1864, 604.

[27] For examples, see the advertisements in *Harper's Weekly,* Sept. 24, 1864, 623–624, and several envelopes in the Durkee Collection.

[28] *Harper's Weekly,* Sept. 17, 1864, 594, Nov. 12, 1864, 722.

[29] *Ibid.,* Sept. 17, 1864, 608, Oct. 8, 1864, 656; *Leslie's,* Oct. 1, 1864, 32, Oct. 22, 1864, 80, Oct. 29, 1864, 96; Weitenkampf, *NYPLB,* 564–567; Folder #4421 in the Library of Congress Print Collection.

[30] *Harper's Weekly,* Oct. 15, 1864, 664–665, 658.

[31] *Ibid.,* Nov. 12, 1864, 723; Weitenkampf, *NYPLB,* 560–561, 563–564, 568–569; Folders #4419 and 4422 in the Library of Congress Print Collection; Auguste Laugel, *The United States During the War* (New York, 1866), 87–88.

[32] *Harper's Weekly,* Nov. 12, 1864, 725, Sept. 24, 1864, 616–617, Oct. 15, 1864, 659. See Weitenkampf, *NYPLB,* 560–569, *passim,* for reprints of Nast's cartoons in the *Weekly.*

[33] *Harper's Weekly,* Sept. 3, 1864, 572, 563; *Paine,* Nast, 98.

[34] *Harper's Weekly,* Aug. 20, 1864, 531, Sept. 24, 1864, 609, Oct. 1, 1864, 627, Oct. 8, 1864, 643, Oct. 15, 1864, 659. Both Lincoln and Grant testified to Nast's effectiveness as a political cartoonist; both testimonials have been widely quoted in the secondary sources but never with citation to the original sources. When asked who was the foremost figure in civil life developed by the war, Grant was supposed to have replied, "I think Thomas Nast. He did as much as any one man to preserve the Union and bring the war to an end"; Paine, *Nast,* 106. Lincoln is supposed to have said: "Thomas Nast has been our best recruiting sergeant. His emblematic cartoons have never failed to arouse enthusiasm and patriotism, and have always seemed to come just when these articles were getting scarce"; Albert Bigelow Paine, "Harper's Weekly and Thomas Nast," in *Harper's Weekly,* Jan. 5, 1907, 17. Lincoln's testimonial bears a resemblance to a letter of introduction to the president that Curtis wrote for Nast: "I have great pleasure in presenting to you my friend, the artist, Mr. Thomas Nast, whose designs in *Harper's Weekly* have been scattered all over the land, and have especially penetrated the lines of the army, showing the country what it is fighting for and in what spirit, and all with a power and felicity the good results of which are known to you. You and the country have no more faithful friend than Mr. Nast." George William Curtis to Lincoln, Lincoln Papers, Library of Congress.

[35] *Harper's Weekly,* Oct. 1, 1864, 632–633, Oct. 8, 1864, 643, Nov. 12, 1864, 728–729.

[36] *Ibid.,* Nov. 19, 1864, 738, Nov. 26, 1864, 768, March 11, 1865, 146. Leslie wrote that Lincoln won the election, not because of outstanding ability or consistency of principles, but because his enemies had made him by their villifications the symbol of resistance to the rebellion; *Leslie's,* Feb. 25, 1865, 353–354.

CHAPTER XIV: ROUNDUP

[1] *Harper's Weekly,* June 18, 1864, 385, 387, Jan. 7, 1865, 2; *Leslie's,* June 18, 1864, 193. Sala mentioned how the New York bookshop owners featured these illustrations in their windows; Sala, *Diary,* 2:319–322; Cary, *Curtis,* 177–179.

[2] *Harper's Weekly,* Dec. 10, 1864, 788–789, Jan. 14, 1865, 28–29; the original sketches are in the Waud Collection.

[3] *Ibid.,* Jan. 7, 1865, 9, Feb. 18, 1865, 108; *Leslie's,* Jan. 14, 1865, 256, Jan. 28, 1865, 296–297, 301, April 8, 1865, 37, April 15, 1865, 49, 55. For photographs of Andersonville prison, see Horan, *Brady,* plates #326–329.

[4] *Leslie's,* April 15, 1865, 49; *Harper's Weekly,* April 15, 1865, 233, 236.

[5] For the photographs, see Miller, *Photographic History,* 3:278–294; Meredith, *Brady,* Lecture Book plates #51, 64, 86, 87. Also see *Harper's Weekly,* May 27, 1865, 324; *Leslie's,* April 22, 1865, 72–73.

[6] *Harper's Weekly,* April 22, 1865, 245, 248–249, 252; *Leslie's,* April 22, 1865, 65, 77, April 29, 1865, 84, 85, 92, May 27, 1865, 152, June 24, 1865, 213; Meredith, *Brady,* plates #110 and 111 and Lecture Book plates #11, 12, 43, 49; Horan, *Brady,* plates, #290–291.

[7] None of the regular sketch artists or photographers were present at the surrender at Appomattox. Sylvanus Cadwallader of the *New York Herald* made a rough sketch of the McLean House while the meeting was in progress, and some time later Alf Waud visited the scene and re-created the moment when Lee mounted "Traveler" to take the news of the surrender back to his army. Without authentic illustrations of the surrender scene available, the situation was ripe for dishonest publishers to issue fraudulent pictures which an enthusiastic public purchased by the hundreds of thousands; Cadwallader, *Three Years with Grant,* 324–325, 328–329.

[8] Harper, *House of Harper,* 232–233; Cary, *Curtis,* 187–189; *Harper's Weekly,* April 15, 1865, 240, April 29, 1865, 261.

[9] *Leslie's,* April 29, 1865, 81.

[10] *Ibid.,* April 29, 1865, 81, 82, 83, 88–89, May 6, 1865, 97, 98, 104–105, May 13, 1865, 120–121, 125, May 20, 1865, 129, 132, 140, May 27, 1865, 148, June 3,

1865, 168–169, June 17, 1865, 197, July 22, 1865, 280–281; *Harper's Weekly,*
April 22, 1865, 260, 264–265, May 6, 1865, 276, 277, 280–281, 284–285, May
20, 1865, 305, 308, May 27, 1865, 328–329, June 3, 1865, 341, 344–345, July 22,
1865, 457; Horan, *Brady,* plates #307, 315–322, 330–334; Peters, *Currier and
Ives,* plate #118; *New York Herald,* April 15, 1865, 1, for a woodcut portrait
edged in black showing—interestingly enough—Lincoln *before* he grew his beard.

[11] *Leslie's,* April 29, 1865, 81; *Harper's Weekly,* June 3, 1865, 340; Weitenkampf, *NYPLB,* 570, 573, 574; Folders #4421 and 4452 in the Library of Congress Print Collection.

[12] There were, of course, exceptions. Late in 1864 General Sheridan supposedly
saved the Army of the Shenandoah with a magnificent breakneck ride to the front,
and at Atlanta General John Logan rode along his lines with great showmanship
to rally his troops. Both events resulted in several illustrations in the grand tradition of the heroic postures; *Harper's Weekly,* July 2, 1864, 424–425, Nov. 5,
1864, 705; *Leslie's,* Oct. 15, 1864, 56–57.

[13] Underhill, *Soldier Boy Samuel,* 131; *Leslie's,* June 10, 1865, 180, 184–185;
Harper's Weekly, June 10, 1865, 351, 356–357.

[14] There are brief mentions of post-war activities in the following sources; for
Lovie, see Wilkie, *Pen and Powder,* 360; for Crane, see *Leslie's,* Aug. 12, 1865,
333; for Simplot, see Wilkie, *Pen and Powder,* 360–361; for Lumley, see the
Lumley Folder in the Art Room of the New York Public Library; for William
Waud, see *Harper's Weekly,* Nov. 30, 1878, 947, and a letter from Frank Weiten-
kampf to Charles K. Bolton, December 13, 1940, in the Alfred R. Waud Folder
in the Art Room of the New York Public Library; and for Becker, see *Leslie's
Weekly,* Dec. 14, 1905, 570, and *American Art News,* Feb. 5, 1910, 5.

[15] For the post-war sketching of these artists, there is material on Forbes in his
Artist's Story, passim; on Davis in Taft, "Pictorial Record of the Old West," 358–
359; *New York Tribune,* Nov. 11, 1894, 7; and *Harper's Weekly,* Nov. 24, 1894,
1114; on Alfred R. Waud in *American Artists and their Work* (2 vols., Boston,
1889), 2:401–409, and the letter from Frank Weitenkampf to Charles K. Bolton
in the Alfred R. Waud Folder in the Art Room of the New York Public Library;
and on Schell in *American Art Annual,* 7:81 (New York, 1909–1910); and
American Art News, April 10, 1909, 7.

[16] Frank Freidel, *The Splendid Little War* (Boston and Toronto, 1958).

A NOTE ON THE SOURCES

Journalistic pictures are one type of historical source material that historians have
generally neglected. The fact that more and more news illustrations, photographs,

and cartoons have appeared in recently-published historical studies indicates their awareness of the pertinence of this material. But they have used pictures only as supplementary illustrations for their texts, and with few exceptions they have not accepted pictures as legitimate primary historical documents. Yet in failing to do so, they have denied themselves access to extremely useful information and insights.

Pictorial reporters, whether they were sketch artists or photographers, have usually been highly-competent observers of the passing scene, men who have been as expertly trained in their particular type of reporting as the correspondents of the daily newspapers. Their pictures have been a distinct factor in the shaping of public opinion. They have often portrayed events more sharply than any written description, including the details which writers have ignored for lack of space or time, together with a single and vivid summary of the total impact of the event. Their portraits of individuals have been clear and precise. Certainly people in the public view, such as a candidate for public office, have been anxious to make as favorable an appearance as possible. Yet most historians have by-passed the "documents" that best describe these impressions. Portraiture of expressions and postures in any situation, whether involving noted persons or not, provides insights into the attitudes of individuals and groups which are not often available in other sources.

Cartoonists have also been highly-qualified commentators whose impact upon the public is probably more generally recognized than that of the pictorial reporters. Political cartoonists have usually been well informed about the subjects they have treated, and their observations are as significant and influential as those of the editorial columnists. Most historians recognize the role of Thomas Nast in the campaign against the Tweed Ring in New York City; but dozens of other political cartoonists have had a similar impact at other times and on different issues. The work of cartoonists whose area of effort has been primarily social rather than political commentary has been just as important. It is difficult to imagine, for instance, historians of the GI's of the Second World War not consulting and using Bill Mauldin's wartime cartoons of Willy and Joe.

There remain the artists whose talents have been purchased by commercial art publishers. As individuals they have not been particularly creative of ideas and images. They have had to meet the demands of the competitive commercial market, and necessarily they have tended to conform to contemporary opinion. But this, indeed, is why their pictures are valuable social documents; they provide insights into conventional contemporary ideas, and for the historian they can be a useful standard by which to compare and judge the work of the more creative artists.

However, there are some indications that pictures are taking their rightful place as legitimate historical sources. The rapid development of social history has stimulated the interest of the historians in the artifacts of society. E. McClung Fleming of the DuPont Winterthur Museum has called attention to the value of the decorative arts as social documents, but he also noted that historians have lagged far behind the archaeologists, anthropologists, and the art historians in their full utilization. ["Early American Decorative Arts as Social Documents," in *The Mississippi Valley Historical Review,* 45:276–284 (September 1958).] The extensive collecting of photographs and prints by a few libraries and historical societies, particularly the Library of Congress, the New York Public Library, and the State Historical Society of Wisconsin, have contributed to a growing interest in pictures as historical documents. The art historians have done good work in the fine arts and occasionally in the commercial and decorative arts, but they have scarcely touched journalistic art.

Nevertheless, historians have been slow to adopt the new material to their own uses. The so-called "pictorial histories" are universally unsatisfactory. In practically every instance, they consist of collections of illustrations and photographs arranged in chronological sequence, and accompanied by a text that usually says nothing at all about the artists, the pictures, or the significance and impact of the pictures. The best effort to date is Robert Taft's *Artists and Illustrators of the Old West* (New York, 1953). But Taft's methodology was basically a biographical treatment which did not require him to evaluate the impact of the pictures.

The late Bernard DeVoto, one of the few historians to consider the problem, took too pessimistic a view of the usefulness of pictures as historical documents. "They splendidly illustrate history," he wrote, "and they contribute to its course but they do not record it by themselves." The main shortcoming of the picture, he argued, was that it "cannot record an *event*. It can look at an arrested moment of an event, it can comment on an event and sometimes interpret one, but it cannot convey one for it must leave out too much—including time, sequence, and development." [Bernard Devoto, "Parks and Pictures," in *Harper's Magazine* 208:13–17 (February 1954).] In the strictest sense of his words, the argument is valid, but it also applies with equal validity to letters, diaries, newspaper and periodical articles, official records of most sorts, and the majority of all the traditional types of historical documents. In essence, DeVoto merely recognized that pictures require interpretation by the historian.

Pictures are basically interpretive documents, becoming more so as one moves from photographs to illustrations to cartoons. The idea is so obvious that it needs statement. What is sometimes not so obvious is that most written documents are also interpretive. The artist is merely a particular type of author who has recorded his impression of a person, event, or incident, sometimes consciously seeking to describe the significance of his subject, sometimes merely trying to record the subject as honestly and objectively as possible. But even in the latter instance, most historians recognize the probability of subconscious bias or misinterpretation. And whether the documents are written or pictorial, they still require interpretation. The historian must evalute their reliability, interpret their significance, arrange them in whatever sequence suits his purpose, and then come to meaningful conclusions.

There is a strong suspicion that the hesitancy of historians to consider pictures and other artifacts as legitimate primary sources stems from their reliance upon the written word. Most historical documents are manuscript or printed, which allows for extensive quoting and paraphrasing while doing research and in the final writing. Written documents also permit a greater precision in footnote citations. But these are both matters of convenience and of conventional methodology, and are not legitimate reasons for the widespread neglect of non-written sources.

Admittedly, there are pitfalls to be watched for in the use of pictures as historical documents. Written language being the medium of the profession, it is necessary for the historian to describe pictures with words. The dangers arise that he will insert ideas more his own than those of the artist and that he will place an interpretation on a picture other than that intended by the artist. But this is a peril just as inherent in the analysis of any written document, and one that is guarded against by the usual means—thorough familiarity with the artist, and evaluation of any one picture in context with earlier and later pictures by the same artist and comparison with other pictures dealing with the same subject.

Journalistic pictures and commercial art present several additional difficulties. Each of these is a part of the public property, a picture created explicitly for public consumption. The motivation or intention of the artist has sometimes been unimportant or only secondary to that of his publisher or of the client for whom he worked. Ostensibly, this should not raise problems for historians experienced in evaluating printed documents written for public consumption. The difficulty, however, stems from the fact that documentation of *any* sort about the great majority of the commercial printers and of many of their clients is not available. Indeed, there was oftentimes never any documentation to begin with. Instructions to artists, cartoonists, and engravers, who have usually remained anonymous, were never written down.

Moreover, journalistic pictures have usually been edited. Photographs have sometimes been clipped or enlarged. The most obvious type of editing is the selection of one or two prints for publication from among the many on the same subject that have usually been available. Illustrations, particularly in the Civil War era, passed through the hands of several artists and engravers from the time they left the sketch artist to the publication of the final illustration, and extensive changes were made in the details and composition of the original sketches. The final products were a composite of the talents and ideas of several artists, and in many instances they also embodied the ideas of editors and publishers. Recognition of this fact complicates the ascribing of authorship and the determining of intention. The historian's solution of the problem hinges upon comparison of the original sketches—whenever they are available—with the published illustrations, and upon a thorough familiarity with the personnel involved in the entire line of production.

The main difficulty is to evaluate the impact of journalistic pictures upon the public. There have been no public opinion polls to measure their influence, and very few contemporary evaluations by competent critics or reviewers. Most people are not consciously aware that their attitudes and ideas have been shaped by cartoons or pictures; certainly, few of them ever record their reactions. Written testimonials about a specific cartoon or picture are relatively rare, though there are probably more for the Civil War era because news photographs and pictures were unique at the time and thus attracted more than the usual attention. Circulation or sales statistics, when they are available for a particular issue or print, are also useful.

In evaluating the impact of images derived from a series of pictures, the problem is complicated by the fact that newspaper reporters, public figures, speakers, and editorial writers often used the same themes, and thus it is extremely difficult to separate the impact of the pictures from the other sources. In this particular study on the Civil War images, several approaches to this problem have been employed. One has been to note the repetition of themes, with particular attention to the time sequence, by the several different types of picture publishers. The printmakers and the publishers of patriotics issued pictures that had to be sufficiently palatable to the public to sell on the market. The assumption has been that the adoption by these commercial publishers of themes originally developed by the artists of the illustrated and comic weeklies, who had more leeway in testing new ideas, indicated the acceptance of the theme by a sizeable segment of the public. The second approach has been to compare the images of the pictures with the attitudes and ideas of soldiers and civilians as determined by their letters and diaries. All of these methods of measuring impact are imperfect, to be sure, but in many respects they parallel the methods by which intellectual historians attempt to evalute the impact of ideas.

Because this is a study of the impact of pictures on the public imagination, published illustrations are the basic source material. The most important of these are the illustrations in *Harper's Weekly, Frank Leslie's Illustrated Newspaper,* and the *New York Illustrated News.* Complete files of *Harper's* and *Leslie's* are available in most of the major research libraries; complete files of the *Illustrated News* are not as readily available, although the New York Public Library has an uninterrupted run. Selected illustrations from these papers have been republished in virtually hundreds of books on the Civil War. Fletcher Pratt's *Civil War in Pictures* (New York, 1955) contains many of the illustrations from *Harper's* and a few from *Leslie's,* and John S. Blay, *The Civil War, A Pictorial Profile* (New York, 1958) has an even broader selection of some 350 illustrations and prints. However, the texts in both Pratt and Blay contain very little information about either the pictures or the artists and publishers who produced them, and both neglect the illustrations in the *New York Illustrated News.*

Complete files of the *Illustrated London News* and the *London Punch* are usually available in the larger research libraries. W. Stanley Hoole has reprinted some of the Frank Vizetelly illustrations from the *Illustrated London News* in *Vizetelly Covers the Confederacy,* Number 4 of the Confederate Centenniel Studies (Tuscaloosa, Alabama, 1957), and most of the *Punch* cartoons pertaining to the Civil War are available in *Abraham Lincoln and the London Punch: Cartoons, Comments and Poems, Published in the London Charivari, During the American Civil War (1861–1865),* edited by William Shepard Walsh (New York, 1909). Files of the *Illustrated Southern News* and the *Southern Punch* are not readily available, as indeed is true for most of the pictures published in the Confederacy. The primary exceptions are the Lincoln cartoons published in the Confederacy, because collectors have located and republished most of these. Examples of Confederate pictures are available in Lamont Buchanan, *A Pictorial History of the Confederacy* (New York, 1951), and there is some scattered information on the southern publishers in Clement Eaton, *A History of The Southern Confederacy* (New York, 1954), and in Mary Elizabeth Massey, *Ersatz in the Confederacy* (Columbia, South Carolina, 1952).

Original copies of the separately-published prints, photographs, cartoons, and "patriotics" are widely scattered in various libraries and private collections. Copies of many of the Currier and Ives prints, together with useful information on the firm's business methods, are included in Harry T. Peters, *Currier & Ives, Printmakers to the American People* (Garden City, New York, 1942), Russel Crouse, *Mr. Currier and Mr. Ives, A Note on Their Lives and Times* (Garden City, New York, 1930), *A Currier & Ives Treasury,* edited by Samuel Simkin (New York, 1955), and an article entitled "Battle Art of Currier & Ives" in *The Old Print Shop Portfolio,* 7:194–216 (May 1948). For the work of other printmakers, one can only examine the collections in the research libraries, particularly that in the Print and Photograph Division of the Library of Congress, and refer to copies republished in some of the secondary works on the war. There is no published collection as such, but the chapter on the Civil War in Roy Meredith, *The American Wars. A Pictorial History from Quebec to Korea, 1755–1953* (Cleveland and New York, 1955) and Blay's *The Civil War, A Pictorial Profile* include many of the prints from the various lithographers.

The basic collection of Civil War photographs is the ten-volume compilation edited by Francis Trevelyan Miller, *The Photographic History of the Civil War,* originally issued in 1911 and republished in 1957 by Thomas Yoseloff of New York and London. The main shortcomings of these volumes are that the photographs are not identified by photographers and also that the photographs themselves fail to duplicate the sharp quality of the original plates. Roy Meredith, *Mr. Lincoln's Camera Man, Mathew B. Brady* (New York, 1946) and James D. Horan, *Mathew B. Brady, Historian with a Camera* (New York, 1955), the two basic sources for information on Brady and his operators, include many excellently-reproduced copies of the Brady photographs. Reproduction of the qualities of the original photographic plates has been best achieved in the magnificent collection of photographs and sketches by the field artists in David

Donald, *Divided We Fought. A Pictorial History of the War, 1861–1865,* edited by Hirst D. Milhollen, Milton Kaplan, and Hulen Stuart (New York, 1952), which also includes many examples of the work of photographers other than the Brady group, and in Bell Irvin Wiley and Hirst D. Milhollen, *They Who Fought Here* (New York, 1959). The standard collection of Lincoln photographs is Frederick Hill Meserve and Carl Sandburg, *The Photographs of Abraham Lincoln* (New York, 1944). For background and technical information on photography during the war, Robert Taft's *Photography and the American Scene, A Social History, 1839–1889* (New York, 1942) is very useful.

The most widely distributed and therefore the most influential of the Civil War cartoons are available in the files of *Harper's Weekly, Leslie's,* the *Illustrated News,* and *Vanity Fair.* Complete files of *Vanity Fair* are not widely available; there is a complete run in the State Historical Society of Wisconsin. However, many of the *Vanity Fair* cartoons have been republished elsewhere. A contemporary evaluation of *Vanity Fair* appeared in the "Reviews and Literary Notices" section of *The Atlantic Monthly,* 10:252–254 (August 1862). For the general history of American comic journalism, there is scattered information in: James Parton, "Caricature in the United States" in *Harper's New Monthly Magazine,* 52:25–43 (December 1875); "Caricature in America" in *All the Year Round,* 41:298–302 (September 1878); William Henry Shelton, "The Comic Paper in America" in *The Critic,* 39:227–234 (September 1901); and William Murrel, "Rise and Fall of Cartoon Symbols" in *The American Scholar,* 4:306–315 (Summer 1935). Copies of some of the separately-published cartoons are available in most of the major research libraries; the Library of Congress Print and Photograph Division has an extensive collection. Extremely useful is Frank Weitenkampf, "Political Caricature in the United States in separately published cartoons: an annotated list" in the *Bulletin of the New York Public Library,* 56:515–528, 557–574 (October and November 1952). Most of the Lincoln cartoons, including British and Confederate caricatures in addition to those published in the North, are readily available in Rufus Rockwell Wilson, *Lincoln in Caricature* (New York, 1953). Stefan Lorant's *Lincoln, A Picture Story of his Life* (New York, 1957) also contains many of the printed Lincoln portraits and cartoons in addition to a full collection of Lincoln photographs.

There are many public and private collections of decorated envelopes and stationery from the period of the war. The one used specifically in this study was the Henry Rogers Durkee Collection, numbering more than 120 examples, in the State Historical Society of Wisconsin. Collectors of these "patriotics" have published many articles together with printed facsimiles, and among the most informative of these are: A. Jay Hertz, "Campaign Covers of the Nineteenth Century" in *The American Philatelist,* 61:948–953 (September 1948); Carroll Chase, "Propaganda Envelopes, Used while the 1851–1857 issues were current" in *The American Philatelist,* 40:16–19 (October 1926); Raymond Marsh, "Some Early Patriotics" in *The American Philatelist,* 64:95–100 (November

1950); Raymond Marsh, "Lincoln Patriotics" in the *Lincoln Herald,* 52:48–53 (December 1950); R. Gerald McMurty, "Lincoln Patriotics" in the *Journal of the Illinois State Historical Society,* 52:123–129 (Spring, 1959); George N. Malpass, "Publishers and Vendors of Civil War Patriotic Envelopes" in *The American Philatelist,* 65:282–293 (January 1952); Catherine S. Overson, "Civil War Envelopes" in *The Magazine Antiques,* 13:490–492 (June 1928); and "Pictorial Envelopes of the Civil War" in the *Bulletin of the Missouri Historical Society,* 5:306–310 (July 1949). The advertisements for the patriotics in *Harper's Weekly, Leslie's,* and the *Illustrated News* are often highly informative.

Four libraries hold the major collections of original field sketches. Examples of these sketches have been reproduced in many secondary works on the Civil War, but the best published collections are Donald, *Divided We Fought,* and Philip Van Doren Stern, *They Were There. The Civil War in Action as Seen by Its Combat Artists* (New York, 1959). The Waud and the Forbes Collections are in the Library of Congress. The Waud Collection contains approximately 2,300 pencil, ink, and wash drawings by William and Alfred R. Waud, and several examples of the original work of Theodore R. Davis, Arthur Lumley, C. E. F. Hillen, who was Leslie's artist with Sherman's army from late 1863 to the fall of Atlanta, and several occasional artists. There are also six letters from or to the Wauds and two wartime photographic portraits of Alfred Waud. The Forbes Collection contains some 300 field drawings and many of the etchings Forbes made after the war for publication as the *Life Studies of the Great Army: A Historical Art Work in Copper Plate Etching Containing Forty Plates* (1876). A full description of all the sketches and etchings in the Collection is in the House of Representatives Report No. 2440, 48th Congress, 2d Session. William Forrest Dawson recently republished the *Life Studies* etchings in *A Civil War Artist at the Front. Edwin Forbes' Life Studies of the Great Army* (New York, 1957).

Winslow Homer's war pictures, particularly his paintings, are located in many of the nation's art galleries and museums. A magnificent collection of his pencil, ink, crayon, charcoal, wash, and water-color field sketches is in the Cooper Union Institute in New York City.

The Alexander Simplot Collection in the State Historical Society of Wisconsin is less extensive than the Waud, Forbes, or Homer Collections, but it is important because until recently its existence was unknown except to the Simplot family. The Collection contains two of Simplot's field sketch books, his incomplete memoirs both in manuscript and newspaper form, and several illustrations of war scenes that he made many years after the war. There is no correspondence other than the draft of a letter to Fletcher Harper, but the notebooks contain valuable information on the prices he received from Harper and Leggett for the sketches they published. There are also several photographic portraits.

The New York Public Library has examples of the original sketches of the most important of Leslie's field artists, including Edwin Forbes, Arthur Lumley,

Henri Lovie, and William Waud. There are also a few George William Curtis manuscripts and some newspaper clippings about the artists.

Other than the stardard biographical dictionaries and cyclopedias, the county histories, and the newspaper obituaries, most of which are listed in the notes, there is only a limited amount of biographical material on the artists and publishers. The brief biographies in these sources of artists like Edwin Forbes, Henry Mosler, Eugene Benson, Winslow Homer, Arthur Lumley, and Thomas Nast usually concentrate on their post-war careers. William Howe Downes, *The Life and Works of Winslow Homer* (Boston and New York, 1911) treats the Civil War period hurriedly and quickly moves on to Homer's career as a seascape painter. Also useful is Frank Weitenkampf, "Winslow Homer and the Wood Block" in the *Bulletin of the New York Public Library*, 36:731–736 (November 1932). Robert Taft did extensive research into the post-war sketching of Alfred Waud, Theodore Davis, and Joseph Becker in preparation for his *Artists and Illustrators of the Old West* (New York, 1953), and for an article entitled "The Pictorial Record of the Old West. IX. Alfred R. Waud and Theodore R. Davis" in *The Kansas Historical Quarterly*, 17:340–359 (November 1949).

There is very little material on the publishers of the illustrated weeklies other than that which appears in the pages of the weeklies before, during, and after the war. The standard sources are Frank Luther Mott's *American Journalism. A History of Newspapers in the United States through 260 years, 1690 to 1950* (revised edition, New York, 1950), and the second volume of his *A History of American Magazines* (3 vols., Cambridge, Massachusetts, 1938). Especially useful is an article by Clement K. Shorter, "Illustrated Journalism: Its Past and Its Future" in *The Contemporary Review*, 75:481–494 (April 1899). Some valuable insights into the personality and career of Frank Leslie appear in Madeleine Bettina Stern, *Purple Passage. The Life of Mrs. Frank Leslie* (Norman, Oklahoma, 1953), and useful information on his publishing techniques in "How Illustrated Newspapers are Made" in *Leslie's*, August 2, 1856; N. P. Willis, "Frank Leslie, a Life Lengthener" an article reprinted in *Leslie's*, December 15, 1860; and Harriet Quinby, "How Frank Leslie Started the First Illustrated Weekly" in *Leslie's Weekly*, December 14, 1905. Joseph Henry Harper has some information on Fletcher Harper and the *Weekly* during the war years in *I Remember* (New York and London, 1934) and *The House of Harper, A Century of Publishing in Franklin Square* (New York and London, 1912). A contemporary appraisal of *Harper's Weekly* appeared in the "Critical Notices" section of the *North American Review*, 100:623–625 (April 1865). Edward Cary's brief biography of *George William Curtis* (Boston and New York, 1894) for the "American Men of Letters" Series is useful because of the inclusion of many of Curtis' wartime letters and for information on his relations with Fletcher Harper and the *Weekly*.

Only a few of the artists published accounts of their war experiences. Edwin Forbes, *Thirty Years After: An Artist's Story of the Great War Told and Illustrated with Nearly 300 Relief-etchings after Sketches in the Field and 20 Half-tone*

Equestrian Portraits from Original Oil Paintings (2 vols., New York, 1890) is particularly valuable because of the frankness with which he reported his own reactions to many of the incidents and scenes he sketched during the war. Alexander Simplot never completed his memoirs, although he published as much as he did write in the *Dubuque Sunday Times* in a series of articles beginning on November 5, 1899. But Simplot relied extensively upon the published reminiscences of the reporters who were with him in the West, especially Franc Wilkie, and as a result the amount of original material is quite limited. Theodore R. Davis published an article entitled "Grant Under Fire" in *The Cosmopolitan*, 14:333–340 (January 1893), largely a study of Grant, but also containing some autobiographical information. The main source of information on the daily activities and the immediate reactions of the artists to the war are the letters they sent to their publishers together with their sketches, excerpts from which were often in *Harper's Weekly, Leslie's,* and the *Illustrated News.* Some of the artists wrote more frequently and freely than others; this was especially true of Alfred and William Waud, Theodore Davis, Henri Lovie, Arthur Lumley, Edwin Forbes, Frank Schell, William Crane, and Joseph Becker. On the other hand, Alexander Simplot, A. W. Warren, John R. Hamilton, J. E. Taylor, and several others were ordinarily more reticent.

The newspaper correspondents sometimes mentioned the artists and their work in their reports to their papers, some of which have been cited in the notes, and after the war in their published diaries and reminiscences. For the Western War from Missouri to Vicksburg, Franc B. Wilkie (*The New York Times*), *Pen and Powder* (Boston, 1888) is very useful because of his frequent references to Alexander Simplot, Henri Lovie, and Theodore Davis. Also important are Albert D. Richardson (*New York Tribune*), *The Secret Service, the Field, the Dungeon, and the Escape* (Hartford, Connecticut, 1865); Thomas W. Knox (*New York Herald*), *Camp-fire and Cotton-field: Southern Adventure in Time of War. . . .* (Philadelphia, 1865); and Junius Henri Browne (*New York Tribune*), *Four Years in Secessia: Adventures Within and Beyond the Union Lines. . . .* (Hartford, Connecticut, 1865). Reminiscences of reporters with the eastern armies who mentioned the work of the artists include Sylvanus Cadwallader (*New York Herald*), *Three Years with Grant, As Recalled by War Correspondent Sylvanus Cadwallader,* edited by Benjamin P. Thomas (New York, 1955); George Alfred Townsend (*New York Herald*), *Rustics in Rebellion, A Yankee Reporter on the Road to Richmond, 1861–65* (Chapel Hill, North Carolina, 1950); and Charles A. Page (*New York Tribune*), *Letters of a War Correspondent,* edited by James R. Gilmore (Boston, 1899). The diaries of three British correspondents also recognize the work and impact of the picturemen. William Howard Russell, *My Diary North and South* (Boston, 1863), contains a number of acute observations, but Russell's characterization of Theodore Davis, with whom he toured the Confederacy at the beginning of the war, was unnecessarily harsh. George Augustus Sala, *My Diary in America in the midst of war* (2 vols., London, 1865), and Edward Dicey, *Six months in the Federal States* (2 vols., London, 1863) are particularly informative about the reactions of the home front to some of the efforts of the artists and publishers. Of the four recent studies of the Civil War reporters, all of which include some material on the arists, the most complete in scope and detail is J. Cutler Andrews, *The North Reports the Civil War* (Pittsburg, 1955), and the most interpretive in terms of the newspapers' "images" of the war is Bernard A. Weisberger's *Reporters for the Union* (Boston, 1953). Louis M. Starr's *Bohemian Brigade: Civil War Newsmen in Action* (New York, 1954) strikes a neat balance between the two studies just mentioned, but Emmet Crozier's *Yankee Reporters, 1861–65* (New York, 1956) lacks adequate citation and documentation to support many of the incidents and facts he narrates.

Some of the letters, diaries, and reminiscences of officers and soldiers are valuable because they include references to specific artists or because they record the reactions of the author to illustrations, cartoons, and the work of the picturemen generally. Others are important because the authors were men with an acute visual awareness, the ability to describe scenes with words that sketch artists portrayed with pictures, and thus are useful for evaluating the effectiveness with which the artists illustrated the scenes and incidents that made a vivid impression upon the soldiers. For both reasons, a great many of these contemporary accounts have been examined for this study, only a few of which have been cited in the notes and only the most outstanding of which are listed here.

Two general studies of the "common soldier" are extremely useful. Bell Irvin Wiley, *The Life of Billy Yank, The Common Soldier of the Union* (Indianapolis and New York, 1952) includes a consideration of the reactions of some soldiers to the work of the artists. Fred A. Shannon, "The Life of the Common Soldier in the Union Army, 1861–1865" in *The Mississippi Valley Historical Review,* 13:465–482 (March 1927) is a concise study of the men in the ranks at ease. Harper, Leslie, and Leggett frequently printed excerpts of letters from soldiers, but as might be expected, the great majority of these are full of praise for the work of the illustrated weeklies. *The Blue and the Gray. The Story of the Civil War as Told by Participants,* edited by Henry Steele Commager (Indianapolis and New York, 1950), and the first volume of Otto Eisenschiml and Ralph Newman, *The Civil War* (2 vols., New York, 1956) are collections of selected excerpts from letters, diaries, and recollections. In most instances, however, the editors have not included the sections that referred to the work of the picturemen, and so it is necessary to go to the originally-published sources.

Several of these sources provide direct "testimony" about the artists and their work. Major Henry Hitchcock knew Theodore Davis and William Waud quite well during Sherman's march from Atlanta to North Carolina, and there are frequent references to both of them in his *Marching with Sherman, Passages from the Letters and Campaign Diaries of Henry Hitchcock, major and assistant adjutant general of Volunteers, November 1864–May 1865,* edited by M. A. DeWolfe Howe (New Haven, Connecticut, 1927). Alonzo H. Quint, the chaplain of the Second Massachusetts Infantry, has several references to specific illustrations and cartoons in *The Potomac and the Rapidan, Army notes from the failure at Winchester to the reenforcement of Rosecrans, 1861–3* (Boston, 1864), and the same is true of the recollections of John D. Billings, *Hardtack and Coffee, or The unwritten story of army life. . . .* (Boston, 1888). General William T. Sherman was unusually frank in expressing his opinion of newspapermen, and many of his comments, which also applied to the artists, can be found in *The Sherman Letters, Correspondence between General and Senator Sherman from 1837 to 1891,* edited by Rachel Sherman Thorndike (New York, 1894); *Home Letters of General Sherman,* edited by M. A. DeWolfe Howe (New York, 1909); and the *Memoirs of Gen. W. T. Sherman. . . .* (revised edition, 2 vols., New York, 1891).

There are three outstanding examples of letters and diaries with high "visual awareness." James Austin Connolly, the "Diary of Major Connolly" in the Transactions of the *Illinois State Historical Society for the year 1928* (Springfield, Illinois, 1928), and recently edited by Paul M. Angle for the Indiana University Press Civil War Centennial Series and republished as *Three Years in the Army of the Cumberland* (Bloomington, 1959) is perhaps the best diary and series of letters to appear from the Western War. Theodore Lyman, *Meade's Headquarters, 1863–1865, Letters of Colonel Theodore Lyman from the Wilderness to Appomattox,* edited by George R. Agassiz (Boston, 1922), and Josiah Marshall Favill, *The Diary of a Young Officer, serving with the armies of the United States during the war of the rebellion* (Chicago, 1909), together provide acute contemporary comments on the war in the East. Also useful to the study were: William Bircher, *A Drummer-Boy's Diary: Comprising Four Years of Service with the Second Regiment Minnesota Veteran Volunteers, 1861 to 1865* (St. Paul, Minnesota, 1889); Jenkins Lloyd Jones, *An Artilleryman's Diary* (Wisconsin History Commission: Original Papers, No. 8, February, 1914); Samuel Edmund Nichols, *Your Soldier Boy Samuel. Civil War Letters of Lieut. Samuel Edmund Nichols, Amherst, '65, of the 37th Regiment Massachusetts Volunteers,* edited by Charles Sterling Underhill (privately printed, 1929); Oliver Wendell Holmes, Jr., *Touched with Fire, Civil War Letters and Diary of Oliver Wendell Holmes, Jr.,* edited by M. A. DeWolfe Howe (Cambridge, Massachusetts, 1946); and Allen Alonzo Kingsbury, *The Hero of Medfield: containing the journals and letters of Allen Alonzo Kingsbury. . . .* (Boston, 1862).

Contemporary accounts from the home front are not as numerous, but several diaries and collections of letters do recognize the work of the picturemen. Two Englishmen, in addition to the journalists Russell, Sala, and Dicey, recorded their impressions: Anthony Trollope, *North America,* edited by Donald Smalley and Bradford Allen Booth (New York, 1951) and Robert Ferguson, *America during and after the War* (London, 1866). For letters and diaries by Americans, Lester Frank Ward, *Young Ward's Diary, A human and eager record of the years between 1860 and 1870 . . . ,* edited by Bernhard J. Stern (New York, 1935) records a young man's reaction to the propaganda of the home front, and is especially interesting because of Ward's later pre-eminence as a sociologist. An older man who was already recognized in his field but who was just as eager in his response to the war was the poet Walt Whitman, and there is some material of interest to this study in *The Wound Dresser. Letters written to his mother from the hospitals in Washington during the Civil War* (New York, 1949) and *The Complete Poetry and Prose of Walt Whitman as prepared by him for the Deathbed Edition* (2 vols., New York, 1949). Also important for the reactions of the home front are the selected letters of a large New York family, Georgeanna Woolsey Bacon and Eliza Woolsey Howland, *Letters of a Family during the War for the Union, 1861–1865* (2 vols., privately printed, 1899), and the third volume of *The Diary of George Templeton Strong,* edited by Allan Nevins and Milton Halsey Thomas (4 vols., New York, 1952). As in the case of the soldiers, the publishers of the illustrated weeklies sometimes printed letters from their civilian readers containing their comments on the work of the picturemen.

Index

INDEX

INDEX

INDEX

INDEX